Nabia Abbott w
young child she v
Middle East to I
British schools a
world war. Later s
United States, wh... 1933 she became the first woman faculty member of the Oriental Institute of the University of Chicago. A leading scholar of Arabic, she was a specialist in deciphering early Islamic papyri. She was the author of seven books and dozens of magazine articles. Nabia Abbott died in 1981.

AL SAQI
BOOKS

Nabia Abbott

Al Saqi Books

Two Queens of Baghdad

Mother and Wife of Hārūn al-Rashīd

With a foreword by Sarah Graham-Brown

British Library
Cataloguing in Publication Data
Abbott, Nabia
The two queens of Baghdad.
1. Khaizurān 2. Zubaidah 3. Caliph's wives——
Biography 4. Arabian Peninsula——Biography
I. Title
953'.02'0922 DS238.A1

ISBN 0–86356–119–5
ISBN 0–86356–031–8 Pbk

First published by the University of Chicago Press, 1946.

This edition first published 1986 by
Al Saqi Books, 26 Westbourne Grove, London W2.

Printed in Great Britain by
Billing and Sons Ltd,
Worcester.

Foreword

Sarah Graham-Brown

Two Queens of Baghdad, published in 1946, is the second of Nabia Abbott's historical biographies of women in the early centuries of Islam. The first, *Aishah—the Beloved of Mohammed*, recounts the life of Mohammed's most influential wife, who after his death played a significant role in political affairs. Through the story of Aishah, Abbott also examines the attitudes of Mohammed and his followers towards women in both public and private life, which were to influence future generations.

In *Two Queens of Baghdad* she continues this theme in her account of the lives of the mother and wife of the most famous of the Abbasid caliphs, Harun al-Rashid, 'hero of many an *Arabian Nights*' tale'.

Abbott felt that Khaizuran and Zubaidah, like Aishah, had not received serious attention from historians and biographers. As she remarks in the preface: 'His (Harun al-Rashid's) recent biographers have tended either to exaggerate or to underestimate the role of these royal women, and all have treated them more or less summarily.'

She therefore sought to use Arab historical sources to create a picture of the life and times of Khaizuran and Zubaidah. In many ways there are sharp contrasts between the two women. Khaizuran came to the court of the Caliph Mansur in Baghdad as a young slave brought from Arabia. She became first mistress and then wife to Mahdi, the next caliph, and later played a significant part in the power struggle between her two sons, Musa al-Hadi and Harun al-Rashid.

Zubaidah, in contrast, was born to court life and high social status. As Harun al-Rashid's wife she too had considerable influence not only within the harem but also in public affairs. She is also remembered for a more practical reason. Immensely wealthy in her own right, she sponsored and financed the building of the water system of Mecca and of stations on the Pilgrim Road from Iraq. The water works, as Dutch scholar Snouck Hurgronje put it, 'made the name of Zubaidah immortal in Mecca'.

Abbott sets the role of these women in the public and private life of the palace against 'the familiar phrase "harem intrigue"'. She argues that 'the many recorded actions of these royal women speak louder and clearer than these overworked words ever did.' Yet in her attempt to demythologize women's role in the court and the harem she encounters some problems with the historical sources she uses. As she observes in the book, contemporary Arab historians eager to remain in favour with the court engaged in self-censorship. Later Arab and Persian writers tend to glamorize and fantasize the admittedly spectacular life of the Baghdad court of Harun al-Rashid's time, which, for all its intrigues, violence, and rivalries, was also the centre of a rich intellectual and creative life. Western writers, she found, had added to the melodramatic distortions and oversimplifications of history.

But where Khaizuran and Zubaidah are concerned, there are also gaps in the record, because both contemporary and later Arab historians wrote under a further constraint: 'To begin with, it was not the proper thing to dwell too much on the affairs of the harem—any harem. Next, from Mansur onward, the caliphs demanded that the royal harem in particular be handled with exceptional care and caution.'

Although the weight of scholarship is evident in almost every part of this book, it is aimed, like *Aishah*, at a wider audience, particularly at 'progressive Muslims', whom Abbott hoped 'both to amuse and instruct'. It was intended to be part of a wider discussion in her work of early Islam and its implications for the role of women in the contemporary world.

But Nabia Abbott was, in the eyes of her contemporaries, first and foremost a scholar. This alone makes her an unusual figure. In 1933 she became the first woman member of the Oriental Institute of the University of Chicago, and in 1963 she was made Emeritus Professor. In a tribute published in the Institute's 1974/5 annual report, Dr Muhsin Mahdi, formerly professor of Arabic and chairman of the university's Department of Near Eastern Languages, commented on 'the discrimination I knew she had faced as a professional woman in those pre-liberation days', and lists her major achievements as 'her pioneering work on the position of women in the Islamic Middle East; her classic study of the rise of the North Arabic script; her massive, painstaking, and path-breaking investigations of Arabic literary papyri, which have already revolutionized the study of the culture of early Islam; . . .'

Abbott's early life seems to have been one of constant movement. She was born in Mardin, in south-western Turkey, on 31 January 1897. Her father was a trader and, while she was still a child, she travelled with her family in a covered wagon in a caravan to Mosul and sailed down the Tigris to Baghdad. The family subsequently moved on to settle in Bombay. It was in India that Abbott received most of her education, attending English schools; during World War I she took a BA degree at Lucknow's Isabella Thorbom College for Girls, graduating in 1919. After the war she spent a brief period in Iraq, where she was involved in the establishment of a women's education programme, a subject that continued to interest her in later years.

Her family then moved to the United States, where she accompanied them and took her masters degree at Boston University, graduating in 1925. She subsequently became first a faculty member and then head of the history department at Asbury College in Wilmore, Kentucky, where she remained until 1933.

When her family moved to Chicago in that year she went to work under Martin Sprengling, professor of Arabic at the Oriental Institute, and began her career there with a study of the Institute's collection of rare early Islamic documents. In order to do this, she immersed herself in the history of early Islamic society, out of which grew her interest in the position of women in that society.

In both the historical biographies, one weakness from a contemporary point of view is the language she uses to describe her female characters, and particularly relationships between men and women. She sometimes seems to have deliberately sought to achieve a tone appropriate to the romantic novels of the day, probably in an effort to reach a wider audience than in her strictly scholarly works. Nonetheless, by introducing women as actors in the life and power struggles of early Islam, and not as mere appendages of men, she contributes to a broadening of historical perspective which even now is refreshing and stimulating.

Her mainly narrative biographical works are complemented by her more analytical general essays and articles on the subject of women in pre-Islamic society and in early Islam. 'Women and the State in Early Islam', published, like *Aishah*, in 1942 (*Journal of Near Eastern Studies* 1: pp. 106–26, 341–68), paints a broader picture and makes explicit some of the arguments that do not always come into clear focus in the biography.

Here she addresses the question of the effects of early Islam on women in terms of both the example provided by Mohammed's own life and the institutionalization of Islam after his death. Although Abbott essentially supports the view that the position of women grew progressively more circumscribed after Mohammed's own day, she argues that there were aspects of his own actions and pronouncements which laid the basis for limits on women's freedom that turned out to be more severe than those which had existed in pre-Islamic days.

In Mohammed's own attitude to women she detects two sometimes contradictory strands. One was a willingness to initiate certain reforms—for instance the ending of female infanticide—while adopting a generally piecemeal and *ad hoc* approach to the whole question of women's rights.

'It is safe to state', she asserts, 'that Mohammed avoided drastic innovations and that he tolerated and adopted such public and private practices as had become well established through long usage, provided these were reasonably compatible with the cardinal doctrine of monotheism and the requirements of a theocratic state' (p. 106). She contends that Mohammed therefore accepted 'the honoured position that the free Arab woman had enjoyed in pre-Islamic Arabia'. This of course must be distinguished from the position of women who were slaves or freed slaves.

But she points out that while Mohammed did initiate some improvements in the economic and legal status of all Muslim women, other aspects of his practice 'left woman forever inferior to man, placed one step below him' (p. 107).

But more crucially she examines the actual status of women in public life in the early days of Islam, arguing that 'it was during this period that the seeds of definite politico-religious discrimination against women were sown' (p. 107).

In the religious domain, women were readily accepted by

Mohammed as converts and received encouragement and even honours. But as Abbott points out, the 'crucial test of woman's real position is to be looked for in the field of active leadership. Was she allowed to fill all or any of the public offices associated with the new religious life?' (p. 111). Her answer is that while Mohammed generally made no objection to, for instance, a woman acting as a prayer leader in her own household, even for both sexes, he did not particularly encourage it and in fact women seldom held any significant public religious position.

In the domain of politics, not surprisingly, Abbott finds the situation still 'less encouraging'. While there were still notable women, Aishah included, who wielded considerable influence and even fought in battles, they could seldom act directly, rather being obliged to seek influence through fathers, husbands, brothers, or sons. Abbott argues that while Aishah's part in the Battle of the Camel (in the year 656) demonstrated that some men were willing to follow the lead of a woman, her defeat and consequent retirement from public life was a setback for her in particular and for women in general.

In the second part of her article she reviews the position of women in the Umayyad period and concludes that over the first century and a quarter of Islam, women's freedom of action and influence in the new state were already in steady decline. But she also takes the view that later restrictions were more the result of socio-economic changes in the rapidly expanding Islamic empire than the consequence of religious tenets as such. It was their interpretation in the light of particular social conditions that was more significant. She sees the moves towards the total seclusion of women of the new aristocracy mainly as the result of the rapid conquests of early Islam, which brought increased wealth and access to female slaves. The latter began to take on the role of concubines, with freeborn wives more and more frequently veiled and secluded 'for reasons of sexual jealousy and social prestige'. These women's links with the outside world thus became attenuated, which in turn made it harder for them to break out of their isolation. Ironically, only slave and bedouin women retained a greater degree of freedom of movement.

Under the influence of these trends, Abbott concludes, 'the royal harem [began] to take on some of the characteristics of a sumptuous female prison guarded by that tragic but sinister figure, the eunuch'.

But in a later article, published in 1956 ('Women', in Ruth Nanda Anshen, ed., *Mid-East: World Center: Yesterday, Today and Tomorrow*; Science of Culture Series Vol. 7, New York 1956, pp. 196–212), she takes issue with the simplistic view common in the West that the seclusion of women barred them entirely from taking any active role in society. Khaizuran and Zubaidah are obvious examples to the contrary, though Abbott acknowledges that their influence and power were mediated through men and largely depended on their patronage.

But she also argues in her 1956 article against the view that the relegation of women to the backrooms of public life was a phenomenon exclusive to Islamic cultures. She points out that 'the Caliph Hadi, who indignantly asked his courtiers what they meant by coming to his mother Khaizuran and making her and her doings the object of their conversation, was only following in the footsteps of Pericles, who, though he publicly defended the free life of his mistress Aspasia, insisted that the best woman is she who is least in man's mouth for praise or blame.'

Abbott also remarks on the ambivalent role of female slaves, some of whom were well educated and accomplished singers as well as courtesans in the royal palace. Many such examples appear in *Two Queens of Baghdad* and in the *Arabian Nights*, 'where girls of natural endowments and liberal education are frequently judged to be the equals of men and on rare occasions declared to be even his superiors.' But, she adds, 'women who cultivate charm and intellect for the sole or prime purpose of amusing man and winning his transient favor rarely reach their full intellectual development.'

Taking a historical overview of women's position in cultures dominated by the three major monotheistic religions, she argues that their oppression has been in many respects similar. 'The status of women in the Middle East has roots that reach back to prehistory. The same major forces controlled her destiny here as, until recently, in the West. Semitic religions and Aryan cultures joined forces to bend and mould her to man's will and desire.' . . .'Equating physical with moral power, man toyed with the idea of his own superiority and willingly succumbed to the "immortal myth" of woman's inferiority . . .

'Judaism, Christianity and Islam turned myth into dogma on the basis of the biblical and Koranic story of the creation and the fall of

Adam and Eve' (p. 196).

She argues that in all three religions essentially the same devices were used to keep women in a position of inferiority: 'the ever-present threat of physical violence too readily executed; energy- and time-consuming excessive child-bearing in the interest of passion, church, or state; denial of free access to the world of books and publications; psychological attitudes that undermine self-esteem and eventually induce in all but the strongest of body and mind a false and vicious inferiority complex' (pp. 198–9). Despite the strength of this condemnation, she defends medieval Islam against some of the misconceptions and oversimplifications of Orientalists in the West, where 'the term "harem" has come to connote everything vicious and to exclude everything wholesome in the relationships of the sexes' (p. 203). Furthermore, she points out that those in the West who, in the eighteenth and nineteenth centuries, began to give thought to the emancipation of women tended to point to Islam as embodying the ultimate in the degradation of women. This, she adds, brought 'denials and apologetics from the Muslim world' and claims of women's superior status under Islam. In her view, this reaction is almost as invidious as the Western claims are false.

Her attitude towards the women's movement in the Middle East in the 1950s radiates hope. She described the movement, with 'its far-reaching implications', as 'the most significant single factor in changing the Middle East, even as the status of woman is everywhere the most significant measure of civilization and human progress'. Seen from the perspective of the 1980s, her analysis seems poignantly over-optimistic, though she was clearly aware that progress towards equality was neither easy nor straightforward.

She judged that the twin factors which had allowed the women's movement, particularly in Egypt and Turkey, to develop and achieve a measure of success were access to education and participation of women in the nationalist struggle. What she was not able to see at that time were the limitations and weaknesses which would be revealed in both mass education and nationalist politics in lessening inequalities for women, and for society as a whole.

Equally, her view of the role of religion as a reforming influence on society along the lines of Muslim thinkers in Egypt such as Mohammed Abduh has proved wide of the mark. 'Apologetics and eclecticism have ever been effective tools of change in Islam, as in its sister faiths and cultures. The West should neither ridicule nor underestimate them, as some tend to do. Used in the current climate of reform, they hold much promise for progressive social action. Nor should one underestimate the will and power of Middle Eastern women to speed this action where the law has not yet caught up with evolving practice' (p. 211).

Preface

THE historical and legendary fame of Hārūn al-Rashīd, the most renowned of the caliphs of Baghdad and hero of many an *Arabian Nights'* tale, has rendered him for centuries a potent attraction for historians, biographers, and littérateurs. Early Moslem historians recognized a measure of political influence exerted on him by his mother Khaizurān and by his wife Zubaidah. His more recent biographers have tended either to exaggerate or to underestimate the role of these royal women, and all have treated them more or less summarily. It seemed, therefore, desirable to break fresh ground in an effort to uncover all the pertinent historical materials on the two queens themselves, in order the better to understand and estimate the nature and the extent of their influence on Hārūn and on several others of the early ᶜAbbāsid caliphs.

As the work progressed, first Khaizurān and then Zubaidah emerged from the privacy of the royal harem to the center of the stage of early ᶜAbbāsid history. Each queen revealed, in turn, a vivid and colorful personality, the first determined to rule the state, the second eager to dazzle court and society. Hārūn himself felt the full impact of both women. But Khaizurān's ruling passion had already left its mark on his father and brother, while Zubaidah's gentler influence was to continue into the reigns of his two sons. Hence, the full and dramatic stories of these queens shed light alike on the character and career of five successive ᶜAbbāsid caliphs. Students seeking to comprehend the various forces that helped to shape the course of the early ᶜAbbāsid Empire will find here, it is hoped, some answers to the many questions that seldom fail to confront them. No longer need they be content or baffled with the familiar phrase "harem intrigue" when the many recorded actions of these royal women speak louder and clearer than these overworked words ever did.

The name of Hārūn al-Rashīd is still a household word in the far-flung Moslem world of today. Zubaidah, too, has her niche in the hall of popular fame. But few are they who can recall even the name of the more aggressive and politically more effective Khaizurān. This is, in part, the natural result of the traditional Moslem aversion to women in public life. Times, however, are changing. Progressive Moslems everywhere are ceasing to allow woman's so-called weakness or sanctity to deprive her of an effective role in the life and thought of their rapidly modernizing world. These progressives, as yet but comparatively few, have the promise of a sizable and ever growing following from among the steadily increasing output of school and college halls. It is hoped that these men and women of vision and these boys and girls of promise will find in this story of the two queens something both to amuse and to instruct.

Times are also changing in the Western world. Old imperialistic nations are adding to their political and economic interests in the Moslem world a growing awareness of its vital and distinctive culture. Two world wars and political Zionism have forced on the New World the discovery of the Arab lands—core of the Moslem world and the historic scene of our story. During World War II, Western archeologists uncovered fresh ruins of Hārūn's palace in his northern capital of Raqqah, now within the Syrian boundary. And, quite recently, Hollywood released its own glamorized version of the romantic Hārūn al-Rashīd—a version in which neither Khaizurān nor Zubaidah had a part. Laymen seeking to go beyond bare ruins and fantastic moving-picture episodes to a fuller and truer knowledge of the historical and historic Hārūn have here, as first guides to their goal, the two women most influential in that monarch's imperial career—two queens who reveal, besides, their own no less significant and romantic stories.

There remains the ever pleasant duty of grateful acknowledgment. Once again Professor Martin Sprengling has put me under deep obligation for his enthusiastic and critical reading of the present study. Director John A. Wilson of the Oriental Institute was generous with pertinent suggestions, which were as gratefully received as the subvention he graciously provided toward publication.

Nabia Abbott

Oriental Institute
May 1946

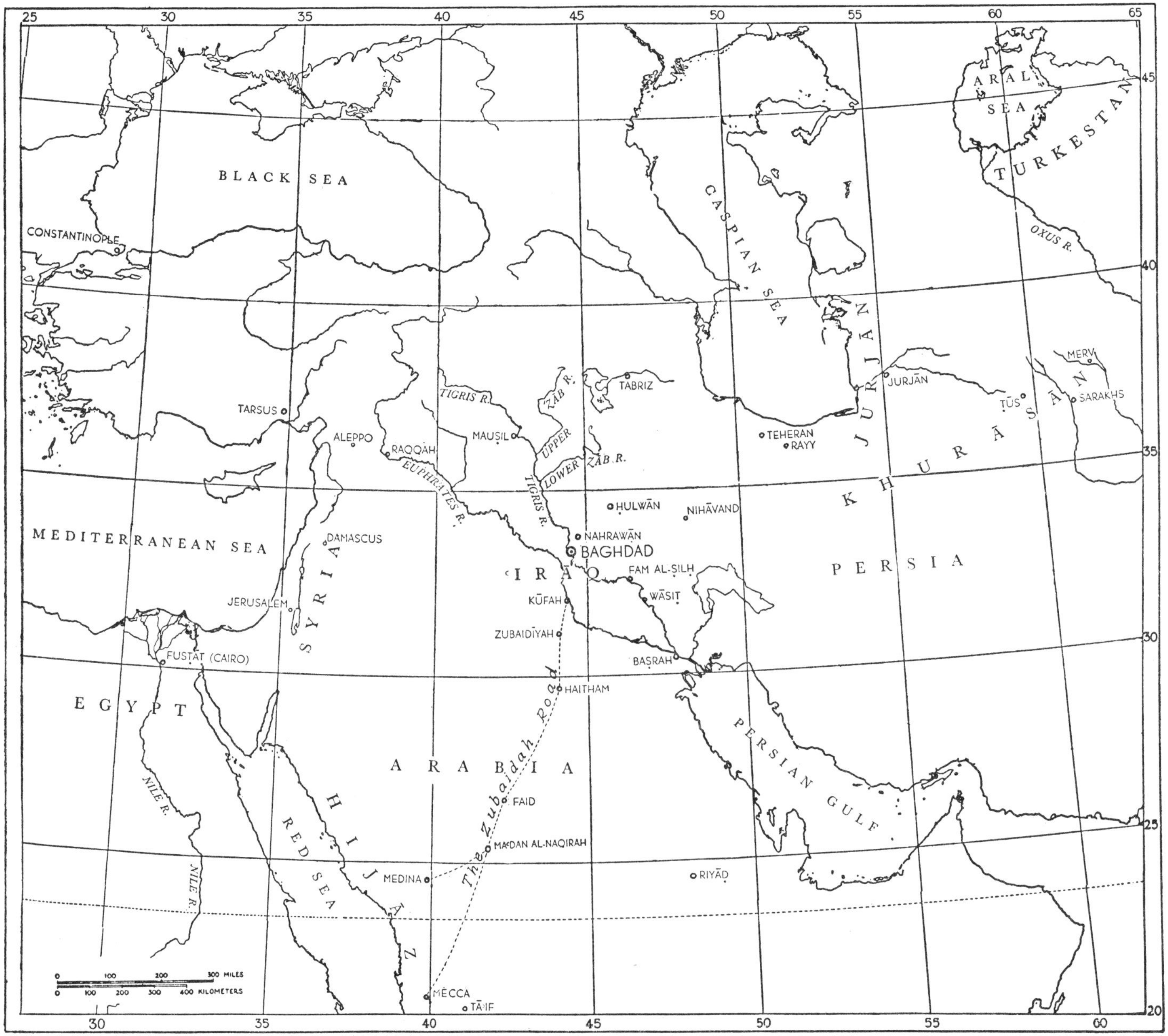

THE EASTERN ʿABBĀSID EMPIRE

Contents

Introduction

I

THE stories of Khaizurān and Zubaidah ran their partly overlapping course in that period of Islamic history conceded by all to be the Golden Age of the ᶜAbbāsid Empire. Golden politically, economically, and culturally, this period stretched from the middle of the eighth to about the middle of the ninth century of our era. It included the reigns of the first nine ᶜAbbāsid caliphs, six of whom were involved, directly or indirectly, with either Khaizurān or Zubaidah or with both of these queens.

The short reign of the first ᶜAbbāsid, Abū al-ᶜAbbās al-Saffāḥ, "The Shedder of Blood" (A.H. 132–36/A.D. 750–54), accomplished the destruction of the Umayyads. It was left for his half-brother, Abū Jaᶜfar al-Manṣūr, "The Victor" (136–58/754–75), to consolidate the dynastic victory. Manṣūr is rightly accounted the greatest of the ᶜAbbāsid caliphs. He brought to his imperial task a great personal talent for sound organization and an untiring industry for effective administration. His vigilant eye watched every avenue of state finance. He realized, better than any of his successors, that "money was not only the sinews of war but an insurance for peace." His farsighted thrift, however, earned for him the title of Abū al-Dawānīq, or "Father of Farthings."[1]

[1] Ṭabarī, *Taʾrīkh* ("Annales"), ed. de Goeje (15 vols.; Lugduni Batavorum, 1879–1901), III, 404–5, 444; Thaᶜālibī, *Laṭāʾif al-Maᶜārif*, ed. P. de Jong

Not the least of his great boons to the dynasty he established was the new, safer, and more central capital —Baghdad, the Round City of Manṣūr. The original unit took several years to build and cost close to five million dirhams.[2] The ambitions that this caliph cherished for the city of his choice and creation are reflected in the names he bestowed on royal palace and capital—the Golden Palace in the heart of the City of Peace and the Palace Immortal without the city wall. Here, then, arose the Round City of Manṣūr, with its huge concentric fortifications, to expand and prosper, to match fame and glory with imperial cities past and to come, and to live forever in memory and legend as the historic capital of the ᶜAbbāsids and the magic city of the *Arabian Nights*.[3]

Vast empire won and new capital established, Manṣūr next used his wealth for the "winning of hearts." This meant securing the prosperity of a strong, united, aggressive political party. It was, however, Manṣūr's favorite son, Mohammed al-Mahdī, "The Well-guided," who was to reap the ultimate benefits of his father's

---

(Lugduni Batavorum, 1867), pp. 16, 81; cf. Theodor Nöldeke, *Sketches from Eastern History*, trans. John Southerland (London, 1892), pp. 107–45.

[2] Muqaddaṣī, *Aḥsan al-Taqāsīm* ("Bibliothica geographorum Arabicorum [*BGA*]," Vol. III [Leiden, 1906]), p. 121; Ṭabarī, III, 326; Ibn Ṭiqṭiqā, *Al-Fakhrī*, ed. Derenbourg (Paris, 1895), p. 220.

[3] For the topography, building, and growth of Baghdad see Abū Bakr al-Khaṭīb, *Taʾrīkh Baghdād* (14 vols.; Cairo and Baghdad, 1931), Vol. I, and the part of this volume translated by Georges Salmon, *L'Introduction topographique l'histoire de Bagdādh* (Paris, 1904); Guy Le Strange, *Baghdad during the Abbasid Caliphate* (Oxford, 1900); Reuben Levy, *A Baghdad Chronicle* (Cambridge, 1929); K. A. C. Creswell, *Early Muslim Architecture* (2 vols.; Oxford, 1932 and 1940), II, 1–38.

great expenditures and vast accumulations. It was for him that Manṣūr bought the succession, at no small figure, from a reluctant but threatened and outwitted cousin. He spared neither pains nor treasure in establishing the prestige of his chosen heir. To accommodate the prince and his large military retinue, Manṣūr ordered the construction of Ruṣāfah, known also as Mahdī's Camp. This royal suburb, complete to palace, garden, and barracks, rose on the eastern bank of the Tigris across from the Round City itself. Finally, Manṣūr left Mahdī an enormous legacy.[4] "Look to this City (Baghdad)," said Manṣūr to his son in his last instructions, "and beware of exchanging it (for another capital). I have accumulated in it for you so large a sum that if the land revenue should fail you for ten years, you will still have enough for the pay of the army, the civil expenditures, the family allotments, and the weal of the border. Watch over it; for as long as your treasury is sound and full you will continue to be mighty. But," he added, "I do not think you will do (as I say)."[5]

Manṣūr's keen prediction proved right. For Mahdī, in the ten-year reign (158–69/775–85) that was allotted him, came to neglect the Round City of Manṣūr for his own suburb of Ruṣāfah. His father's well-considered disbursements he replaced with lavish expenditure. The contents of the overflowing treasury of the "Father of

[4] Ṭabarī, III, 345, 347, 352, 364; Masᶜūdī, *Murūj al-Dhahab* (*Les Prairies d'or*), ed. C. Barbier de Meynard (9 vols.; Paris, 1861–77), VI, 222; cf. his *Kitāb al-Tanbīh wa al-Ashrāf* (*BGA*, Vol. VIII [Leiden, 1893]), p. 342; Ibn Khallikān, *Wafayāt al-ᶜAyān* ("Biographical Dictionary"), ed. and trans. W. M. de Slane (4 vols.; Cairo, 1925–30), IV, 353; *Fakhrī*, p. 235.

[5] Ṭabarī, III, 444; cf. *ibid.*, p. 404.

Farthings" soon flowed back into the wide channels of empire. But it was largely Mahdī's personal temperament together with the expansive spirit of the times that opened up several avenues of liberal spending that verged on prodigality. One such outlet centered round Mahdī's social and family life The economically administered court of Manṣūr, where levity dared not raise its head, yielded to sumptuous living. While theologians, scholars, and serious-minded poets provided intellectual stimulation, Ovidian bards, court jesters, musicians, and singing girls catered to the emotions. All were royally rewarded. There was next the demand of the royal harem itself, with its multiple wives and numerous concubines who vied among themselves and strove to match the scale set them by the royal master.

Mahdī himself was incapable of saving for a near future that promised to grow evermore prosperous. The promise was fulfilled in the reigns of his son, Mūsā al-Hādī, "Moses the Guide" (169–70/785–86), and Hārūn al-Rashīd, "Aaron the Rightly Guided" (170–93/786–809). Hārūn, despite a reign of magnificent display and spectacular liberality, is said to have left his heirs a legacy of over 900,000,000 dirhams, or 48,000,000 dinars, believed, in either case, to be the greatest sum left by an ᶜAbbāsid caliph.[6] It was in this literally golden age that

[6] *Ibid.*, p. 764; H. F. Amedroz and D. S. Margoliouth, *The Eclipse of the Abbasid Caliphate* (7 vols.; Oxford, 1920–21), I, 238; IV, 268; cf. Masᶜūdī, *Tanbīh* (*BGA*, Vol. VIII), p. 342; Thaᶜālibī, *Laṭāʾif al-Maᶜārif*, pp. 71–72; Ibn Khallikān, IV, 353; Suyūṭī, *Taʾrīkh al-Khulafāʾ* (Cairo, 1305/1888), p. 116. See below, pp. 36–37, for the rate of exchange. The sums mentioned vary somewhat.

Mahdī's Khaizurān and Hārūn's Zubaidah held lavish court at Baghdad.

It was not only in matters of finance that Manṣūr prepared the way for his heir. He himself acted as Mahdī's mentor and preceptor and surrounded him with men of administrative ability and strength of character. Among his several parting precepts to his son was the following: "Put not off the work of today until tomorrow; attend in person to the affairs of state; and sleep not (at your post) even as your father has not slept since he came to the caliphate, for, when sleep closed his eyes, his spirit remained awake."[7] Nevertheless, this fond father was not blind to the weak points—serious defects these from the parent's point of view—of his son's character, namely, liberality, sociability, and a fondness for the fair sex. Perhaps he hoped that the type of men he associated with Mahdī would restrain him as caliph. Chief among these were the Barmakid (Barmecide) governor, Yaḥyā ibn Khālid, and Mahdī's secretary, Abū ᶜUbaid Allah ibn Yassār.

Coming on the political scene with the ᶜAbbāsids was the Persian family of Khālid ibn Barmak, destined to play a significant role in the administrative and cultural evolution of the early ᶜAbbāsid Empire. The able and industrious Khālid rose rapidly to power. He and his son Yaḥyā rendered Manṣūr strategic service, the father in the financial administration of the empire and the son with Prince Mahdī in Khurāsān. In Abū ᶜUbaid Allah, Mahdī had a faithful and serious-minded minister who

[7] Ṭabarī, III, 448.

had won Manṣūr's approval and kept an eye on Mahdī's companions and expenditures. In his next wazir, Yaᶜqūb ibn Dāʾūd, Mahdī found not only an able servant but also a congenial spirit who flattered the inclinations of the caliph and succeeded in obtaining for himself the entire administration of state. Mahdī, therefore, threw overboard his father's parting instructions to attend to the affairs of state in person. The blind poet, Bashshār ibn Burd, partly out of personal grievance and partly out of public indignation, wrote a scathing verse that not only denounced the caliph and his wazir but had public and dynastic implications. "O sons of Umayyah," cried this poet, "wake up! Too long have you been asleep. Verily, Yaᶜqūb ibn Dāʾūd is the caliph. O people, your caliphate is ruined! Look for the caliph betwixt the wineskin and the lute."[8]

The early ᶜAbbāsids were patrons of learning and culture according to their light. This light grew progressively powerful until it shone with dazzling brilliance in the reign of Maʾmūn, the last caliph of our story. Keen rivalry existed among the different provinces of the empire for intellectual leadership and recognition. ᶜIrāq, already in the lead in late Umayyad times and now itself the imperial province, yielded place to none. Within her own borders the long-rival cities of Baṣrah and Kūfah proclaimed their superior merits and staged some spectacular contests. But, as all roads soon led to

[8] *Ibid.*, pp. 487–90, 508–10; Ibn ᶜAbdūs al-Jahshiyārī, *Kitāb al-Wuzarāʾ wa al-Kuttāb*, ed. Hans V. Mžik (Leipzig, 1926), pp. 185–86. For variation of verse see Abū Faraj al-Isbahānī, *Kitāb al-Aghānī* (20 vols.; Būlāq, 1285/1868), III, 71; Khaṭīb, VII, 262–63; Ibn Khallikān, IV, 354; *Fakhrī*, pp. 247–50.

the new wonder city of Baghdad, leading ᶜIrāqī scholars and poets, like others, found themselves in the beckoning capital. Some of the most brilliant of intellect became attached to the court of one or more of the early caliphs. The most distinguished scholars were sought after as tutors for the numerous princes in the palace. Once in favor, a poet had an excellent opportunity to acquire a small fortune, especially if he displayed both wit and talent. For, with the exception of Manṣūr, these caliphs of the Golden Age and of our story literally showered the poets with tens of thousands of the coin of the realm for an apt phrase or verse at just the right place and moment.

Royalty's great interest in poetry and poets had a source of motivation over and above personal literary tastes and dynastic cultural patronage. From pre-Islamic times the poets were akin to the soothsayers and prophets in that they were believed to be spirit-inspired. As such they were a powerful element in the generation of emotion as a springboard for public action. The prophet Mohammed, fearing this very power, cast reflection on them, but in time he, too, came to have his own court poets. The poets once again gloried in their privileged position as formers and molders of public opinion. Honest eulogist and dishonest flatterer flourished side by side. The quality of neither the honesty nor the flattery was ever strained, since it blessed both poet and patron, the one with fame and fortune, the other with power and glory. Many a poet, therefore, will be met with in the course of our story.

Music was early frowned upon by the strictly orthodox and soon became a subject for controversy. But while this controversy raged among the theologians, music itself made headway and prospered. Professional musicians were, as a class, under a social and moral stigma. Nevertheless, the sophisticated capitals of province and empire developed a measure of bohemianism among the upper classes who mingled freely with these artists. At the court one finds princes and princesses engaged in the art of poetry and music. Quite a few of these showed remarkable gifts, inherited as frequently as not from their talented mothers—concubines whose readiness with verse or skill of voice and fingers charmed the hearts of caliphs. The Qurʾān expressly forbids intoxicating drinks. But the prophet Mohammed was known to have used some grape and date juices. This proved an entering wedge, for fermented wines passed frequently for simple juices. In the controversies that raged over music and drink, ʿIrāq was partial to wine and the Ḥijāz to song. At the court of Baghdad slave women completed the famous trio.

The social and moral standards which came to prevail at the court of the early ʿAbbāsids are to be understood in the light of certain institutions and the general weakness of human nature which, with luxury and ease, tends on the whole to degeneration. The institutions involved were the trio of polygamy, concubinage, and seclusion of women. The seclusion of the harem affected the free-born Arab woman to a greater extent than it did her captive or slave-born sister. The choicest women, free or slave, were imprisoned behind heavy curtains and locked doors, the strings and keys of which were intrusted into the hands of that pitiable creature—the eunuch. As the size of the harem grew, men indulged to satiety. Satiety within the individual harem meant boredom for the one man and neglect for the many women. Under these conditions, as in like or parallel circumstances in human history, satisfaction by perverse and unnatural means crept into society, particularly into its upper classes.[9] Not that all or even the majority of this high society was personally involved, but there were princes and poets, generals and judges, whose clandestine conduct colored the tone of that society and on occasion, as will be seen later in the story, helped to direct the very course of Islamic history.

Feeding the tastes and vanities of both men and women were the resources and products of the wide empire and beyond. The slave trade, extensive in its ramifications, developed into a thriving industry. Human flesh was sorted, graded, and put on the market. The bulk of the stock was sold at auction at the first opportunity and found its way into domestic service or the crafts. The cream that was separated out was held for the luxury trade and consisted usually of young eunuchs and gifted slave girls, both of whom went through a thorough physical grooming. Those who showed musical talent were sent to the leading musical institutions of the Ḥijāz for long and exacting training. So it happened

[9] For sex morality cf. Jāḥiẓ, *Kitāb al-Ḥayawān* (7 vols.; Cairo, 1323–25/1905–7), I, 48–81; Zamakhsharī, *Rauḍ al-Akhyār al-Muntakhab min Rabīᶜ al-Abrār* (Cairo, 1280/1863), pp. 180–95; Rāghib al-Iṣbahānī, *Kitāb Muḥāḍarāt al-Udabāᵓ wa Muḥāwarāt al-Shuᶜrāᵓ wa al-Bulaghāᵓ* (2 vols.; Cairo, 1287/1870), I, 64, 136; II, 143–64; Nuwairī, *Nihayāt al-Arab fī Funūn al-Adab* (Cairo, 1342——/1923——), II, 198–210.

that a connoisseur of slaves often spent large sums of money on the professional education of his slave boy or slave girl before they were ripe for the lucrative market. Great as was the supply of slaves, the demand for these choice ones was always greater. It is for this item of the slave trade, this polished black or white gem, that caliphs and nobles paid the fabulous sums mentioned in our story.

II

The political and domestic roles of Khaizurān and Zubaidah reflect and continue the development of woman's position in the early Islamic state. Khadījah, Mohammed's first wife, was his staunch supporter who fully shared his confidence. Aishah, his favorite wife, played the major part in the first civil war of Islam. Several of the Umayyad queens had great personal influence on their husbands; others added grace and luster to the court.[10]

There was in latter Umayyad times a current belief that an ᶜAbbāsid born of a Ḥārithite woman would establish an ᶜAbbāsid dynasty. The woman of the "prophecy" was Raiṭah the Ḥārithite. One of her three sons, ᶜAbd Allah the Younger, later became the first ᶜAbbāsid caliph, Saffāḥ. Some accounts make her the mother of a second ᶜAbd Allah whom they identify with the caliph Manṣūr. This is certainly an error, as will be seen presently. Outside the probable dynastic significance of her

[10] Cf. Nabia Abbott, "Women and the State in Early Islam," *Journal of Near Eastern Studies* (formerly *AJSL*), I (1942), 106–26, 341–68; *Aishah, the Beloved of Mohammed* (Chicago, 1942).

tribal connection, Raiṭah the Ḥārithite is little heard of in ᶜAbbāsid records.[11]

Umm Salāmah, the artistocratic Makhzūmite wife of Saffāḥ, fared better than did his mother at the hands of the historians. The story of their marriage is reminiscent of that of the wealthy widow Khadījah to the needy youth Mohammed. Umm Salāmah had outlived two distinguished Umayyad husbands. One day she chanced to see the youthful Abū al-ᶜAbbās and was intrigued by his handsome appearance. She inquired about him and was informed of his genealogy. She then sent him a proposal of marriage through one of her freedwomen. The young man pleaded his poverty. But the rich widow had foreseen that obstacle and had sent with her messenger the funds needed for the wedding. The young man was willing. Umm Salāmah, seated on her bridal couch, her person literally covered with jewels, graciously received her groom and won his favor. He promised her, on oath, never to marry another woman or even to take a concubine. And he kept his promise. During the extremely difficult years that followed, in which the ᶜAbbāsids plotted for the caliphate, he, the future Saffāḥ, took no decisive measure without Umm Salāmah's advice and approval. Their only son died young, but a daughter, Raiṭah, later married her cousin, the caliph Mahdī.[12]

Great as was her stock of jewelry at the time of her

[11] Yaᶜqūbī, *Taʾrīkh* ("Historiae"), ed. Houtsma (2 vols.; Lugduni Batavorum, 1883), II, 369; Ṭabarī, III, 88, 2499; Ibn ᶜAbd Rabbihi, *ᶜIqd al-Farīd* (3 vols.; Cairo, 1293/1876), II, 352; Khaṭīb, I, 63–64; Ibn Khallikān, II, 103, 109.

[12] Masᶜūdī, *Murūj*, VI, 110–12; Ibn ᶜAbdūs, p. 91; Ṭabarī, II, 840; *Aghānī*, IX, 131; but cf. *ᶜIqd*, III, 52.

marriage to Saffāḥ, fate enabled the latter to intrust Umm Salāmah with the rich loot acquired from the fallen Umayyads. His uncle ʿAbd Allah, the governor of Syria, strove to exterminate the fallen Umayyads. He acquired, in the process, great quantities of valuables and jewels, including a special heirloom of the royal harem. This was a sleeveless jacket with a row of large rubies down the front and back. It had belonged to ʿĀtikah, wife of the caliph ʿAbd al-Malik, and was inherited by her niece ʿAbdah, wife of the caliph Hishām. Umm Salāmah must have seen and admired, if not indeed coveted, it. When ʿAbd Allah sent his ill-gotten loot to Saffāḥ, the latter turned it over to Umm Salāmah. She at once missed ʿAbdah's jacket and induced Saffāḥ to write for it. ʿAbd Allah substituted another jacket, which Umm Salāmah recognized as belonging to one of Hishām's concubines. Again ʿAbd Allah was ordered to send ʿAbdah's jacket, and this time he claimed he did not know where it was. Umm Salāmah demanded that ʿAbdah herself be sent to her. The ill-fated ʿAbdah was started on her journey but never reached her destination. Presently Manṣūr succeeded Saffāḥ, grew suspicious of the ambitious ʿAbd Allah, and brought about his downfall. His hoard of wealth and jewels was sent to Manṣūr. And there, among them, was ʿAbdah's jacket. In time the heirloom came into the possession of Manṣūr's favorite granddaughter, Queen Zubaidah, who, as will be seen later, made excellent use of it.[13]

[13] Ṭabarī, III, 51, 90, 102, 126; Ghuzūlī, *Maṭāliʿ al-Budūr fī Manāzil al-Surūr* (2 vols.; Cairo, 1299/1882), II, 139–40.

There were some in Saffāḥ's court who could not appreciate his fidelity and devotion to his wife. Once Khālid ibn Ṣafwān made bold to broach the subject to his royal master. He could not understand why the caliph contented himself with one woman when his vast empire offered so rich a variety. He dwelt on the characteristic charms of more than a dozen types of alluring beauties. Saffāḥ listened to the tempter with avowed pleasure. Khālid departed, fully expecting a royal gift to follow him. Saffāḥ, in the meantime, fell to thinking of Khālid's words. Presently Umm Salāmah entered and immediately sensed something was wrong. Before long Saffāḥ, yielding to her persistent questioning, told her the entire story. So it happened that, instead of the expected gift-bearing messengers of Saffāḥ, a murderous-looking group of men sent by the infuriated Umm Salāmah presented themselves before Khālid's door. He locked himself out of their reach just in time.

Three days later he was summoned once again before Saffāḥ, who asked him to repeat his delightful talk of their previous meeting. Khālid suspected that Umm Salāmah was listening. He proceeded, therefore, to tell an altogether different story, the gist of which was that monogamy was the wisest marriage policy. Hearing laughter from behind the curtains, he added, "I also told you that the Makhzūm are the flower of Quaraish and that you, possessing the flower of flowers (the Makhzūmite Umm Salāmah), need not covet any other woman, free or slave."

"You speak the truth indeed," came Umm Salāmah's approving words from behind the curtain. Saffāḥ's protests availed him nothing. Umm Salāmah now rewarded the "truthful" Khālid with a generous gift.[14]

Saffāḥ, the Shedder of Blood, was himself cut down in the prime of life by the smallpox. To many in high places and in the ᶜAlid opposition his death was a ray of hope for the security of their own lives. To Umm Salāmah, however, his passing-away brought a great sorrow and drove all laughter from her heart.[15]

Manṣūr, elder half-brother to Saffāḥ but born of a Berber slave girl named Sallāmah, succeeded to the throne, with a nephew, also born of a concubine, as second in the line of succession. The ᶜAlids taunted the new caliph with being the son of a concubine. Manṣūr, in his turn, replied with a long list of distinguished sons of concubines, starting with Ishmael, the son of Abraham by Hagar. The ᶜAlids claimed the caliphate on the basis of their descent from Fāṭimah, the daughter of the prophet Mohammed. They found that basis challenged by Manṣūr and his successor on the grounds that a woman can neither inherit nor acquire the supreme power and that, therefore, she cannot transmit it. Such ideas were bound to enhance the prestige of royal concubines. Some of these would naturally intrigue to secure the succession for their offspring. Manṣūr, therefore, helped to confirm ideas and practices already current under the later Umayyads and to make of these an ᶜAbbāsid dynastic

[14] Masᶜūdī, *Murūj*, VI, 112–18; Ibn al-Jauzī, *Kitāb al-Adhkiyā*ᵓ, trans. O, Rescher (Galata, 1925), pp. 168–72; Ibn Ḥijjah (on margins of Rāghib. *Muḥāḍarāt* [Cairo, 1287/1870]), II, 214–44.

[15] *Aghānī*, IX, 131; Ibn al-Jauzī, *Akhbār al-Ẓurraf wa al-Mutāmājinīn* (Damascus, 1347/1928–29), p. 74.

policy. Henceforth the sons of slave mothers were to be no longer taunted with that fact, while a sort of ᶜAbbāsid "Salic Law" functioned in matters of succession.[16]

Nevertheless, Manṣūr was fully aware of the political significance of marriage alliances. His wives represented leading tribes and families. Political considerations prevented him from at least one marriage of inclination. Furthermore, he denounced political marriage alliances among the ᶜAlids and among his own ambitions generals.[17]

The most vivid of Manṣūr's wives was Arwā, better known as Umm Mūsā, whose lineage went back to the kings of Himyar. Their marriage took place before the ᶜAbbāsid conspiracy had progressed enough to bring Manṣūr into prominence. Umm Mūsā demanded, as a condition to her marriage, a written agreement that her suitor would take neither wife nor concubine for as long as she lived. Later, as caliph, Manṣūr regretted his promise and tried repeatedly to have it legally voided. But Umm Mūsā always knew when a judge was being approached for that purpose, and her bribes never failed to reach the magistrate in question. In the end she named the chief justice of Egypt as the only judge to whom she would submit her case. He was, therefore, brought from his distant province to ᶜIrāq to try the case between the royal couple. Umm Mūsā produced her

[16] Masᶜūdī, *Murūj*, VI, 157–58; cf. his *Tanbīh*, p. 540; *Aghānī*, XV, 33; Ṭabarī, III, 87, 209–13.

[17] Ṭabarī, III, 114–15, 175–76, 185, 187–89, 442–43; *ᶜIqd*, III, 53; Balādhurī, *Ansāb*, V (Jerusalem, 1936), 111; Masᶜūdī, *Murūj*, VI, 182, 223–24.

marriage contract as evidence, and the just judge decided the case in her favor.[18]

This determined queen, who insisted on her own contractual rights, showed an unusual interest in woman's welfare. She established an endowment for the benefit of that unfortunate member of the Moslem harem—the concubine whose children were all girls. She herself presented Manṣūr with two sons: Mohammed—the future Mahdī—and Jaᶜfar. They were the only sons Manṣūr ever considered for the succession.[19]

After Umm Mūsā's death, in the tenth year of his reign, Manṣūr was offered a hundred virgins by his sympathetic subjects. His harem, therefore, was large and his sons many. Yet he was not unduly influenced by the women, since he seldom allowed the pleasures of the harem to interfere with his conduct of state affairs.[20]

Manṣūr allowed ᶜAbbāsid women freedom when no adverse political complications were involved. He permitted two princesses to accompany the expedition of 139/756 against the Byzantines. Again the ᶜAbbāsid Princess Asmā helped, in 145/762, to defeat an ᶜAlid rebellion at Medina. Motivated by a personal hatred for the leader, Mohammed, she contrived the unfurling of the ᶜAbbāsid standard from the tall minaret at Medina, where Mohammed and his men awaited Manṣūr's

[18] Jāḥiẓ (pseud.), *Kitāb al-Maḥāsin wa al-Aḍdād*, ed. van Vloten (Leiden, 1898), p. 232; Kindī, *Kitāb al-Wulāh wa Kitāb al-Quḍāh* ("Governors and Judges of Egypt"), ed. Guest (Leiden and London, 1912), pp. 274–76.

[19] Ṭabarī, III, 400, 442, 752; Jāḥiẓ, *Maḥāsin*, p. 232.

[20] Ṭabarī, III, 306, 308, 362–63, 442–43; *ᶜIqd*, III, 53; *Aghānī*, IX, 49, 134; Yaᶜqūbī, II, 468, 471.

forces. The ᶜAlids, therefore, concluded that the ᶜAbbāsids had made an effective entry into the city. Further demoralized by Asmā's well-placed criers of "flight," they deserted Mohammed in large numbers, leaving him to fight a heroic but helpless battle that ended in his martyrdom. Asmā's house and those of a few others were declared points of refuge.[21]

Such indirect service as any woman rendered the state, Manṣūr was, no doubt, glad to accept. He kept his own harem, however, in the background and out of all state affairs. He watched the growth of Mahdī's harem and took note of that prince's weakness for the fair sex. Shouldering his parental responsibility to the last, he included in that now famous set of last instructions to his heir this word of warning: "Beware of taking the women into your counsel and your affairs. But," added this shrewd judge of men, "I think you will take them in."[22]

Such, then, were some of the varied highlights of this Golden Age of the ᶜAbbāsids. Manṣūr the Victor set the stage for high drama at the imperial city of Baghdad. He played the hero's role in Act I and turned the limelight on his son Mahdī, who in turn made way for his heirs, Mūsā al-Hādī and Hārūn al-Rashīd. But sharing the center of the stage, providing both variety and contrast, came, among others of the fair sex, the two most remarkable women of early ᶜAbbāsid times. First in this unfolding drama was Khaizurān, slave-concubine of

[21] Ṭabarī, III, 125, 244–45, 253; Yaᶜqūbī, II, 452–53.

[22] Ṭabarī, III, 444.

Mahdī and mother of his two heirs. Second on the scene was Zubaidah, born to the purple, granddaughter of Manṣūr, royal cousin and consort of Hārūn al-Rashīd, and sharer of his historical and legendary fame.

In the following pages an attempt will be made to tell the stories of these two queens of Baghdad in as far as the historical records have preserved them.

PART I

Khaizurān

I

Mistress of the Harem

MANṢŪR had not neglected Mahdī's private family life. The young prince received his first concubine, Muḥayyāt, when in his early teens; for he himself was born in 126 or 127/744 or 745, and by 142/759–60 Muḥayyāt had already given him a son who died, however, in infancy.[1] Slave girls used to be bought in her name and presented to Mahdī, probably with the idea of evading Manṣūr's attention. The first of these girls to find favor with the youthful prince was Raḥīm, mother of his oldest surviving child, ᶜAbbāsah.[2] Raḥīm herself is little heard of, but her daughter was destined for both great and tragic events in the years to come.[3] The determination of the exact date of her birth hinges

[1] Ṭabarī, *Taʾrīkh* ("Annales"), ed. de Goeje (15 vols.; Lugduni Batavorum, 1879–1901), III, 526; Ibn Shākir al-Kutubī, *Fawāt al-Wafayāt* (2 vols.; Būlāq, 1283/1866), II, 280; Ibn ᶜAbd Rabbihi, *ᶜIqd al-Farīd* (3 vols.; Cairo, 1293/1876), III, 53; Abū al-Faraj al-Isbahānī, *Kitāb al-Aghānī* (20 vols.; Būlāq, 1285/1868 [Vol. XXI (Leiden, 1888)]), IX, 49, makes her Manṣūr's concubine, which must be an error.

[2] Ibn Qutaibah, *Kitāb al-Maᶜārif*, ed. Wüstenfeld (Göttingen, 1850), p. 193; *ᶜIqd*, III, 53.

[3] Cf. below, pp. 195–97.

on knowing the exact date of the birth of her half-brother Mūsā, the future Hādī, who is said to have been a year younger than she.[4] However, the birth dates of neither Mūsā nor his younger and more famous brother Hārūn, the future Rashīd, can be definitely determined at this stage of our knowledge. With this stubborn problem of the birth date of the two princes is linked the question of the date of the first appearance of their mother, Khaizurān, on the historic scene.

When first met with, Khaizurān is the slave girl of a Thaqafite Arab. Her unbounded ambition was perhaps reflected in her dreams. In an age when the art of the interpretation of dreams was much in vogue, she found a ready listener in her master, who became convinced of her royal future. But the physical charms of the young girl, "slender and graceful as a reed," as her name, Khaizurān, implies, must have been an even more convincing argument than her wishful thinking and dreaming. Presently, her master brought her from Jurash in the Yaman to the great slave market at Mecca, where she was purchased by a slave-trader.[5]

She is next seen before the caliph Manṣūr, who is inspecting and questioning her with interest, but neither the place nor the date of that incident is mentioned. If one assumes Mecca to be the place, then the incident can be dated to one of three of Manṣūr's pilgrimages to

[4] Ṭabarī ("Chronique"), Persian recension by Belᶜamī, trans. M. Hermann Zotenberg (4 vols.; Nogent-le-Rotrou, 1874), IV, 464.

[5] Jāḥiẓ (pseud.), *Kitāb al-Maḥāsin wa al-Aḍdād*, ed. van Vloten (Leiden, 1898), pp. 232–33; Abū Bakr al-Khaṭīb, *Taʾrīkh Baghdād* (14 vols.; Cairo and Baghdad, 1931), I, 83; Yāqūt, *Muᶜjam al-Buldān* (*Geog. Diet.*), ed Wüstenfeld (6 vols.; Leipzig, 1924), III, 489.

that city, that is, to the year 140, 144, or 147.[6] Earlier pilgrimages are ruled out by Mahdī's youth and later pilgrimages by other factors, as will be seen presently. Though some give Hādī's birth as of Shawwāl, 144 (January, 762),[7] most of the early historians give his age at his death in Rabīᶜ I of the year 170 (September, 786) as anywhere from twenty-three to twenty-six years.[8] This would throw the year of birth back to 147 and 144, respectively. But inasmuch as the Pilgrimage is in the last month of the year, Manṣūr could not be considering Khaizurān at Mecca in these years themselves if either year is to be considered the birth date of Hādī. Hence the year 140 would be more likely for a Meccan transaction.

But the record is so worded as to leave the impression that Mahdī was along with his father at the time of the purchase of Khaizurān. It does not seem that Mahdī accompanied his father to Mecca in 140. He was at Rayy from 141 to 144 and again from 146 or 147 to 151. He was in the capital and on the northern Mesopotamian frontier sometime in the interval between these two periods.[9] Bits of information gleaned from various

[6] Masᶜūdī, *Murūj*, IX, 64.

[7] This date is arrived at by calculating from date in *ibid.*, VI, 261.

[8] Ṭabarī, III, 579–80; Ibn Athīr, *Al-Kāmil fī al-Taʾrīkh* ("Chronicon"), ed. C. J. Tornberg (14 vols.; Upsaliae at Lugduni Batavorum, 1851–76), VI, 69; Khaṭīb, XIII, 22; cf. also Yaᶜqūbī, *Taʾrīkh* ("Historiae"), ed. Houtsma (2 vols.; Lugduni Batavorum, 1883), II, 461; Ibn Qutaibah, *Maᶜārif*, p. 193; *ᶜIqd*, III, 53.

[9] Ṭabarī, III, 133–34, 143, 364; Hamzah ibn Ḥasan al-Isbahānī, *Taʾrīkh Sinī Mulūk al-Arḍ* ("Annalium"), ed. J. M. E. Gottwaldt (2 vols.; Lipsiae, 1848), I, 220; Ibn Khaldūn, *K. al-ᶜIbar wa Dīwān al-Mubtadaʾ* (7 vols.; Būlāq, 1284/1867), III, 187, has the year 147 instead of 144.

sources and periods throw only a wavering light on the vexed question of the birth date of the princes. Khaizurān is said to have accompanied Mahdī on the way out to Rayy while expecting her firstborn. Hādī and Hārūn are both said to have been born at Rayy and in quick succession.[10] The dates for Hārūn's birth, strange as it may seem, vary all the way from 145 to 150.[11] Hādī and Hārūn could have been born at Rayy in 144 and 145, respectively, if one assumes that Khaizurān entered Mahdī's harem as early as 141, when Mahdī conducted an expedition into Khurāsān.

The other alternative is that Khaizurān was bought in ᶜIrāq between 144 and 146 and that she accompanied Prince Mahdī on his second expedition to Rayy, where her two sons were born in 147 and 148 (or after for Hārūn), respectively. This alternative, though the more probable, is not altogether free from doubts. The late birth date for Hārūn is said to be a fabrication of the Barmakids so as to claim foster-relationship between Hārūn and Faḍl the Barmakid.[12] Again, it makes Hārūn but a youth of fifteen or less at the time of his military exploits of 163/780 on the Byzantine frontier.[13] Furthermore, the later dates raise the question of age seniority in heirship to the throne, leaving unexplained the prefer-

[10] Ibn Abī Usaibīᶜah, *ᶜUyūn al-Anbāʾ fī Ṭabaqāt al-Aṭibbāʾ*, ed. August Müller (2 vols.; Cairo and Königsberg, 1882–84), I, 153, 149.

[11] E.g., Ṭabarī, III, 738; Ibn Athīr, V, 448; VI, 73; Masᶜūdī, VI, 287–88; Ibn ᶜAbdūs al-Jahshiyārī, *Kitāb al-Wuzarāʾ wa al-Kuttāb*, ed. Hans V. Mžik (Leipzig, 1926), p. 155; Ibn Qutaibah, *Maᶜārif*, p. 194; Khaṭīb, XIV, 6.

[12] Ṭabarī, III, 599.

[13] *Ibid.*, pp. 495 ff.; Ibn Athīr, VI, 41–42.

ence of Khaizurān's younger sons over their older half-brothers. On the other hand, if Khaizurān was already in the royal harem as early as 141, then her sons were Mahdī's oldest boys. There would be, therefore, that excuse for placing them ahead of his next sons, even though these were born of his royal cousin and legal wife, Raiṭah.[14]

Mahdī was married to Raiṭah in 144 after his return from Khurāsān.[15] She gave him two sons, ᶜUbaidallah and ᶜAlī, born in 145 and 147, respectively.[16] Though both boys grew to manhood, held important positions, and outlived their father,[17] yet neither of them, despite their mother's royal descent, was ever considered for the caliphate.[18] Nor is Raiṭah ever represented as in active competition with Khaizurān. This is all the more remarkable when it is remembered that Raiṭah was Mahdī's only *wife* until 159, that she had Manṣūr's confidence, and that Mahdī himself was not known to have crossed her or ignored her expressed wishes.[19] This may be an indirect testimony to the paramount influence that Khaizurān early exerted on Mahdī, as it may also point to Raiṭah's tacit recognition of the futility of challenging that influence.

When Manṣūr questioned Khaizurān as to her origin,

[14] Cf. above, p. 11.

[15] Ṭabarī, III, 143; Yaᶜqūbī, II, 450; Masᶜūdī, VI, 112.

[16] Khaṭīb, X, 311; XII, 54.

[17] Ṭabarī, III, 501, 522, 607; Yaᶜqūbī, II, 485; Ibn Qutaibah, *Maᶜārif*, pp. 192–93.

[18] Cf. Mubarrad, *Al-Kāmil*, ed. W. Wright (Leipzig, 1864), pp. 389–90.

[19] *Aghānī*, IX, 127–28; Ṭabarī, III, 550–51; cf. below, p. 51.

she replied, "Born at Mecca and brought up at Jurash (in the Yaman)."

"Have you any relatives?" continued the caliph.

"I have none but Allah; my mother bore none besides me."

The caliph must have been well impressed. "Here, boy!" he called out to one of the youthful attendants, "take her to Mahdī and tell him that she is good for childbearing." Though Manṣūr's keen eye selected the young girl, it was not his purse that paid for her. That privilege was seemingly left for Mahdī himself.[20] Details of Khaizurān's physical charms, beyond that implied in her name, seem to be totally lacking. As to her racial origins, the earliest records are content to leave her as "Khaizurān, a woman of Jurash."[21] Later sources make her a Greek captive from Kharshanah[22] or of Berber origin.[23] There is little reason to credit the Greek origin, as this has risen obviously from a misreading of the Arabic word meaning "a woman of Jurash." The Berber origin, on the other hand, may have some foundation, since Berber slaves were thought to make very pleasant and desirable concubines.[24]

Khaizurān found favor with Mahdī from the start.

[20] Jāḥiẓ, *Maḥāsin*, pp. 232–33; Khaṭīb, XIV, 431; Ibn al-Jauzī, *Kitāb al-Adhkiyāʾ*, ed. O. Reschere (Galata, 1925), p. 321.

[21] E.g., n. 5 above; Ṭabarī, III, 599; Ibn Athīr, VI, 73; Masʿūdī, VI, 261.

[22] Ḥuṣrī, *Zahr al-Adāb wa Thamar al-Albāb* (on margins of *ʿIqd* [Cairo, 1293/1876]), I 222; Yāqūt, II, 423. H. St. John Philby, *Harun al-Rashid* (New York and London, 1934), p. 20, has confused her with Shaklah.

[23] Suyūṭī, *Taʾrīkh al-Khulafāʾ* (Cairo, 1305/1888), p. 109; Dimishqī, *Akhbār al-Duwal* (Oriental Institute MS No. A12041), p. 147.

[24] Cf. *ʿIqd*, III, 283; Aḥmad Amīn, *Ḍuḥā al-Islām* (Cairo, 1933), p. 86.

The eagerness with which she anticipated the birth of her first child and her hopes that it would be a boy are both reflected in the stories that have survived regarding the birth of Mūsā, her firstborn. A personal visit to a doctor for a physical examination to determine pregnancy was, of course, out of the question for a young and favored woman of the royal harem. But Khaizurān found a way to be assured of the advent of the hoped-for child as soon as medical science could detect it. She secretly sent her maid with specimens to the camp doctors and eagerly awaited the results of their verdict. ᶜĪsā, a venturesome apothecary who had attached himself to Mahdī's camp and palace, returned the verdict that the specimen indicated pregnancy and added, for good measure, that the expected child would be a boy. The delighted Khaizurān waited some time to be sure of her condition before she sent ᶜĪsā his first of a series of gifts that were to follow. Ṭaifūr, a freedman of hers, wishing to do his own doctor, ᶜAbd Allah al-Ṭaifūrī, a favor, asked Khaizurān to consult him, too. The honest ᶜAbd Allah confirmed the pregnancy but denied that the sex of the child could be known. Khaizurān took note of his honesty and sent him also a gift. Further, as a grateful offering to God for the expected blessing, she manumitted several slaves. Mahdī's joy, it is said, was greater even than hers. Time passed, and Mūsā arrived, to the great delight of both parents. Khaizurān did not forget her "prophet"-apothecary. She now informed Mahdī of his earlier prediction. ᶜĪsā was called in and questioned and found to be deficient as a physician, as standard tests went. Nevertheless, he was retained for the infant prince; but with him was retained also the honest ᶜAbd Allah.[25]

By now the story of the prediction was known to all the court physicians. The Syrian doctor Jūrjis ibn Jabrāʾīl,[26] one of the ablest of the profession, belittled the prediction and its maker and thereby won Khaizurān's enmity. Soon her second child was on the way, and Jūrjis suggested to Mahdī that ᶜĪsā be put to the test. Again ᶜĪsā predicted a man-child, and again his prediction came to pass with the birth of Hārūn. Hence, Mahdī, too, came to look upon him with favor and addressed him no longer as ᶜĪsā but by the honored title, Abū Quraish, that is, "Father of the Quraish," the noble tribe of the Prophet and of the caliphs themselves. Abū Quraish in time confessed good-naturedly that he had no special prophetic or medical knowledge—that his first prediction was but a casual remark and his second an uneasy chance on a lucky guess.[27] In the meantime he rose to power and wealth. That must have been a trial for the Syrian doctor, who had to accept him as a professional equal and eventually take second place to this favorite of Khaizurān's.[28] Jūrjis' son, Bakhtīshūᶜ, was to inherit this unhappy position in the reign of Mahdī. He found Khaizurān and Abū Quraish too powerful a combination and begged leave to depart from the court at Baghdad to his city of Jundī Sāpūr.[29]

[25] Al-Qifṭī, *Taʾrīkh al-Ḥukamāʾ* (Leipzig, 1903), pp. 430–31; Ibn Abī Usaibiᶜah, I, 149, 153; Abū Faraj, *Mukhtaṣar al-Duwal* (Bierut, 1890), pp. 220–21.

[26] Ibn Abī Usaibiᶜah, I, 123.

[27] Qifṭī, p. 430; Abū Faraj, *Mukhtaṣar al-Duwal*, p. 221.

[28] Ibn Abī Usaibiᶜah, I, 149.

[29] *Ibid.*, p. 126; Qifṭī, p. 101.

It was not until after the birth of her two sons, Mūsā and Hārūn, that Khaizurān informed Mahdī of her family—a mother, two sisters, and at least one brother—who were still at Jurash. It will be remembered that at the time of her purchase she had stated she was her mother's only child. She evidently had wished to make her way unencumbered by family ties. The brother is referred to as Ghiṭrīf ibn ᶜAṭā, and Khaizurān herself is sometimes called the daughter of ᶜAṭā. Ghitrīf, furthermore, claimed descent from the Banū Ḥārith.[30] Whether Manṣūr had anything to say about this new development is not known. Mahdī, however, had the whole family brought to him, presumably to Rayy. Khaizurān not only had kept their existence her secret all these years but had seemingly made no attempt to improve their condition. For when by Mahdī's order the governor of Jurash sent his own men to bring Ghiṭrīf to him, they found him an ill-clad farm hand who had been previously manumitted by his master. Ghiṭrīf, therefore, had to be provided with suitable clothing before he could be sent to Mahdī's court.[31]

Khaizurān's family, transferred so dramatically from poverty and servitude to affluence and royal connections, began to profit steadily and increasingly from that lady's influence and high standing with Mahdī. Though nothing definite is known of the mother's reactions to this happy turn of the wheel of fortune, one can imagine with what pride and satisfaction she looked upon her offspring, now the favorite of the court. Salsal, the older

[30] Yāqūt, *Geog.*, III, 489; Masᶜūdī, VI, 261; cf. Ibn Athīr, VI, 83.

[31] Yaᶜqūbī, II, 481.

of the two girls so recently transplanted, was soon in favor with another of the caliph's sons, Jaᶜfar, half-brother of Mahdī.[32]

To Jaᶜfar and Salsal were born a daughter and a son. The boy was named Ibrāhīm, but the girl's name is variously given as Sukainah[33] or Amat al-ᶜAzīz, this last meaning "Handmaid of the Almighty." She was soon a favorite with her grandfather, Manṣūr, who, on account of her freshness and plumpness, gave her the pet name Zubaidah, or "Little Butter Ball,"[34] by which name she was destined to become famous as the queen of her royal cousin, "the good Hārūn al-Rashīd." The date of her birth, like that of Mūsā and Hārūn, is not known, except for the fact that she was at least a year or so younger than Hārūn. In 145/763–64, Manṣūr dispatched her father, Jaᶜfar, and the general Ḥarb ibn ᶜAbd Allah to Mauṣil. Here the general built a new palace, in which, it is stated, Zubaidah was born. Ḥarb died in 147, and it is not likely that Jaᶜfar occupied this palace before Ḥarb's death.[35] At any rate, Zubaidah's birth cannot be placed in 145, since the earliest date for Hārūn's birth is the last month of that same year.[36] The records are

[32] Jāḥiẓ, *Maḥāsin*, p. 233; cf. Ibn Qutaibah, *Maᶜārif*, p. 192, where the girl's name is given as Salsabīl.

[33] Jāḥiẓ, *Maḥāsin*, p. 233.

[34] Cf. Ibn Khallikān, *Kitāb Wafayāt al-Aᶜyān* ("Biographical Dictionary"), trans. W. M. de Slane (4 vols.; Paris, 1843–71), I, 533.

[35] Ibn Athīr, V, 437; for Ḥarb cf. Yāqūt, *Geog.*, II, 234; Ibn Taghrībirdī, *Nujūm al-Zāhirah* ("Annals"), ed. W. Popper (Berkeley, Calif., 1909——), I, 397.

[36] Horovitz, in *Encyclopaedia of Islam*, IV, 1235, gives A.H. 145 as the date of her birth. This is obviously a misinterpretation of Ibn Athīr, V, 437.

strangely silent on the activities of her mother, Salsal, who lived to see her daughter as queen-consort and queen-mother, outlived her sister Khaizurān, and witnessed the tragedy of her grandson Amīn some half a century later.[37]

Khaizurān's younger sister, Asmā, grew up at court unattached until the year 159, when she captured Mahdī's heart for a brief period, as will be seen presently, and then disappeared again from the records. Ghiṭrīf, it appears, coveted the governorship of the Yaman and achieved it later under peculiar circumstances.[38] These years, it will be remembered, saw the building of Baghdad and of Ruṣāfah across the river, where Mahdī took his residence after his triumphal return from Khurāsān in 151/768. Casual references to places in the new capital, suburb, and surroundings would seem to indicate that both Khaizurān and her brother had estates assigned them in these regions.[39] Manṣūr's presence probably restrained Khaizurān's ambitions for her family. Be that as it may, Ghiṭrīf and his family came more to the fore in the reigns of Mahdī and Hādī and especially in the reign of Hārūn, when Khaizurān herself was at the height of her power.

Khaizurān bore Mahdī a third son named ʿĪsā, of whom, however, very little is known beyond the implied fact that he was dear to his father and that the

[37] See below, p. 218.

[38] Khaṭīb, I, 83; cf. below, pp. 88–89.

[39] E.g., Khaṭīb, I, 83, 125–26; Guy Le Strange, *Baghdad during the Abbasid Caliphate* (Oxford, 1900), pp. 130, 191–93.

garden town of ᶜĪsabādh in the suburb outside eastern Baghdad was named after him.[40]

Just as Khaizurān's sons were the most favored by their father, so also was her only daughter, named Bānūqah or Bānūjah, that is, "Little Lady." The date of her birth is not known. But as she is reported to have died young, and that before the death of the poet Bashshār ibn Burd in 166/782–83, who was among those who consoled Mahdī on his loss,[41] her birth must be placed about the last half of the preceding decade. She was a pretty brunette of fine stature who seems to have had her way with both parents; for, young though she was, she had her own palace, and, girl though she was, her father took her with him on his trips. To escape scandalous tongues, she traveled in disguise, belted and turbaned as a page and girt with a sword. This, however, did not deceive the keen observers of Baṣrah who saw her one day riding in style between the caliph and his captain of the guard and took note of her budding figure.[42]

Mahdī grieved over the death of "Little Lady" to an unheard-of extent. In a land where girls came into this world for the most part unwelcomed and departed al-

[40] Yāqūt, *Geog.*, III, 752; Balādhurī, *Futūḥ al-Buldān*, ed. de Goeje (Lugduni Batavorum, 1886), p. 296; *ᶜIqd*, II, 229; cf. Le Strange, *op. eit.*, p. 194.

[41] Khaṭīb, VII, 118; *Aghānī*, III, 72; Ibn Khallikān, I, 255. Since Bashshār died *before* the fall of the wazir Yaᶜqūb ibn Dāʾūd, which, according to Ṭabarī, III, 506, took place in 166, this last date is to be preferred to 167 or 168 in considering the death of either the girl or the poet.

[42] Khaṭīb, VII, 118; Ṭabarī, III, 543–44; Ibn Athīr, VI, 58 (where the name is misread as "Yāqūtah"); Ibn Qutaibah, *Maᶜārif*, p. 193; *ᶜIqd*, III, 53; Le Strange, *op. cit.*, pp. 226–27. The name is obviously a corruption of the Persian *banu-cha*, that is, "Little Lady," or "Little Princess."

most unmourned, Madhī, the devoted and bereaved father, appeared publicly to receive the condolence of the people. The public came in great numbers to comfort their sovereign, while poets and scholars vied, one with the other, for appropriate and eloquent expression of sympathy.[43] The young princess was the first of the ᶜAbbāsids to be buried in the eastern cemetery north of Ruṣāfah, where later her mother was to join her and lend her name to the place, which came to be known as the Khaizurān Cemetery.[44]

Among other concubines whom Prince Mahdī acquired comparatively early in life was al-Baḥtarīyah, noble-born daughter of the Persian rebel against whom Mahdī was first sent to Khurāsān. The defeated rebel, realizing all was lost, sucked the poison in his ring and died a suicide. His harem and the harems of others of his followers were captured and the inmates distributed as slaves to the victors. Al-Baḥtarīyah and a child Negress named Shaklah were then acquired by the prince. The former found favor with the conqueror of her father, for she bore him a son named for his grandfather, Manṣūr, and two daughters, Sulaimah and ᶜĀliyah. Nothing more is known of Sulaimah, but the other two will be met with again.[45]

Mahdī presented the child Shaklah to his concubine Muḥayyāt, who, discovering a musical talent in the

[43] Ṭabarī, III, 544; for others' efforts cf. *Aghānī*, XXI, 120; Jāḥiẓ, *Kitāb al-Bayān wa al-Tabyīn* (Cairo, 1313/1895–96), II, 36.

[44] Khaṭīb, I, 125; *ibid.*, trans. Georges Salmon (Paris, 1904), p. 173; Ibn Khallikān, II, 678; Le Strange, *op. cit.*, p. 191.

[45] Ṭabarī, III, 137, 140; Ibn Qutaibah, *Maᶜārif*, p. 193; cf. below, pp. 36 and 157.

child, sent her to the famous school of Ṭāʾif in the Ḥijāz for a thorough musical education. Years later Mahdī, then caliph, chanced to see the now grown-up and accomplished maid in Muḥayyāt's quarters and took a fancy to her, whereupon Muḥayyāt graciously presented her to him. She gave Mahdī his powerful and dark-skinned son Ibrāhīm (162–224/779–839), who inherited his mother's musical talents and who, as poet, scholar, musician, and countercaliph, will figure repeatedly in this story.[46]

Khaizurān's harem worries do not seem to have arisen in connection with any of these earlier copartners with her in Mahdī's affection, including even the royal wife Raiṭah, as already seen. Her real source of danger was the ever present singing girl, for Mahdī was an enthusiastic patron of music and musicians. Himself gifted with a fine voice,[47] he soon drew to his court the best musical talents of the empire and inaugurated, alas for the shades of Manṣūr and the spirits of the pietists, the Golden Age of Arabian music. To his court came Ibrāhīm al-Mauṣilī, a Persian domiciled in Mauṣil. He was destined, by reason of his musical and social talents, to become in time Hārūn's boon companion par excellence and sharer, like Zubaidah, of his legendary *Arabian Nights'* fame. His professional fame was to be eclipsed only by that of his son, Isḥāq (150–235/767–

[46] Ṭabarī, III, 140, 917; Ibn Khallikān, I, 16–20. *Aghānī*, IX, 48–49, speaks of Muḥayyāt as Manṣūr's concubine, but cf. *ʿIqd*, III, 53.

[47] Ibn Khallikān, III, 464.

850), considered, for all time, the greatest of Islamic musicians.[48]

But Mahdī's early patronage of the art of music was not altogether free from the effects of the social stigma that was attached to the musicians, nor yet was it totally free from the conviction that music, or at least certain types of music, excited a pernicious influence on man, particularly on the young. So Mahdī the gifted, while he himself enjoyed others' musical talents, frowned on the practice of the art by noble Arabs and royal Hāshimites and absolutely forbade the gifted Ibrahīm, Ibn Jāmi^c^, and others to sing before his sons and heirs, Mūsā and Hārūn. When these artists knew no better than to disregard the injunction, trusting no doubt to secrecy, they were flogged for their folly. Ibrāhīm, in particular, received an unmerciful thrashing, was imprisoned, and was banished for a time, though others continued to entertain the court.[49]

No more charming and, therefore, no more dangerous entertainers were to be found anywhere than the glamorously beautiful, richly gifted, and highly accomplished singing girls of the court—the best of their kind throughout the far-flung empire. Mahdī, generous and warmhearted by nature, except where pride and faith were involved, bestowed rich gifts and warm affections on his singing girls. These came to him either as the par-

[48] *Aghānī*, V, 2–48, and Index; Khaṭīb, VI, 175–78; Ibn Khallikān, I, 20–22; III, 464; cf. H. G. Farmer, *A History of Arabian Music* (London, 1929), pp. 93, 100 ff., esp. pp. 116–17 and 124–26.

[49] *Aghānī*, V, 5–6; VI, 74.

ticularly choice offerings of his obliging or scheming courtiers or through the services of a shrewd slave connoisseur. Khaizurān, occupying the proud position of recognized favorite, must, on occasion, have had her fears of a probable fall. More than one tale is told of how now one, now another, charmer climbed for a while to the same proud station but was never the equal of Khaizurān in occupying it alone.

Among the earlier of these charmers was the songstress Maknūnah, who took pride in her slender hips and high chest. Mahdī, while yet prince, bought her for the high figure of 100,000 silver dirhams and kept the transaction secret from his stern and thrifty father. She found such favor with the prince that Khaizurān used to say, "No other woman of his made my position so difficult." She gave Mahdī his daughter ᶜUlaiyah (160–210/776–826, not to be confused with her older half-sister, ᶜĀliyah), who inherited her parents' musical talents along with a flair for a gay and exciting court life, of which more will be told later.[50]

Madhī bought, about the same period, yet another brilliant songstress trained at Medina and much sung by the poets. This was Baṣbaṣ ("Caress"), for whom he is said to have paid no less a price than 17,000 gold dinars (some 120,000 silver dirhams). She is sometimes mentioned, but seemingly erroneously, as the mother of ᶜUlaiyah, unless one is to assume there were two daughters of Mahdī so named.[51]

[50] *Ibid.*, III, 83–95; XIII, 114–15 (where the confusion with Baṣbaṣ is referred to); Farmer, *op. cit.*, p. 119. Cf. below, pp. 154–56 and 206.

[51] Some of the stories told of ᶜUlaiyah are irreconcilable as to the dates and even the character of the girl; the assumption, therefore, may prove a

Two more songstresses joined Mahdī's harem, Ḥullah and Ḥasanah, both of whom are described as beautiful and expert at their profession. Ḥasanah was, like Maknūnah, to give Khaizurān some uneasy moments. She and Khaizurān are sometimes grouped together as the most favored of Mahdī, who on occasion was torn between his affections for both of them.[52] Mahdī shows this same tendency to be swayed by two loves on yet another occasion involving a second pair of concubines, Ḥasnā and Malkah. Ḥasnā entered the room *first* but was soon followed by Malkah. Mahdī called on the girls themselves to decide with which one of them he was to spend the afternoon's siesta. Ḥasnā replied with this Qur᾽ānic verse: "Those who go before, they are those brought near." And Malkah, not to be outdone, offered: "The last is for thee better than the first."[53] The record loses interest in Mahdī's dilemma and goes on instead to cite the poets on the theme of being torn between two loves.[54] Whether the Ḥasnā of this pair is confused with Ḥasanah of the Khaizurān episode cannot be determined with certainty. It is probable that Ḥasanah entered Mahdī's life comparatively late. She outlived

---

fact (see preceding note and Farmer, *op. cit.*, p. 132). A gold dinar in Manṣūr's time equaled seven silver dirhams (Qālī, *Kitāb al-Amālī* [Būlāq, 1324/1906], III [*Dhail*], 41). The ratio fluctuated, generally increasing, so that in Ma᾽mūn's time a dinar equaled fifteen dirhams (Zaidan, *Ta᾽rīkh al-Tamaddun al-Islāmī* [5 vols.; Cairo, 1922], II, 53, 57).

[52] *ʿIqd*, III, 53; Ḥuṣrī, III, 226–27; Rāghib al-Iṣbahānī, *Kitāb Muḥāḍarāt al-Udabā᾽ wa Muḥāwarāt al-Shuʿrā᾽ wa al-Bulaghā᾽* (2 vols.; Cairo, 1287/1870), II, 39.

[53] Sūrahs 56:10 and 93:4.

[54] Rāghib, *Muḥāḍarāt*, II, 29.

Mahdī, in whose death, according to some versions, she was unintentionally but tragically involved.[55]

Raiṭah, as already stated, was Mahdī's only legal wife until he became caliph. Soon after that event he proceeded to take his full quota of four legal wives. His intentions seem to have been to liberate Khaizurān and make her his second legal wife, a position that would be more in keeping with his plans for the succession. For Mahdī was taking steps, soon after his accession, to secure the succession for Khaizurān's two sons, Mūsā and Hārūn.[56] The early annals relate under the year 159/775–76 the brief and factual statement that in this year Mahdī manumitted Khaizurān and married her.[57] More gossipy sources recording anecdotes for entertainment, and frequently touching them up for the effect desired, tell quite a tale in connection with this important event in Khaizurān's private life and royal career. Mahdī, this story goes, sent Khaizurān on the pilgrimage, promising to marry her on her return. While she was gone, he formed a sudden attachment for her younger sister, Asmā, whom he married, settling on her a marriage portion of one million dirhams. The news, of course, reached Khaizurān. When Mahdī realized that Khaizurān was on her way back, he went out to meet her. "What is this affair of Asmā?" she demanded. "And how much did you settle on her?"

"Who is Asmā?" asked the pretending Mahdī.

"Your wife," insisted Khaizurān.

55 Cf. below, pp. 74–76.

56 Ṭabarī, III, 467–68; Ibn Athīr, VI, 28–29.

57 See previous note and ᶜ*Iqd*, III, 53.

"If Asmā was my wife, she is now divorced," said Mahdī.

"You divorced her, then, when you heard of my return."

"Since you know (it all), well, then, I gave her a marriage portion of one million and made her a gift of a second million."

Then, adds the narrator, Mahdī married Khaizurān.[58]

Since in Islamic law a man may not have two sisters as co-wives, Mahdī's original intentions toward Asmā must have had their reservations.

That same year Mahdī contracted yet another marriage, this time with a noble Arab woman, Umm ᶜAbdallah.[59] The next year he rounded out his quota of four legal wives by his marriage to the ᶜUthmānid Ruqaiyah.[60] The records have little to say of these two wives, whose marriages were, in all probability, convenient political alliances. Raiṭah as the senior wife and Khaizurān as the favorite wife continue to be the two most important figures in Mahdī's harem.

Two stories, separated by more than ten years, have been handed down about Raiṭah. The first dates to the last year of Manṣūr's reign and would seem to indicate that Manṣūr considered Raiṭah a trustworthy and stouthearted woman. For, before he started on his last and fateful pilgrimage, he intrusted her with the keys to the royal treasury. He gave her specific instructions that a certain room was to be opened, in the event of his

[58] Jāḥiẓ (pseud.), *Maḥāsin*, p. 233.

[59] Ṭabarī, III, 466; Ibn Athīr, VI, 27.

[60] Ṭabarī, III, 483; Ibn Athīr, VI, 72.

death, by her and Mahdī alone. When after Manṣūr's death these two did open the room in question, they discovered a vault containing the grim remains of a large group of ᶜAlid victims of ᶜAbbāsid persecution and treachery. Raiṭah's reaction is not recorded, but Mahdī was very much shocked by the sight. He ordered a large pit to be dug to serve as a common grave.[61]

The second incident also has its grim aspects. By the end of his reign Mahdī was quite active in the persecution of heretics. Among his victims were a noble Hāshimite and his harem. There were two daughters and a wife who were imprisoned and later brought for questioning, either before Mahdī or before Hādī. They were then intrusted to Raiṭah, who denounced them for their evil ways (alleged heresy and incest) and sent them out of her presence with a pious curse. The wife and older daughter were later tortured to death.[62]

That Khaizurān was able to hold her own and come out of various critical harem situations always the victor, despite the steady competition of the ever present songstress and the noble Arab woman, argues for qualities over and above physical appeal and charm. That she had a nimble and witty brain may be gathered from her general career. What education, if any, her former master had given her, she probably put to good use. It is more likely that she was, by and large, self-educated. The city of Mecca offered opportunities,

[61] Ṭabarī, III, 445–46. Theodor Nöldeke, *Sketches from Eastern History*, trans. John Southerland (London, 1892), p. 123, cannot bring himself to believe this gruesome story; but cf. Zaidan, *Taʾrīkh al-Tamaddun al-Islāmī*, IV, 89–91; and below, p. 219.

[62] Ṭabarī, III, 449–51; Ibn Athīr, VI, 60.

even for a slave girl, to sit at the feet of some of the day's most learned or prominent theologians. Once in the palace, there was plenty of leisure to improve one's mind, if one had a mind to do so. Many were the opportunities to familiarize one's self with poetry and the literature of the day. In Khaizurān's particular case, she came to acquire a reputation for learning and literary talents. She is said, for instance, to have learned Tradition from Awzāʿī (d. 157/744), a noncompromising theologian.[63] However, she is associated with but two traditions. The one has specific bearing on the political situation at the time of Hārūn's accession and will be referred to later. The other was a harmless enough one that she learned from Mahdī himself: "He who fears Allah, Allah will watch over him in all things."[64]

Evidence of her literary talent is just as scanty. So far, but one very ordinary verse has been attributed to her in two versions and on different occasions. According to the earlier of the two versions, Khaizurān sent a virgin maid bearing a cup inscribed with a verse by her as a gift to her son Hārūn al-Rashīd, who was just recovering from some indisposition.[65] The sentiment of the verse is: "Get well soon and enjoy drinking out of the cup." The second and later version is a different story. It is Mahdī who has been indisposed. Khaizurān sends him a crystal cup with a drink of her own choosing

[63] Ṭabarī, III, 579; Ibn Athīr, VI, 67; for Al-Awzāʿī cf. Ṭabarī, III, 2514, 2519; Khaṭīb, VIII, 227; IX, 158–59; Nawawī, *Kitāb Tahdhīb al Asmā* ("Biographical Dictionary"), ed. Wüstenfeld (Göttingen, 1842–47), pp. 382–84; Ibn Khallikān, II, 84.

[64] Khaṭīb, XIV, 430–32, is the brief entry given to Khaizurān.

[65] Rāghib, *Muḥāḍarāt,* I, 261.

by the hand of a virgin maid of exceeding beauty. The verse on the cup starts out with the same line as in the first version but ends: "When you have recovered your health and have improved it further by this drink from this cup, then be gracious to her who sent it, by paying her a visit after sunset." Mahdī, runs this account, was so delighted with gift and poem that he called on his lady and spent two whole days in her company.[66]

Granted either or both versions, this verse is still very slim evidence of any poetic talent. Others of Mahdī's concubines were ready with song and poem as the occasion demanded. Poetry was on everyone's tongue. Khaizurān, in all probability, was more adept at quoting than at composing verses. Mahdī, on the other hand, was adept at both, to judge by a number of his verses, some of which were addressed to Khaizurān herself. While he was away at a pleasure resort, Mahdī longed for his favorite's company, and so he wrote her an elegant verse that started, "We are in great joy, but no joy is complete without you," and ended, "Then hasten, nay, if you are able, fly, to us with the zephyr."[67]

There are sufficient indications that Khaizurān's pronounced gifts were in fields other than those of learning and literature. They lay rather in the realm of personality and character, not that her gifts along these lines were unique, single or in combination, but that they fitted well at most points into the pattern of Mahdī's

[66] Al-Ibshīhī, *Al-Mustaṭraf* (2 vols. in 1; Cairo, 1305/1890), II, 49.

[67] *Fawāt al-Wafayāt*, II, 281; cf. Jāḥiẓ, *Al-Bayān wa al-Tabyīn* (3 vols. in 1; Cairo, 132/1914), III, 185–86; *Aghānī*, XII, 99; XXI, 133.

own personality and character.[68] Both were amiable and both enjoyed gay and lavish court life. What is even more to the point, they both enjoyed the same brand of wit and humor. To these add the facts of Khaizurān's ambition, tact, and mettle, on the one hand, and Mahdī's easygoing, pleasure-loving temperament, on the other, and presently it begins to be understood how Khaizurān retained her position of favorite and came to exercise so great an influence on Mahdī and, through him, on the empire.

A story is told which seems to illustrate how this former slave girl, favorite concubine, and now first queen of Mahdī's court learned at first the art of courtly etiquette and came in time to exercise, not without tact, the undisputed role of leadership in the royal harem. The senior ᶜAbbāsid princess, Zainab bint Sulaimān, was a woman highly esteemed by all her numerous royal cousins. She had witnessed the growth of the ᶜAbbāsid movement and the foundation of that dynasty. Mahdī had early instructed his favorite Khaizurān to fashion her conduct and deportment after the pattern of this leading and honored princess. Khaizurān must have made an apt and willing pupil. The relationship of the two women, therefore, seems to have been more than cordial, for when Khaizurān, as queen, held a salon for the royal princesses, the place of honor was always reserved for the Lady Zainab.

On one such occasion Khaizurān was informed that a beautiful woman dressed in shabby clothes sought audience with her. The woman was admitted to the

[68] For which cf. Jāḥiẓ, *Kitāb al-Tāj* (Cairo, 1914), pp. 84–85.

royal gathering and questioned as to her identity. She revealed that she was Muznah, a widow (daughter, according to some) of the ill-fated Umayyad caliph, Marwān II. Poor and destitute, she had come to claim protection "until Allah saw fit to do what he pleased." Her story and condition touched the heart of Khaizurān, whose eyes filled with sympathetic tears. But Zainab, recollecting past events in which she had petitioned the then fortunate Muznah in vain, now hardened her own heart. "May Allah not lighten your burden, O Muznah! Do you not remember when I came to you at Ḥarrān requesting the body of Ibrāhīm the Imām, when you upbraided me and gave orders that I be turned out saying, 'What have the women to do with mixing in the affairs of the men?' " Zainab's reaction can be better understood when it is recalled that Ibrāhīm, who had been murdered at Ḥarrān, was the acknowledged leader of the ʿAbbāsids and the father-in-law of Zainab herself.[69] Muznah now humbly confessed that she believed that Allah was indeed punishing her for that very misdeed, adding, "But you (Zainab) seem to favor it, since you are urging the Lady (Khaizurān) to imitate it when you should be encouraging her to do good and to refrain from returning evil for evil." Muznah departed in tears. But Khaizurān, touched as she was, did not wish to oppose Zainab openly. She therefore signaled to some of her maidens to lead Muznah secretly to her own apartments, where later she provided for her comfort.

That evening Mahdī dined with Khaizurān. She related the episode to him and won his spontaneous and

[69] Cf. Ṭabarī, III, 2520.

enthusiastic approval of her part in it. Mahdī, at the same time, condemned Zainab for the uncharitable stand she had taken. He went a step further. He saw to it that Zainab and Muznah met once again at a gathering of the princesses when the place of honor was accorded to the latter. Mahdī himself engaged Muznah in conversation on past events, at which she so excelled that presently no one else in that royal assembly dared venture a word. The caliph, much impressed and amazed, exclaimed, "O cousin, were it not that I do not wish to associate the people to which you belong with our affairs, I would indeed marry you!" She was then invited to remain at his court and was acccorded the rank and allowance of a royal princess, which she enjoyed until her death early in the reign of Hārūn al-Rashīd.[70]

Another anecdote illustrates Khaizurān's imperious and fiery temper that might have gotten her into serious trouble with anyone other than Mahdī. The story, here summarized, is told by the historian Wāqidī, who frequented Mahdī's court:

> I went one day to Mahdī, who called for his inkwell and notebook and wrote down some of the things I related to him. Presently he rose to leave but told me to wait until his return. He went to the harem but soon returned full of rage. I asked him the cause of this sudden change, and he said that he went to Khaizurān, who flew at him and even tore his clothes, exclaiming, "O you picker of left-overs! What good have I ever received at your hands?"
>
> "And it was I" (continued the roused Mahdī) "who bought her from a slave-trader, and she has seen from me what she has seen (of great benefit and favor), and I have made her two sons heirs to my throne! Am I, then, a picker of left-overs?"

[70] Masʿūdī, VI, 234–40; for a later and obviously much-distorted version of this story see Ibn Ḥijjah, *Thamarāt al-Awrāq*, I, 248–51.

Wāqidī tried to calm his caliph by citing various traditions bearing on the general weakness and perversity of woman's nature. He ended up with the classic Moslem verdict on the weaker sex by quoting a tradition linked with the biblical story of the creation of Eve and attributed to Mohammed himself: "Woman is like the rib (out of which she was created). If you straighten her, you break her; if you enjoy her, you do so accepting her crookedness."[71] Mahdī was easily calmed, and he rewarded his counselor with two thousand dinars.

When Wāqidī returned home, he found a servant of Khaizurān's who gave him this message from her: "I heard all that you said to the Commander of the Believers. May Allah reward you." Accompanying the message was a gift of gratitude of some suits of clothes and a cash sum that was just ten dinars short of what Mahdī had given him, "because she liked not to match the king's gift."[72]

Court jesters and court poets are quick to sense harmony or discord among their patrons. A trick played on Mahdī and his Khaizurān by the Negro court jester and poet, Abū Dulāmah,[73] is eloquent testimony to the harmony, based on a similar vein of humor, that existed between the royal couple. Numerous anecdotes are told of Abū Dulāmah and Mahdī, and on almost every oc-

[71] Bukhārī, *Ṣaḥīḥ*, ed. Krehl (4 vols.; Leiden, 1862–1908), III, 440; cf. Thaʿlabī, *Qiṣaṣ al-Anbiyāʾ* (Cairo, 1314/1897), p. 17.

[72] Khaṭīb, XIV, 431; Gabriel Audisio, *Harun al-Rashid* (New York, 1931), pp. 25–26, relates another incident, perhaps only a later and more embellished version of this story itself.

[73] *Aghānī*, IX, 120–40; Khaṭīb, I, 87; VIII, 488–93; Ibn Khallikān, I, 543–39; Aḥmad Farīd Rifāʿī, *ʿAṣr al-Maʾmūn* (Cairo, 1927), II, 300 ff.

casion the jester comes out the richer for his buffoonery.[74] The practical joke that this jester, with the aid of his wife, Umm Dulāmah, played on the royal pair took the following form. Abū Dulāmah went sorrowful and weeping before Mahdī and informed him that Umm Dulāmah was dead and that he had not the wherewithal to outfit and bury her. Mahdī was touched and made him a generous gift of clothes, ointments, and money. In the meantime Umm Dulāmah, far from being dead, was herself bewailing the death of Abū Dulāmah to Khaizurān, who, no less touched than Mahdī, gave her also a generous gift. When later Mahdī and Khaizurān were together, each told the story as they believed it and soon realized that it was another of Abū Dulāmah's tricks which, nevertheless, they enjoyed heartily.[75] Abū Dulāmah, on another occasion, made one and the same request from both Raiṭah and Khaizurān, namely, that they give him one of their slave girls to amuse him, since he was through with the old hag who was his wife. The royal ladies, who were at the time on a pilgrimage, promised to grant his request, but either forgot or delayed the gift on their return. He, therefore, addressed an identical verse to each by way of a reminder and presently received his girls.[76]

Several of the first-class poets of Mahdī's court contributed quite a bit of amusement for Mahdī's harem.

[74] E.g., *Aghānī*, VIII, 107; IX, 133–34; Ibn al-Jauzī, *Akhbār al-Ẓurraf*, pp. 73–74; Ibn Ḥijjah, II, 227–28, 235–36.

[75] *Aghānī*, IX, 131; Rāghib, *Muḥāḍarāt*, I, 339–40. This story appears in the *Arabian Nights*, with much embellishment, as a joke played on Hārūn and Zubaidah.

[76] *Aghānī*, IX, 134–35, 137–38.

There was Bashshār ibn Burd, able poet and original critic, whose love lyrics were eagerly sought by the ladies. Blind from birth or childhood, he had ready access to the harem, at its inmates' specific request. But his indiscreet expressions eventually caused Mahdī to forbid his visits, as he had already forbidden his composing any more love lyrics.[77] To this offense Bashshār added yet another. Indignant at the studied neglect he experienced at the hands of Mahdī through the instigation of his wazir, Yaᶜqūb ibn Dāʾūd, he satirized both in a scathing verse already referred to in this study.[78] Yaᶜqūb, it is believed, forged in the poet's name an even more offensive verse that cast reflections on Mahdī's sporty and immoral life and ended with "May Allah give us another in his stead and thrust Mūsā back into the womb of Khaizurān."[79] Mahdī's wrath can well be imagined. The poet was accused of heresy and condemned to death by flogging.[80]

If the blind Bashshār lost his head because it was too full of love lyrics and politics, another great poet, Abū al-ᶜAtāhiyah, was to keep his on his shoulders under six capricious and exacting caliphs. Though he, too, was open to accusations of heresy, his ready tongue saved his life on dangerous occasions. Greatly gifted, with poetry his natural speech, he used his panegyrics to good purpose. His happy eloquence was the despair of envious poets, themselves in the first ranks of their profession; while his biting satire drove lesser lights and

[77] *Ibid.*, III, 41, 55, 65; Ḥuṣrī, II, 18, 26.

[78] See above, p. 6.

[79] Ṭabarī, III, 538; Ibn Khallikān, I, 256.

[80] Cf. above, p. 32.

fainter hearts to seek refuge in flight from the capital.[81] His name and fame endure not only because he was the poet of half-a-dozen caliphs but because he wrote, on the one hand, stern ascetic verse and, on the other, bold, passionate lyrics addressed to ᶜUtbah, a slave girl in Mahdī's harem.

ᶜUtbah and a slave companion, Khāliṣah, must have been very young when they came into possession of Umm Salāmah, wife of Saffāḥ. From her they passed on to her daughter Raiṭah, wife of Mahdī. They became women of influence in the domestic affairs of the palace, in the service of both Raiṭah and Khaizurān, and after them in that of Zubaidah.[82] The fair ᶜUtbah seems to have found personal favor with Mahdī himself.[83]

Abū al-ᶜAtāhiyah later related to his son and friends how his affair with ᶜUtbah got its start. The story—and a good one it is—runs something like this. The young poet with two other youthful companions and litterateurs left Kūfah to seek fame and fortune at the capital city of Baghdad. Being total strangers in the teeming city, they hired a room near a city bridge and its mosque and loitered around in the hope of making some worthwhile connections. Days passed and nothing happened. With the foolhardy daring of ambitious and spontaneous youth, they conceived the idea of addressing love verses to these two inmates of Mahdī's harem, who were

[81] Khaṭīb, XIII, 388–89; Ibn Khallikān, I, 395; *Aghānī*, XVI, 148; for biographies cf. *Aghānī*, III, 126–83; *Khatīb*, VI, 250–60; Ibn Khallikān, I, 202–10; Rifāᶜī, II, 261–73.

[82] Mubarrad, *Kāmil*, pp. 55, 737; Masᶜūdī, VI, 248.

[83] Ibn Qutaibah, *Kitāb al-Shiᶜr wa al-Shuᶜarā᾿* (Leiden, 1902), p. 498.

accustomed to going to the bazaars accompanied by a number of servants on shopping trips for the palace. So said one of the youths, "Hereafter, I am in love with Khāliṣah," and Abū al-ᶜAtāhiyah joined in with, "And I am in love with ᶜUtbah." Then they composed verse after verse addressed to the maids, and each managed to send or bring his production to his "beloved" who, on occasion, accepted the verse and, on others, turned the youths away. But youths like these do not give up easily.

The affair, started so cavalierly and with such ulterior motives, developed into a major passion with the poet, without, however, striking a responsive cord in ᶜUtbah's cold heart. It achieved, nevertheless, its initial purpose. For this poet made no secret of his love or verses, much to the continual annoyance of ᶜUtbah herself. The following translation quoted in part, though too free with the letter of the verse, does, nevertheless, catch some of the spirit of one of the poems:

I wrote to ᶜUtbah and said Oh Love! think,
And assuredly know that on the brink
Of Jehennam I stand, trembling and lone,
And all on account of your heart of stone;
My eyes swim in tears, like fountains they gush,
In them, I'm immers'd, so fiercely they rush!
Her cold heart was touch'd, she anxiously said,
"Does anyone know, or dumb as the dead,
Have you secret kept, of what you have told
In verses to me of your love so bold?"
Now what could I say? I must own the truth,
Yet I felt shamefac'd, just like one uncouth,
To own thus, that I instead of conceal,
In madness, to all, my love did reveal!
"You wretch," she exclaim'd, then saying no more,

And thus I am left, disconsolate, lone.
Oh, ᶜUtbah, belov'd! your heart is of stone.[84]

Abū al-ᶜAtāhiyah, having first thought of ᶜUtbah as a means to reaching Mahdī, now began to think of this caliph as a means to obtaining ᶜUtbah, be she willing or not. He approached his friend, the singer Yazīd Ḥaurā, who was a favorite with Mahdī, to plead his case. Yazīd dared not speak so directly to the caliph on this subject. He, however, advised his poet friend to compose a verse which he would then set to music and sing before Mahdī. This was done, and Mahdī promised to help. A month went by, and the eager poet repeated the process through the good services of Yazīd. Mahdī now summoned ᶜUtbah, told her the story, and asked what she wished to do, promising at the same time that he would show great favor to the two of them if she accepted the poet. ᶜUtbah asked leave to consult with her mistress, that is, Raiṭah. Time passed and nothing happened. The impatient poet once more reached the ear of the caliph through verse and song. ᶜUtbah was again called in and questioned. "I mentioned the affair to my mistress," said she, "and she did not approve. Let the Commander of the Believers do as he pleases."

"Certainly," said Mahdī, "I will not do anything she dislikes."[85]

The poet, despairing for the time, returned later to

[84] Haroun M. Leon, "Abu l-ᶜAtahiya, 'al-Jarrar,'" *Islamic Culture*, V (1931), 632; for the original Arabic cf. Ibn al-Muᶜtazz, *Ṭabaqāt al-Shuᶜarāᵓ al-Muḥadathīn*, ed. A. Eghbal ("Gibb Memorial Series," Vol. XIII [1939]), p. 105; Ibn Khallikān (Cairo, 1310/1892–93), I, 71, and De Slane's translation, I, 203, for a brief prose rendering.

[85] *Aghānī*, III, 74–75; cf. Ḥuṣrī, I, 293–94.

the attack. And Mahdī, it seems, had a mind this time to grant the poet's request, but ᶜUtbah, no longer hiding behind her mistress' wishes, spoke her mind. "Commander of the Believers, treat me as becomes a woman and a member of your household. Would you then give me over to an ugly man who sells jars and seeks to profit by his verse?" The caliph was thus prevailed upon to spare ᶜUtbah this fate. Nevertheless, Abū al-ᶜAtāhiyah continued to sing her praises. She complained this time to Khaizurān, with whom Mahdī found her in tears. The poet was called in and confronted with some of his audacious verses and, for once, was unable to extricate himself. The lover-poet was then flogged for his persistence, but, meeting ᶜUtbah on the way, he pointed to the plight she had brought him and so sent her weeping again to Khaizurān. Mahdī repented his deed and sent the poet fifty thousand dirhams, which he immediately distributed to those at the royal gate. Mahdī took him to task for this, and he answered, "I wish not to consume the price of my beloved"; so Mahdī gave him another fifty thousand and forbade him, this time, to give it away.[86] Yet, even flogging did not cure him. He continued to make verses on ᶜUtbah, for which he was presently exiled. But he could not keep away and returned though only to be imprisoned. His friends, however, pleaded for and secured his release.[87]

The experiences of Bashshār and Abū al-ᶜAtāhiyah at the hands of Mahdī for their verses on members of that caliph's harem were not the kind to invite imitation. It is, therefore, not surprising to find that other poets left

[86] Masūᶜdī, VI, 241–43; *Aghānī*, XIX, 153; but cf. Ḥuṣrī, I, 297.

[87] Ḥuṣrī, I, 295–96; *Aghānī*, III, 145, 151; V, 6.

the royal harem, including Khaizurān, alone unless it was to pronounce some innocent couplet, now and again, in reference to her favored children. One such verse states that there are none, among the sons of all the caliphs, like the sons of Khaizurān.[88] When her young daughter, Banūqah, died, one of the poets in his verse of condolence referred to the child as having been the joy of both Mahdī and Khaizurān.[89] Yet another verse, quoted quite frequently by the sources, is one that congratulates Khaizurān on the occasion of the nomination of Hārūn as heir, which event made her the mother of two prospective caliphs. It comes, it seems, from the court poet, Marwān ibn Abī Ḥafṣah. "O Khaizurān, rejoice thee, and again rejoice; for thy two sons have come to rule the people."[90] Yet, even this verse was frowned upon by Mūsā al-Hādī, who advised a reciter to hold his tongue and not mention his mother's name for good or for evil.[91] Khaizurān herself does not seem to have courted publicity through the poets.

Interesting and significant as was Khaizurān's role in Mahdī's harem, it was not for this alone that she won a lasting place in Islamic history. It was, rather, the direction she gave to the political course of the ᶜAbbāsid Empire, chiefly through her energetic intrigues in the succession of her sons, that brought her a more or less sinister fame. It is, therefore, to this wider phase of her activities that the reader's attention is next called.

[88] Khaṭīb, XIV, 430.

[89] *Aghānī*, XXI, 120.

[90] Ṭabarī, III, 591–92; Masᶜūdī, VI, 269; Suyūṭī, *Taʾrīkh*, p. 111, and H. S. Jarrett's translation (Calcutta, 1881), p. 291.

[91] Ṭabarī, III, 591–92.

II

Power behind the Throne

KHAIZURĀN'S steadily increasing influence over Mahdī is hardly to be questioned. But the extent to which this influence found expression, direct or indirect, on the course of his empire and its immediate administration is difficult to gauge with any certainty, for the records refer to her influence mostly in general terms. It is to be further noted that such references are frequently first mentioned by the historians not under the reign of Mahdī but under that of Hādī as a sort of preliminary introduction to and explanation of the mother-son tragedy that was soon to follow. "Khaizurān," runs one of these accounts, "in the first part of Hādī's reign used to settle his affairs and to deal with him as she had dealt with his father (Mahdī) before him in assuming absolute power to command and forbid."[1] This could mean that she "commanded or forbade" Mahdī's acts, or that, regardless of Mahdī, with or without his knowledge, she acted autocratically and dictatorially on her own, or that she indulged in both these

[1] Ṭabarī, III, 569–71; Ibn Athīr, VI, 68; Masʿūdī, VI, 268–69; *Fakhrī*, p. 261; Ibn Khaldūn, III, 217.

practices. However, when search is made for specific incidents that would illustrate the possession and exercise of such powers, the net result of the search is meager, particularly in Mahdī's own reign. This, again, could mean that Mahdī allowed her a free hand and that the historian's brief and general statement reflects her generally well-known power. Or, again, it may be one more example of how most of the Moslem historians tend to pass over such unpalatable reference to woman's rule as briefly as possible. Frequently they ignore it altogether, unless, or until, it cannot be any longer so slighted or ignored. Such was the case with Khaizurān and Hādī.[2] It is quite conceivable that, had not Khaizurān clashed so severely with Hādī, her political influence in Mahdī's reign would have been totally ignored by the historians.

The first definite reference to Khaizurān's influence in politics is in connection with the imprisonment of Yaḥyā, the son of Khālid the Barmakid. Yaḥyā was imprisoned and heavily fined for misuse of power in the province of Fars. It was then that Khaizurān pleaded his case on the basis of foster-brotherhood between her son, Hārūn, and Yaḥyā's son, Faḍl. Mahdī, again easily influenced, released Yaḥyā and reinstated him in his post.[3]

A second specific instance of her political influence is associated with forced labor and an attempted miscarriage of justice. It is to be noted that the unholy alliance

[2] Even in this glaring case, historians like Yaᶜqūbī make no reference to her power, while Masᶜūdī and Ibn Khaldūn first mention it in connection with the events of Hādī's reign.

[3] Ibn ᶜAbdūs, p. 175; cf. below, pp. 63 and 198.

between politics and the administration of justice had already, in the days of Manṣūr, become the bane of honest men and judges. The famous jurisconsult, Abū Ḥanīfah, had begged to be excused from serving as judge in Baghdad but was pressed into service. His subsequent strike, imprisonment, and speedy death must have helped to put refusal to serve out of the minds of other candidates.[4] Sharīk ibn ᶜAbd Allah, judge of Kūfah in both Manṣūr's and Mahdī's reigns, claimed that he so served under compulsion. Skeptics, watching him waiting on Khaizurān as she was on her way back from the pilgrimage, probably in 158, scoffed in verse at this "compulsion."[5] Yet the following story is told of how Sharīk came to serve Mahdī.

Sharīk came into Mahdī's presence one day, and that caliph offered him one of three choices: to serve him as judge, to instruct his children, or to partake of a meal with him. Sharīk held his peace as he thought it over. Did he fear a poisoned morsel? One wonders! When he spoke at last, he chose the meal. Then Mahdī himself directed the chef to prepare him a dish of varied brains mixed in sugar and honey. The chef was somewhat alarmed, for he remarked that the old man—Sharīk was in his early sixties—would be forever undone after such a meal. Sharīk ate the prepared dish and thereafter consented to be both tutor for the princes and judge for their father. He was then put on the public pay roll, but the unhappy man felt he had failed the faith.[6]

[4] Ṭabarī, III, 371, 458, 465, 469, 484, 501, 503; Ibn Khallikān, I, 622–23.

[5] Khaṭīb, IX, 285; Yāqūt, *Geog.*, III, 246.

[6] Masᶜūdī, VI, 226–27; Ibn Khallikān, I, 622–23; Suyūṭī, *Taʾrīkh*, p. 108.

Whatever the properties of the sweet brain dish, Sharīk does not seem to have lost either his will-power or his sense of value and justice in the exercise of his function as tutor and judge. For it is related that one day one of Mahdī's sons (unnamed) came to Sharīk and asked to be informed about a certain tradition. Sharīk ignored him. The youth repeated his question, adding, "It seems that you belittle the sons of the caliphs."

"No," answered Sharīk, "it is rather that learning is considered much too precious by the learned for them to waste it." Then the youth, who had hitherto sat haughty and at ease—an attitude not befitting a pupil seeking knowledge—accepted the intended rebuke, kneeled before his instructor, and repeated his question. "It is thus (humbly) that knowledge is to be sought," said Sharīk, and presumably gratified the prince's desire for that pearl of great price.[7]

This, then, was Sharīk, the judge of Kūfah, with whom Khaizurān's agent clashed. It is to be remembered that a royal wife generally used up for herself, her retinue, and her establishment large quantities of cloth for clothes, draperies, and furnishings. It is further to be remembered that the ladies of the palace sought to acquire the best and to vie one with the other in ostentatious display of their rich silks, brocades, and tapestries. Khaizurān's agents, therefore, traveled in search of the best materials and workmanship. The weaving and embroidering industries flourished. In particular demand at the court were the *ṭirāz*, cloth or robes ornamented with gold and embroidered calligraphic bands,

[7] Suyūtī, *Taʾrīkh*, p. 108.

displaying some distinctive mark or sentiment, in phrase or verse, that took the royal fancy. They seem to have become quite the fashion with the early ᶜAbbāsids.[8]

Khaizurān had sent one of her agents to supervise the cloth and embroidery production of the factory at Kūfah and had written the then governor of the city, Mūsā ibn ᶜĪsā, to see that no obstacles were put in the agent's way. Mūsā must have complied with her instructions, since the agent, who was a Christian, by the way, was everywhere obeyed in Kūfah. Feeling secure, he behaved haughtily and went about dressed in fine clothes. Worse than that, he pressed artisans into forced labor at the factory. One day Judge Sharīk happened to see this agent, who had with him a man in handcuffs. The man cried out for help to the judge. "I am a worker in fine brocades. Artisans like me are (normally) hired for a hundred (dirhams) a month. But this man here seized me four months ago and has kept me a prisoner at the factory, giving me only my (daily) food. I have lost track of my family. Today I escaped from him, but he pursued and overtook me." The judge questioned the official, who sought security in the repeated phrase, "He is in the Lady's service," the Lady being, of course, Khaizurān. The agent, furthermore, ordered the judge to send the handcuffed artisan to prison. Instead, the good judge Sharīk released the man and sentenced the queen's agent to a public flogging.[9] Here the record stops, tanta-

[8] Florence E. Day, "Dated Ṭirāz in the Collection of the University of Michigan," *Ars Islamica*, IV (1937), 421–22, and references there cited; R. B. Serjeant, "Materials for a History of Islamic Textiles up to the Mongol Invasion," *Ars Islamica*, IX (1942), 55–84. See Ibn Khaldūn, I, 222–23.

[9] Khaṭīb, IX, 288.

lizingly omitting the sequel, for sequel there must have been when Khaizurān no doubt heard of the affair. At one time, Mahdī seems to be threatening the judge with the dreaded accusation of heresy;[10] but since the relative chronology of these events is not at all clear, it is impossible to know if the two events were directly connected. Mahdī could have made the threat at the time he himself was trying to induce Sharīk to enter his service.

The good judge seems to have escaped the pitfalls of his office in Mahdī's reign. He was, however, deprived of his judgship in the reign of Hādī. Was this, then, Khaizurān's revenge?

This scarcity of specific instances to illustrate the exercise of absolute power by Khaizurān in her husband's lifetime can mean that her actual power in the high politics of that period was limited and that such power as she had and exercised centered mainly in palace and harem affairs. It is a well-known fact that throughout the Islamic world, past and present, woman's most honored and powerful role is not that of wife but of mother. Khaizurān, the wife, no doubt used her woman's charm and tact to accomplish her ends with the devoted and easygoing Mahdī. But Khaizurān, the mother, intended to control her offspring more openly and directly. Mahdī, she cajoled and flattered. Hādī and Hārūn, she hoped to "command and forbid." Was it not because she had found favor with their royal father that they, her sons, were singled out for the heirship to the glorious caliphate? Thus Khaizurān, slave, concubine, and queen-consort, most probably looked upon her

[10] *Ibid.*, p. 294; cf. ᶜ*Iqd*, I, 186–87; III, 305–6.

future queen-motherhood as the climax of her ascending career.

In the meantime the affairs and management of the young princes must be taken in hand. Parents have from time immemorial claimed impartiality in their affection for their children. Favoritism, glaringly evident to the outsider, is vehemently denied by the involved parent, or it is occasionally explained as justified by some personality or character trait of an offending child. Child psychology and psychoanalysis have revealed the beginnings of parent-child antagonisms or the children's jealousy and consequent hatred of one another in the parents' unconscious neglect of an older child on the advent of a baby brother or sister. If the older child happens to have the misfortune of a physical handicap together with a naturally sensitive or envious temperament, and if, furthermore, a royal crown is at stake, then these are the ingredients to delight a witch's heart as she throws them into her caldron of trouble, there to boil and bubble. Trouble for Prince Hādī had already started brewing in his father's lifetime.

Khaizurān's eager anticipation of the coming of her firstborn has been already related.[11] The physicians who were then engaged to watch over the health of the child served him throughout his life. The honest doctor, ᶜAbd Allah al-Ṭaifūrī, relates how the birth of Hārūn brought ill-luck to Mūsā, since Hārūn was showered with favors to the exclusion of his older brother. This, the physician felt, affected his own position unfavorably, until Mūsā was old enough to comprehend what was happening.

[11] See above, p. 27.

Thereafter, Mūsā was more generous to him than was the queen-mother Khaizurān. The physician's prestige rose again as his charge became heir to the throne. The young prince acquired a harem, among them Amat al-ᶜAzīz, who was dearer to him than the apple of his eye, and who followed his example, nay, even outdid him, in her great generosity toward the physician ᶜAbd Allah.[12]

Mūsā al-Hādī started life with the physical handicap of an unattractive mouth. His upper lip is definitely stated to have been short and contracted, so that the young boy had difficulty in making both lips meet. The sight must have annoyed his parents. Mahdī appointed a special servant to watch the child and remind him to close his mouth. Soon the boy came to be known by the unsavory nickname of "Mūsā-shut-your-mouth."[13] How much damage the initial handicap and this blunt reminder of it did to the growing boy's ego will have to be left to the imagination. The boy was fair, tall, and heavily built, and in these he was not so different from his younger brother, Hārūn. The records describe him as physically brave and courageous. They credit him with assured self-confidence, energy, and resolution. To his somewhat partial physician, ᶜAbd Allah, he seemed the most noble in self-respect, a most gracious and sociable character, most equitable and just. Most of the sources are agreed on his great generosity, but there is a differ-

[12] Ibn Abī Uṣaibiᶜah, I, 153–54. This account, strange enough, makes this one woman the mother of all of Hādī's nine children, who himself died aged, at the most, twenty-six years (cf. below, pp. 66 and 97).

[13] E.g., Ṭabarī, III, 580; Ibn Athīr, VI, 69; Thaᶜālibī, *Laṭāʾif al-Maᶜārif*, p. 31; Ibn Taghrībirdī, I, 459; Suyūṭī, *Taʾrīkh*, p. 109. But cf. Qifṭī, p. 219, where the loyal but partisan Ṭaifūrī denies this defect in Hādī.

ence of opinion as to the sweetness of his nature and the tractability of his temper. He is described as a short-, hot-, and ill-tempered youth, impatient and quarrelsome, jealous and suspicious, a man of strong desires, hard of heart, and full of cunning withal.[14] How many of these qualities did he inherit with the none too gentle ᶜAbbāsid blue blood that ran in his veins or the none too modest plebeian strain that the cunning Kkaizurān injected into that blood stream? And, again, how many of them were forced upon him by the none too enviable position of being the older but the less-favored son? The answers must be left with the controversy of heredity versus environment.

It is quite conceivable that a son with all or most of those qualities would clash with his mother's aims and temperament more so than with his more easygoing and indulgent father, who referred to him in pride and affection as "my dear son," as he watched the sturdy youth, clad in heavy armor, spring smartly onto his mount.[15]

Mahdī did not neglect the education and training of his first heir, especially in the earlier years of his own reign. He sought out men of good reputation and fame as instructors for his sons, and himself set them the example of patronizing and honoring the scholars of the day. Hādī, whose intellectual endowment was not inconsiderable, had a taste for learning, particularly in literature. Later, he came to have for one of his best and

[14] Ṭabarī, III, 586, 596; Masᶜūdī, VI, 262; VIII, 294; Jāḥiẓ, *K. al-Tāj*, p. 35; Khaṭīb, XI, 150–51; Ibn Abī Uṣaibiᶜah, I, 156; *Fakhrī*, p. 258.

[15] Ṭabarī, III, 170.

almost inseparable companions ᶜĪsā ibn Daʾb,[16] an outstanding scholar from the province of Ḥijāz. When it came to matters of religious policy, Mahdī himself instructed his son to follow his own example in weeding out heresy; and Hādī, who took quite an interest in religious debates, had every intention of following, in this respect, in his father's footsteps.[17]

The younger prince, Hārūn, received his first instruction and training at the hands of that pillar of the early ᶜAbbāsid state, Khālid the Barmakid and his family, particularly his son Yaḥyā. It is claimed that there were several cases of foster-relationships between three generations of ᶜAbbāsids and Barmakids. The first goes back to Saffāḥ and Khālid, each of whom had a daughter who was nursed by both mothers.[18] The second is Hārūn and Faḍl, the son of Yaḥyā, while a third generation of foster-relationship is claimed for Hārūn's son, Amīn, and a son of Jaᶜfar the Barmakid. A less frequently mentioned foster-relationship is that between Hārūn and Jaᶜfar. This, however, is further complicated by the statement that Jaᶜfar's own mother died while he was yet an infant and that he and Hārūn were then both nursed by Fāṭimah, wife or concubine of Yaḥyā, who thus became foster-mother to both. She was known as Umm Jaᶜfar and was addressed by Hārūn al-Rashīd himself as Umm al-Rashīd.[19]

[16] Jāḥiẓ, *K. al-Tāj*, pp. 116–17; Ṭabarī, III, 589–90, 592–93; Masᶜūdī, VI, 263–64, 277; Khaṭīb, IX, 306; XI, 150–51.

[17] Ṭabarī, III, 588.

[18] *Ibid.*, II, 840; Ibn ᶜAbdūs, pp. 105, 155, 175.

[19] ᶜ*Iqd*, III, 28–29.

Aside from the foster-relationships, Yaḥyā was for a great deal of the time in the 140's with Prince Mahdī in Khurāsān. The two families had every opportunity and incentive for close contact. Khālid and his son Yaḥyā were for most of the time in favor not only with Prince Mahdī but with the more critical and exacting caliph Manṣūr. Therefore, the statement that Mahdī's young son was committed to the excellent care of the Barmakids[20] seems quite plausible. At a later period in the young prince's life, both Khālid and Yaḥyā were more specifically associated with Hārūn than with Mūsā al-Hādī. The experienced Khālid accompanied the youthful Hārūn on his Byzantine campaigns, while his son Yaḥyā was Hārūn's special secretary and "wazir" as early as 161/777–78.[21] It was because of the foster-relationship and this more important and intimate administrative connection, in which Prince Hārūn sat, figuratively speaking, at the feet of the shrewd diplomat and able statesman, Yaḥyā ibn Khālid, that Hārūn used to address the latter as "Father."[22]

Yaḥyā, aside from his genius for government, had a keen sense of responsibility. He displayed an inordinate capacity for industrious attention to the routine administration of the western provinces intrusted to his care in the name of Hārūn. The young Hārūn, on the other hand, preoccupied with the pleasures of life, cared not to be weighted down with the cares of government. He gave Yaḥyā a free hand. The arrangement suited

[20] Ṭabarī, III, 498; Yaʿqūbī, II, 490.

[21] Ṭabarī, III, 492, 497.

[22] Cf. below, pp. 113, 133, and 193.

both prince and administrator, as it seems also to have met with the approval of Mahdī and Khaizurān. As these four key figures of the court drew closer together, Prince Hadī was left to the company and care of lesser personages and to his own uneasy thoughts and fears.

When it came to the social and moral training of the now more mature princes, Mahdī sought to substitute the force of example by that of precept and met with the usual success, or rather failure, in such cases. Though he surrounded himself with musicians, dancers, and singers, he forbade these artists the lucrative pleasure of entertaining his sons and heirs. Reference has already been made to the imprisonment and flogging of the gifted musicians Ibrāhīm and Ibn Jāmiᶜ.[23] Other incidents are not lacking which prove that, on the whole, Hādī's choice of social companions did not meet with his father's approval. He resorted to the rod so as not to spoil the child; but its use was by proxy. Since obviously the dignity of heirship precluded a public flogging, it was not the heir but his less fortunate companions who took the painful chastisement. ᶜAbd Allah ibn Mālik, Mahdī's captain of police, used to be ordered to administer the stripes. Prince Hādī would then ask him to be lenient with his friends, but ᶜAbd Allah would pay no attention, fearing more the present displeasure of Mahdī than the likely future wrath of Hādī as caliph.[24] Not even flogging seems to have been effective in keeping Ibrāhīm ibn Dhakwān, better known as Ibrāhīm al-Ḥarrānī, from Hādī's company. He had been intro-

[23] Cf. above, p. 35.

[24] Ṭabarī, III, 583; Ibn Athīr, VI, 70; *Fakhrī*, p. 258.

duced to the young prince through one of his instructors. Mahdī had forbidden him the prince's company, but the latter would not leave Ibrāhīm alone.[25]

Khaizurān, in this same fateful decade of the prince's life, concerned herself with plans for their harems. True to Eastern and Islamic custom, family life began early for both princes. Hādī is on record as being prolific in offspring. Short as his life was, he left seven sons and two daughters, all born of concubines. Brief and confused as are generally the entries on the caliph's harems, the references to Hādī's harem are among the briefest, but with their full share of confusions and contradictions.[26] At least some half-dozen different concubines are to be distinguished. Some he bought himself; others were presented to him. Among the latter was one Amat al-ᶜAzīz, who had belonged to Rabīᶜ ibn Yūnus, the powerful and ambitious chamberlain of Manṣūr and Mahdī. Exceedingly beautiful of face and figure, she was first presented by Rabīᶜ to Mahdī, who, seeing her youth and beauty, thought she was more fit for his young son Mūsā al-Hādī. She found favor with the prince, but the chamberlain, if the stories told later of this "triangle" are true, had great reason to regret making this gift to royalty.[27] She bore the prince his two oldest sons. The next concubine, Raḥīm, is said to have been the mother of yet another son, Jaᶜfar, of whom more later. The rest of his harem are just names,

[25] Ṭabarī, III, 583; *Fakhrī*, p. 263.

[26] Ṭabarī, III, 580; *ᶜIqd*, III, 53–54; Ibn Abī Uṣaibiᶜah, I, 153–54.

[27] Ṭabarī, III, 597–98; Masᶜūdī, VI, 266; cf. below, p. 86.

"maids" or "mothers of children," that can well be passed over.

It is to be understood that acquiring a wife was a much more serious undertaking than stocking-up on concubines who could be discarded, given away, or even killed without any questions raised. A wife had her legal rights to property settlement. She had "family connections," which frequently ramified far and deep into the ever sensitive tribal situation. Partial as were the rules of divorce to the man, even a legitimate divorce of a royal queen would have social and political repercussions. There was, furthermore, the question of royal dignity to consider. Since remarriage was never legally forbidden to the divorced wives of the caliphs, a caliph who divorced his wives might be put to the personal humiliation of seeing them the wives of other men of high or low station. He could, of course, autocrat that he was, flog, imprison, or even execute any daring enough to take this perfectly legal, but not proper, step. But there will still remain an element of personal humiliation. These considerations were to lead, in the none too distant future as history goes, to fewer and fewer royal marriages. With few exceptions the royal concubine reigned almost supreme in the caliphal palace. Here and there an exceptional "mother of children" achieved, like Khaizurān, manumission and legal matrimonial status.

It is, therefore, not surprising, considering these general factors and Hādī's youth and short reign, to find that he had but two legal wives, both of whom were his cousins. One, Lubābah, was the daughter of Jaᶜfar, son of the caliph Manṣūr.[28] She was, therefore, half-sister to Zubaidah but no direct relation to Khaizurān. The second was ᶜUbaidah, daughter of Ghiṭrīf and, therefore, niece of Khaizurān.[29] No date is given for either marriage. The probability is, since Hādī was older than Hārūn, that one or both of his marriages took place before Hārūn's marriage in 165/781–82, to his double cousin Zubaidah, offspring of his paternal uncle Jaᶜfar and maternal aunt Salsal.[30] Khaizurān could thus point, with pride and satisfaction no doubt, to two daughters-in-law who were also her nieces. ᶜAzīzah, a second daughter of Ghiṭrīf, who had been first married and divorced by an ᶜAbbāsid prince, was later married by Hārūn, Zubaidah notwithstanding.[31] The date of this marriage, too, is not stated, and it may have taken place after Khaizurān's death. Most tantalizing is the historian's silence on the intimate relationship of aunt and nieces who were also related as mother and daughters-in-law. How did Khaizurān, who sought to rule her men, react to Hārūn's passionate love for his favorite, Zubaidah? Did this young and spoiled princess royal take orders from her scheming and aggressive aunt and mother-in-law? For seven years powerful mother and favorite wife shared Hārūn's fame and affection, yet there seems to be not a single statement or anecdote that links their names together, and there is but one that links Khaizurān and ᶜUbaidah.[32]

[28] Jāḥiẓ, *Maḥāsin*, p. 235.

[29] Ṭabarī, III, 590–91; *Aghānī*, XIII, 13.

[30] Cf. above, pp. 29–31.

[31] Ṭabarī, III, 757.

[32] See below, p. 89.

The clash of wills and temperaments among the members of the royal family became apparent in the development of the succession question. Hādī was appointed sole heir in 160/776[33] and, as such, stayed closer to the capital than his younger brother, Hārūn, who was soon sent on expeditions against Byzantium. Hārūn's spectacular military successes and resulting favorable treaty of 165/782 with the Empress Irene[34] were dramatized at Baghdad and considerably raised that young prince's political stock, climaxing, in 166/782–83, with his appointment as second heir to the throne, with the title of Al-Rashīd, that is, "The Rightly Guided."[35] Hādī, who had every prospect of a long life and several sons already to his credit, could hardly be expected to be enthusiastic over Hārūn's heirship, especially as he felt that the undercurrents of harem and court were against him.

Father and son drifted farther apart. Presently it was decided to send Prince Hādī to distant Jurjān east of the Caspian Sea. Mahdī relented in his opposition to Ibrāhīm al-Ḥarrānī, whom he now allowed to accompany Hādī. There is some evidence that the caliph and his son held conflicting views on the policy to be pursued in Jurjān.[36] Perhaps Ibrāhīm was in part responsible for Hādī's ideas. At any rate, there soon came from Jurjān reports about him that once more displeased Mahdī. He,

[33] Ṭabarī, III, 472–76; Ibn Athīr, VI, 29–30.

[34] Ṭabarī, III, 494–95, 503–5; Ibn Athīr, VI, 40–41, 44.

[35] Ṭabarī, III, 506; Ibn Athīr, VI, 45–46.

[36] ᶜ*Iqd*, I, 70 ff., esp. pp. 78–79.

therefore, recalled Ibrāhīm, but Hādī held him back. Eventually, Mahdī sent word to Hādī himself to send him Ibrāhīm or else be excluded from the heirship. In the face of such threats, Hādī reluctantly parted with his companion.[37] In the meantime, Mahdī had determined on placing Hārūn ahead of Hādī in the line of succession. He sent, in 169/785–86, leading members of the royal family to inform Hādī of the change and to secure his acceptance of the new order. Hādī refused his consent. Mahdī next sent a group of freedmen to bring the disobedient son back home. Hādī fought the messengers and refused to answer his father's summons. Mahdī now decided to go and subdue his stubborn son himself and so started on that fateful trip.[38]

Mahdī and his army left the capital on the Tigris for the distant Jurjān, where Prince Hādī had been stationed since 167/783–84. Accompanying the irate father on this mission of discipline and displacement for the first heir to the throne was Hārūn, the central figure around which capital and harem plots had been and still were revolving. And with Hārūn went his "father," Yaḥyā the Barmakid. Rabīᶜ ibn Yūnus, the powerful chamberlain, was left at the helm of the political wheel in Baghdad. The march was a long one, but Mahdī had no intention to force it, for there was good hunting on the way, and hunting was a favorite sport with the caliph.

A number of good stories are told of how Mahdī, while on the hunt, would be separated from his companions to

[37] Ibn ᶜAbdūs, p. 198; *Fakhrī*, p. 263.

[38] Ṭabarī, III, 523; Ibn Athīr, VI, 54.

wander alone in the forest and come back with some thrilling or amusing experience. More than one such tale has a kinship with the "King Alfred and the Cakes" theme. One, in particular, is rich in Islamic flavor. Mahdī arrived alone at a Bedouin's tent and announced himself as a hungry guest. The Bedouin remarked on the alertness, strength, and noble appearance of his unknown guest, to whom he offered his humble fare of bread and whey. This, Mahdī devoured with a real hungry man's relish of any food, adding, "Bring forth whatever (else) you have." Out came the juice of the grape. Host and guest each drank a glass, after which Mahdī asked, "Know you who I am?"

"Nay, by Allah," answered the Arab.

"I am one of the special servants (of the caliph)," Mahdī informed him.

"May Allah bless you in your position (of service) and grant you long life whoever you are," said his host as he passed him the second cup.

This, too, Mahdī drank and again asked, "O Arab, know you who I am?"

"Yes," answered his host; "you just mentioned you were of the special service."

"It is not so."

"Who, then, are you?"

"I am one of Mahdī's generals."

"Welcome! make yourself at home. Your visit is indeed a pleasure," said his host, and passed him the third cup of wine, after drinking which Mahdī repeated his initial question and received the answer, "Yes, you claim you are one of Mahdī's generals."

"It is not so," said Mahdī. "I am the Commander of the Believers in person." Whereupon the Bedouin Arab tied up his wineskin.

"Give us another drink," called out Mahdī.

"Nay, by Allah, not a mouthful more shall you have!"

"And why so?" asked guest Mahdī.

"We gave you one drink," replied his host, "and you claimed you were of the special service. We humored you and gave you a second cup, and then you claimed you were one of Mahdī's generals. We put up with that, too, and gave you a third drink, and you next claimed that you were the Commander of the Believers in person. Nay, by Allah, it is not safe to give you a fourth cup, for then you will claim to be the Prophet of Allah himself."

Mahdī broke into hearty laughter. Presently the royal hunting party caught up with its caliph. The Arab, realizing now that this was indeed the caliph, ran for his life, fearing the caliph's displeasure for his last remark. He was overtaken and brought back, and there followed the usual "happy ending," with the Arab showered with rich gifts of clothes and money. This particular one, getting over his surprise and finding his tongue again, said to his royal guest, "I bear witness that you are truthful, even if you were to make the fourth and the fifth claims," i.e., claim to be Prophet and God. At this, Mahdī was so convulsed with laughter that he almost fell off his charger. He closed the episode by taking the Arab into his personal service.[39]

[39] Masᶜūdī, VI, 229–31; Zamakhsharī, *Rauḍ al-Akhyār* (Cairo, 1280/1863), pp. 200–201. For other hunting stories of Mahdī cf. Masᶜūdī, VI, 227–

Not all of Mahdī's hunting adventures were to end as happily. Out on the unpleasant business of chasing down a stubborn and rebellious son, Mahdī thought to break the long march with a pleasure hunting-trip on the side. The army was at Māsabādhān, and the near-by village and woods of Radhdh seemed to offer good sport. As frequently happened with Mahdī, he was soon isolated from his party. His hounds got wind of an antelope and gave chase. Mahdī charged after the hounds. The prey rushed against the gate of some ruins, the hounds dashed after it, and Mahdī's bucking, unruly horse rushed after them, crashing the caliph against the ruined gates and into instantaneous death. A tragic but clean end,[40] that is, if this story of the hunting accident is to be believed; not that the story itself is impossible, but because it is but one of several stories of "accidental death" for this caliph.

Poison and not the hunt is the active agent in these other stories. The briefest version here is that one of Mahdī's concubines sent a rival of hers some poisoned food by the hand of a maidservant who knew all the time that the gift was poisoned. Mahdī happened to waylay the girl and eat of the poisoned dish, the girl being much too frightened out of her wits to warn the caliph that death lay in the morsel.[41] A fuller version of

28; Ibn Khallikān, I, 524–25; Ibn al-Jauzī, *Akhbār*, pp. 73–74; Alī ibn Ẓāfir al-Azdī, *Badāʾiʿ al-Bidāʾah* (Cairo, 1278/1861), pp. 186–87; Khaṭīb, VIII, 491–92.

[40] Ṭabarī, III, 523–24; Ibn Athīr, VI, 54; Yaʿqūbī, III, 484; Ibn Khaldūn, III, 214.

[41] Ṭabarī, III, 524; Ibn Aṭhīr, VI, 54.

this story names the concubine and details the tale. The envious and murderous concubine turns out to be Ḥasanah, met with earlier in these pages. She plucked out the stem of a pear carefully, inserted the poison, and replaced the stem. Then she placed the polished, tempting fruit uppermost in the dish and sent it on its death-dealing way. Mahdī, sitting in a tower of the palace at Māsabādhān, saw Ḥasanah's maid pass below with her attractive tray of fruit. Since pears happened to be a special favorite with him, he called to the girl, reached out for the best fruit, which was the poisoned pear, and ate it. No sooner had he finished eating, than he cried out with pain. Ḥasanah, awaiting other results, heard the anguished cry and was soon informed of what had taken place. She came weeping and beating her face and crying out in her emotional despair, "I desired you for myself alone, and now I have killed you, O my master!"[42]

Still another story that involves Ḥasanah and this ill-conceived and ill-fated expedition runs as follows. When Mahdī prepared to depart to Māsabādhān, he desired his favorite concubine, Ḥasanah, to accompany him. She sent this word to Mahdī's chief of court astrologers: "You advised this expedition for the Commander of the Believers and have thus burdened us with a journey we have not taken into account. May Allah hasten your death and rid us of you!" The maid brought back this in answer: "I did not advise this expedition. As for your curse, God had already decreed my speedy death. So make not the mistake of thinking it an answer to your

[42] Ṭabarī, III, 524; Ibn Athīr, VI, 54–55.

curse. Rather, prepare for yourself plenty of dust and, when I die, place the dust on your own head." His cryptic message became clear to her when Mahdī's death followed that of the court astrologer by twenty days.[43]

Astrologer or no, Mahdī himself, insist the records, got advance notice of his final call. While in Māsabādhān, the caliph woke up one early morning hungry and called for food. Having eaten, he entered a courtyard to resume his sleep and gave orders not to be disturbed. Presently, his companions were awakened by his loud crying. They hastened to him, and he asked, "Did you not see what I saw?"

"We did not see anything," they said.

"There stood at the gate a man," said the caliph, "whom I would not fail to know were he one among a thousand, nay, among a hundred thousand men." He proceeded to recite verses that left no doubt in his hearer's minds but that he believed he had seen the angel of death at the gate. Ten days later he was dead.[44]

Cryptic pronouncements, troubled dreams, poisoned dainties, and the accidents of the chase—all tell a tangled tale that still remains to be disentangled. Mystery and suspicion still hang around the death of Mahdī, who was laid to his final rest in the far-off village of Radhdh, hastily buried under the shade of a walnut tree.[45] Prince Hārūn, son of Khaizurān, and Prince ᶜAlī,

[43] Abū Faraj, *Mukhtaṣar al-Duwal* (Beirut, 1890), pp. 219–20.

[44] Ṭabarī, III, 525–26; Ibn Athīr, VI, 54; Yaᶜqūbī, II, 484–85; Masᶜūdī, VI, 258–59.

[45] Tabarī, III, 526; Yāqūt, *Georg.*, IV, 393.

son of Raiṭah, performed the last services for their departed father.

Nowhere is there any record of how their royal mothers received the news of the death of their joint husband. But it is on record that Mahdī's concubines, and particularly Ḥasanah, mourned him greatly. As the carriages of the returning harem, all in deep mourning, reached Baghdad, the poet Abū al-ᶜAtāhiyah was moved to spontaneous verse. His lines began by contrasting the women departing in brocades and returning in sackcloth, dwelt on the transitoriness of life for one and all, and ended with the advice to weep for one's own destiny if one must weep at all.[46]

Mahdī's death ended one period of Khaizurān's life at the same time that it ushered her into another. Behind her was youth, success, and happiness. Ahead of her lay maturity, power, and tragedy. For death, having arrived on the royal stage, decided to tarry a while longer.

[46] Ṭabarī, III, 525; Yaᶜqūbī, II, 485; Masᶜūdī, VI, 225–26.

III

Humiliation

THE period between the passing-away of one monarch and the accession of the next is, under the best of conditions, a time of stress and strain in royal household, kingdom, or empire. In the Islamic state it is generally critical enough to warrant all precaution and secrecy until the announcement, "The King is dead," can be followed immediately by "Long live the King!" It is better still, if the new monarch is on hand to receive in person the allegiance of court, army, and people. The death of a caliph away from his capital calls for quick and astute action on the part of the empire's statesmen, if transition from one reign to the other is to be accomplished peacefully. When harem intrigue and rival claimants are also on the burdened scene, the transition period may mean the signal for swift death for one or more royal prince, riot in the streets of the capital, or open revolt there and in the distant parts of the empire.

When Manṣūr died on the Pilgrim Road, the chamberlain Rabīᶜ ibn Yūnus kept the caliph's death secret until Mahdī at Baghdad could take the situation well in hand. Now, once more, it fell to Rabīᶜ, this time himself at Baghdad, to hold together the reins of empire in a situation that was even more dangerous. For as Mahdī made his unexpected exit off the crowded stage, he left behind him rival heirs and ambitious widow to continue with a play that had already run its first act of tragedy.

There were, in fact, three complicated scenes overlapping in time though far distant in space. At Māsabādhān, Hārūn fell back on the experienced and trusted Yaḥyā the Barmakid, who, now that Mahdī was gone without having altered the succession, advised his young charge to abide by the succession as it stood and allow Hādī to ascend the throne. That determined upon, Hārūn was to send, with utmost speed, the news of Mahdī's death, together with the insignia of the caliphate and the assurance of his own allegiance, to his brother Hādī, who was then farther east in Jurjān. The army that had started out with Mahdī was to receive some cash payment and return home to Baghdad. Hārūn and Yaḥyā, too, were to return to the capital as fast as possible.[1]

As the capital received the news of the caliph's death, riots broke out in the city. Khaizurān sent for both Rabīᶜ and Yaḥyā. Rabīᶜ answered her summons and was placed by her in control. But Yaḥyā kept aloof, fearing Hādī's displeasure, should he, Yaḥyā, appear to be working with Kaizurān. For Hādī suspected her as being behind the plot to replace him by her favorite

[1] Ṭabarī, III, 544–46; Ibn Athīr, VI, 58–59; Masᶜūdī, VI, 261; Thaᶜālibī, *Laṭāʾif al-Maᶜārif*, p. 79.

Hārūn, who was also Yaḥyā's political charge. Rabīᶜ and Yaḥyā, however, seem to have been on friendly terms. The riots were quelled and the army was quieted by three years' pay. Baghdad awaited the arrival of the new caliph.

Hādī, in the meantime, had, on the receipt of his brother's message, ridden literally posthaste for the capital. He covered the long distance in twenty days. He had lost no time in expressing, even before his arrival, his great displeasure at Rabīᶜ's response to Khaizurān and promised that chamberlain a speedy death. Yaḥyā, on the other hand, was commended for not answering the queen's summons. Rabīᶜ trembled for his fate and came to take counsel with Yaḥyā, who advised that Rabīᶜ send out his son Faḍl, with appropriate gifts, to welcome and congratulate Hādī. Rabīᶜ's wife approved of the advice. So dangerous was the situation, however, that Rabīᶜ thought it best to make out his will and intrust it to his friend Yaḥyā. The latter, though willing to help, would not take this new responsibility alone, and so Rabīᶜ's wife had to share it with him. Faḍl met the returning Hādī at Hamadhān and presented his gifts, congratulations, and explanations, which were received with favor, for the time being at least. Presently, at Baghdad, Rabīᶜ himself tendered his allegiance and made his excuses in person. Just what line these excuses took, the record does not tell. But they must have been convincing enough, since Hādī decided to make Rabīᶜ his first wazir, as he had already decided to let Yaḥyā continue to administer the provinces of his brother Hārūn, who was now the first heir to the throne.[2]

There is no record of the first meeting between Kkaizurān and her caliph-son, Hādī. Outwardly, at least, a truce must have been declared between the two, for the records are agreed that, for the first few months of his reign, Hādī allowed his mother all the freedom and privileges she had enjoyed under his father. She had, in calling Rabīᶜ and Yaḥyā to her presence, assumed an aggressive role from the start. Rabīᶜ, when he made his explanations to the returned Hādī, must have had to account for his relationship with Khaizurān, since it was that one fact more than any other that had roused Hādī's death-threatening wrath against him. Rabīᶜ may even have had a hand, at this initial interview with the new caliph, in smoothing out some of the differences that separated mother and son. One looks in vain at this point for a clarifying statement that might explain, in part at least, events past and to come. The Moslem historian yields here to his natural temptation for brevity, generalization, and ambiguity when it comes to dealing with the harem.

Did Hādī appoint his wazir in good faith or with mental reservation? Was the liberty he allowed his mother Khaizurān one of choice or of compulsion? Did the mutual co-operation, at this stage, of the two brothers have any ulterior motives with either one or both? To what extent was Hādī himself under the influence of his own harem? These and other questions cry out for

[2] Ṭabarī, III, 546–48; Ibn Athīr, VI, 59–60; Masᶜūdī, VI, 265; Ibn ᶜAbdūs, p. 197.

answers as the tragic events of Hādī's short reign of a little over a year take their course. The answers, however (as the reader may have guessed by now), are not at all easy to get, and such as are given are in general neither sufficient nor clear cut, for the early Moslem historians are, for the most part, annalists and not analysts. They receive and record with meticulous care and with little partiality different versions of the same event. When it comes to probing for motives, their natural good sense warns them of the dangers and pitfalls ahead. They sidetrack the issue, hint now and again at this or that motive, and exit from what frequently is a blind alley with "Allah alone knows best."

The gaps left and the contradictions preserved by the annalist have been, and still are, a temptation to let one's imagination and inclination settle such questions positively and for all time. But an objective view calls for caution and results in sober statements of probability over against the more flashy assertion of this subjective certainty. Moslem writers, giving free play to imagination and inclination, have, through the centuries, woven *Arabian Nights'* legends around the name of Hārūn al-Rashīd. This they have done with such abandon that these legends are easily recognized and so are discounted. The *Arabian Nights'* tales are read with profit not for historical truth but for general entertainment. A more dangerous source of the distortion of history creeps in when Western writers, also allowing free play of imagination and inclination, present the results of their efforts as ascertained history. This brief digression was called for by the following passages from two popular authors on Hārūn al-Rashīd.

> As for Yahia and Harun, dazed by the turn of events, they consulted together feverishly. Should they risk a march against Hadi? That would be a bold stroke, for he had the law on his side. . . . . In the face of this serious dilemma, Yahia the Barmecide flashed his political genius. He counselled feigning submission and loyalty. The important thing just then was to save their heads; the future could be attended to later.[3]

> By no single act of all his brilliant career did Harun better vindicate his worthiness of the imperial sceptre than by thus renouncing it in the interests of civil peace. The army was his for the commanding, and he disbanded it. His elder brother was at his mercy, and he placed him on the throne. His mother sought to thrust greatness on him, but he preferred to abide by the verdict of Fate. Of few can it be said so truly that he was born great.[4]

Thus, the "literary" efforts of two biographers leaves the reader the choice of Hārūn as a "Dr. Jekyll" *or* a "Mr. Hyde," with each of these characters seemingly unknown to the creator of the other. Both biographies make good reading, but more for pleasure than for historical instruction. In the present study a conscious effort is being constantly made to keep close to the sources. Thus, in the case on hand, the records testify to Yaḥyā's political genius and to his counsel of submission and loyalty, but with the feigning left out. Again the records substantiate Hārūn's actual moves but leave no room for "renouncing the imperial sceptre," which was not quite within his grasp *de facto* or *de jure*.

[3] Gabriel Audisio, *Harun al-Rashid* (New York, 1931), pp. 30–31.

[4] H. St. John Philby, *Harun al-Rashid* (New York and London, 1934), pp. 30–31.

That is, Hārūn and his counselor, Yaḥyā, were not the rogues that the first account would make them, nor was Hārūn the unselfish noble soul that the second account paints. Yaḥyā's political sagacity is unquestioned. His policy and advice need no ulterior motives for their explanation. Hārūn's acceptance of them was due partly to his own reluctance to assume responsibility and partly to the force of habit of yielding to Yaḥyā's leadership for a decade and more.

But to return to the set of questions that started this line of thought. Viewing these in the light of events before and after, it does not seem at all impossible that the initial strain and stress of the reign being over, the major characters involved all breathed a sigh of relief. The probability is that they accepted the situation at the time as it stood—as somewhat better than one and all had had reason to expect. Hādī had his throne and Hārūn his heirship; Rabīᶜ and Yaḥyā were both in office; and even Khaizurān kept the power she had feared to lose. All might have been smooth sailing for the ship of state had Khaizurān, in the months that followed, tempered her love of power with either the patient wisdom of Yaḥyā or the happy indifference credited to Hārūn. And again all might still have gone well even after the break between mother and son, had not Hādī alarmed, not so much his brother, Hārūn, but that brother's political mentor, Yaḥyā, by the attempt to replace Hārūn by his own young son, Jaᶜfar, in line as heir apparent.

In these few months before serious trouble began to raise its head again, Hādī settled down to his new role as caliph. This role he filled with such great dignity in public that even a foster-brother, though perfectly at ease with him in private, trembled with awe at the caliph's majesty.[5] He heard petitions in person, it would seem, almost daily.[6] When once three days had passed without this function, his minister intercepted him on a visit to his mother, who was indisposed at the time, and reminded him of his duty. Hādī sent this word of excuse to Khaizurān: "ᶜUmar ibn Bazīᶜ has reminded us of a duty toward Allah which is more obligatory for us than our duty toward you. So we turned to it. But we shall visit you on the morrow, Allah willing."[7]

Among those who thought that they had reason to fear the vengeance of the new caliph was the captain of police, ᶜAbd Allah ibn Mālik, one of whose duties had been to flog those of Prince Hādī's companions who had not met with Mahdī's approval.[8] Hādī retained the captain in his office, though later he took him to task for his past. But the captain argued quite effectively along these lines: "Now that you are the Commander of the Believers yourself and I am your captain of police, would you wish me to set aside your commands in favor of those of your son?"

"No," said the sensible caliph.

"As I now serve you, so I served your father."

Hādī was pleased and dismissed his good and faithful servant with a gift. But the latter feared that his enemies—especially those whom he had flogged, but who were now in high office—would turn the caliph,

[5] Ṭabarī, III, 586.

[6] *Ibid.*, 584.

[7] *Ibid.*, pp. 582–83; Ibn Athīr, VI, 70.

[8] Cf. above, p. 65.

while in his cups, against him. Hādī sensed this fear. He therefore made a personal visit to the captain's house, broke bread with him there, made him a second royal gift, and so dispelled all his anxiety.[9]

All work and no play may have been Manṣūr's motto. It was not that of his son or grandsons. Hādī, on his return to the capital, spent his first full night and day in the company of his favorite concubine, receiving no one in audience.[10] Soon after, he assembled his former boon companions, and, in this, first Rabīᶜ's son Faḍl and then Yaḥyā assisted him. The former planned the return of the exiled musician, Ibn Jāmiᶜ, as a pleasant surprise for the new caliph, while Yaḥyā was specifically asked by Hādī to help him locate Ibrāhīm al-Mauṣilī for him.[11] The poets, too, always on hand, had lost no time in singing the usual praises for a new caliph. Among the readiest to sing his praises were the talented spendthrift, Salm al-Khāṣir,[12] and the more famous miser and poet, Marwān ibn Abī Ḥafṣah.[13] The former's policy was to have poems on hand for any emergency, even to the point of preparing elegies for those still much in the flesh.[14]

Soon after his arrival at Baghdad, Hādī had left the capital city to take up his residence in the near-by suburb of ᶜĪsābādh outside eastern Baghdad, where

[9] Ṭabarī, III, 458, 583; Ibn Athīr, VI, 70–71; *Fakhrī*, pp. 258–59.

[10] Ṭabarī, III, 548.

[11] *Aghānī*, VI, 73; Ṭabarī, III, 573; cf. above, p. 35.

[12] Cf. *Aghānī*, XXI, 210–29; Rifāᶜī, II, 349–53.

[13] *Aghānī*, IX, 41, 47; XXI, 128; Ṭabarī, III, 593–94.

[14] *Aghānī*, XXI, 121.

Mahdī had built his Palace of Peace and Hādī himself his White Palace.[15] No specific reason is given for the move, but perhaps it was to avoid too close supervision by his mother. The distance, however, was short enough to permit of frequent messenger service and visits when needed. It was here, then, that Hādī spent most of the time, at work or at play, of his short reign.

The first signs of trouble after this brief lull in the diplomatic storm gathered around the newly appointed Rabīᶜ ibn Yūnus. Soon after Hādī moved to ᶜĪsābādh, he removed Rabīᶜ from the wazirate in favor of Ibrāhīm al-Ḥarrānī. Rabīᶜ was appointed to head the bureau of registration, but his son, Faḍl, had the important office of chamberlain, with orders not to turn the public away from the caliph.[16] Rabīᶜ himself explained his demotion and the greater misfortune that befell him a little later to his co-operation with Khaizurān at the time of the death of Mahdī. He felt, perhaps with reason, that Hādī had not really forgiven him for that move. Still, there are some evidences of other complications, particularly in connection with Rabīᶜ's former slave girl, Amat al-ᶜAzīz. Rabīᶜ may or may not have mentioned this girl, now the favorite of Hādī. But his enemies carried word to Hādī that Rabīᶜ had said that he had never loved a slave girl better than he had loved this one. This so aroused Hādī's ire and jealousy that he determined to do away with Rabīᶜ. A plot was afoot to have him waylaid and killed, but news of it leaked out to him. He changed his

[15] Ṭabarī, III, 548, 502; Khaṭīb, I, 97; XIII, 22.

[16] Ṭabarī, III, 585, 598; Ibn ᶜAbdūs, p. 197; *Fakhrī*, pp. 261–62.

route and escaped the waiting assassins' poisoned knife but only to receive, at the hands of Hādī himself, the cup of poisoned honey and then go home to die. All this took place within a few months, but how few is nowhere stated. Hence, Rabīᶜ's death is placed by some in A.H. 169 (A.D. 785/86) and by others in 170. Hārūn was at the last rites and recited the prayers over the body, but Hādī did not attend the funeral.[17]

Rabīᶜ's removal from the wazirate could not have been particularly welcome either to Khaizurān or to Yaḥyā. His removal from life must have been more than alarming to both of them. Whether it came before or after Khaizurān's open break with Hādī is not known, but the probability is that it came after that break, which itself took place four months after Hādī's accession.[18] In these four months Khaizurān, the records agree, assumed and exercised great powers in the administration of state affairs. She imposed her will and her decisions on her son and made excessive demands on him for her own and other's benefits. At first, he refused her nothing.[19] One day she sent him her maid, Khāliṣah, with a request for clothing. Hādī ordered a whole storehouse full of clothes to be handed over to her.[20]

Another incident points in the same general direction.

[17] Masᶜūdī, VI, 265–66; Ṭabarī, III, 597–99; Ibn Athīr, VI, 60; Ibn Khallikān, I, 525–26.

[18] Ṭabarī, III, 569; Ibn Athīr, VI, 68.

[19] Ṭabarī, III, 569, 571; Ibn Athīr, VI, 68; Masᶜūdī, VI, 268–69; *Fakhrī*, 261; cf. above, p. 54.

[20] Ṭabarī, III, 569.

Khaizurān's favor, as is to be expected, was sought after and exploited by some of the leading Hāshimite princesses, including the ranking Princess Zainab. These frequently acted as intermediatory intercessors for a cause which or for a person who needed to reach the caliph's ear. A curious detail, preserved or interpolated, is found in connection with an event that would seem to have taken place after the break between mother and son. In the ᶜAlīd rising that led to the Battle of Fakhkh in the Ḥijāz some nine months after Hādī's accession, the ᶜAbbāsid prince, Mūsā ibn ᶜĪsā, fighting in Hādī's forces, put a key prisoner to death on his own initiative. Hādī was displeased with Mūsā for this, but the latter pleaded thus: "O Commander of the Believers, I gave thought to his case, and said to myself, 'Aishah and Zainab will come to the Mother of the Commander of the Believers and weep before her and plead with her, and she will then speak on his behalf with the Commander of the Believers, who will, therefore, set him free.' "[21] Evidently Mūsā ibn ᶜĪsā, who had had an earlier experience with Khaizurān, did not quite credit the full break between mother and son and described here the "normal" procedure of roundabout harem intrigue with Khaizurān for a central figure.

Soon, however, Hādī began to hedge, as is clear from the following episode. One day while he was calling on Khaizurān, she asked him to appoint her brother, who was now also his father-in-law, governor of the Yaman. Hādī put her off with, "Remind me of it before my cups." He went home, dined, and called for his drink.

[21] *Ibid.*, pp. 551, 556, 560.

Presently, Khaizurān sent him one of her maids to remind him of the request. "Return," Hādī ordered the maid, "and say 'Choose for him either the divorce of his daughter ᶜUbaidah or the governorship of the Yaman.' " The maid understood no more of this than the words "choose for him," and that alone was the message she delivered to her mistress. Khaizurān returned word, "I have already chosen for him the governorship of the Yaman." So Hādī divorced ᶜUbaidah on the instant by simply repeating the divorce formula. Presently, he heard loud cries from the harem and went to inquire into their cause. Khaizurān tried to explain, but her son insisted it was her own choice. "That was not the message that was delivered to me," she informed him. There followed a sequel the "humor" of which can be understood to the full only by a Moslem society. Hādī, having rushed, as it turned out, prematurely, into divorcing his wife, wanted company in his misery and ordered every single one of his boon companions present to divorce a wife. This each did with a sword hanging over his head.[22] The sequel to this sequel is not recorded, but the reader is free to use his imagination.

Insatiable sycophants began to crowd around Khaizurān. These hoped to achieve their ends and ambitions by imposing on her vanity and her seemingly unlimited influence with Hādī. Soon there was a line of retainers, nobles, and generals that trailed its way to her gates to flatter and to angle for patronage. Hādī heard, saw, and blustered. "Do not," he sent word to his mother, "overstep the essential limits of womanly modesty and

[22] *Ibid.*, pp. 590–91; *Aghānī*, XIII, 13.

overdo in person the role of the generous donor. It is not dignified for women to enter upon affairs of state. Take to your prayer and worship and devote yourself to the service of Allah. Hereafter, submit to the womanly role that is required of your sex."[23] But Khaizurān heeded not these warning signs of danger ahead and rushed headlong into a major catastrophe.

It so happened that the storm burst in connection with a request on behalf of the captain of police, ᶜAbd Allah ibn Mālik, who, as already seen, had every reason and intention to serve Hādī as faithfully as he had served Mahdī. What the favor was that Khaizurān sought from Hādī for ᶜAbd Allah has escaped the record. At any rate, Hādī could not see his way to granting it and so made excuses to his mother. These she ignored as she persisted with, "You absolutely must grant my request."

"I will not do it," said Hādī stubbornly.

"But I have already assured ᶜAbd Allah ibn Mālik of it," continued the equally stubborn but none too wise Khaizurān.

The storm finally broke. "A plague upon the son of the strumpet," shouted Hādī in his rage. "I know it is he who is behind this; but, by Allah, I will not grant it to you."

"Then, by Allah," flashed back Khaizurān, "I shall never again ask anything of you."

Hot with rage, the son flung back defiantly, "And, by Allah, I care not!"

Greatly angered, Khaizurān rose to depart.

[23] Ṭabarī, III, 569, 571.

"Stay where you are," roared out Hādī, "and heed my words. I swear it, by Allah, and on the forfeiture of my descent from the Messenger of Allah, that if I hear that any one of my generals, retainers, or servants is at your door, I shall strike off his head and confiscate his property. Let him then who will, take that course. What is the meaning of all these daily processions back and forth to your door? Have you no spindle to keep you busy or Qurʾān to remind you (of Allah) or house to shield you? Beware and again beware! Open not your doors hereafter to either Moslem, Christian, or Jew."

Khaizurān departed in a high passion, knowing not whither she went.[24]

This stormy outburst, instead of clearing the atmosphere, proved but a prelude to a series of other outbreaks on the different parts of the political horizon.

Following the drastic step he had taken with his mother to its next logical move, Hādī summoned his generals and started by putting this question to them: "Who is better, I or you?"

"Most certainly you, O Commander of the Believers," they answered.

"And who, then, is better, my mother or your mother?"

"Assuredly your mother," they made reply.

"Then which of you," continued Hādī, "would like to have the men speak of his mother's affairs saying, 'So-and-so's mother did thus and so,' and 'So-and-so's mother said this and that'?"

[24] *Ibid.*, p. 570; Ibn Athīr, VI, 68; Masᶜūdī, VI, 269–70; *Fakhrī*, pp. 261–62; Ibn Khaldūn, III, 217.

"Not any one of us would like that," they readily answered.

"Then, what mean you by coming to my mother and by making her and her doings the object of your conversation?" When they heard this, they ceased their visits to her altogether.

Khaizurān was deeply hurt at this public humiliation coming after her own ominous scene with her son. She separated herself from him and vowed she would never again speak to him. "Thereafter," adds the record, "she spoke no word to him, bitter or sweet, and entered not his presence until death visited him."[25]

Mother and son were now openly at war; and each plotted the undoing of the other. The first round, only partially successful, went to Hādī; the second, swift and final, brought victory to Khaizurān. Between the two rounds the fate of Yaḥyā and of Hārūn al-Rashīd hung in the balance.

That Hādī was, to start with, somewhat resentful of Hārūn and not quite easy in mind as to his intentions seems to be warranted from the following episode, which took place early in the reign. Hārūn was one day announced while Hādī was holding court at ʿĪsābādh. Among those present and in high favor with Hādī was Zubaidah's full brother, Ibrāhīm, and Hādī's own right-hand man, Ibrāhīm al-Ḥarrānī, both sitting to the left of the caliph. Hārūn was admitted and took his seat at a respectful distance to the right. Hādī stared at him for some time in silence and then said: "O Hārūn, it seems to me that you allow yourself to dwell too much on the

[25] Ṭabarī, III, 571; Ibn Athīr, VI, 68; Ibn Khaldūn, III, 217.

fulfilment of the dream[26] and to hope for that which is not now within your reach. Remember, too, that 'one must first pluck the thorns from the tragacanth' "—an Arabic proverb that means the undertaking is exceedingly difficult.[27]

Hārūn knelt on both knees and answered: "O Mūsā, the haughty are humbled, the humble are raised (to honor), and the unjust are deceived. I do certainly hope that the caliphal authority will (in time) devolve upon me. I will then be equitable to those whom you have oppressed and generous to those whom you have cut off (from your generosity). I will place your sons above my own and give them my daughters in marriage. I will bring that to pass which is worthy of the memory of the Imām Mahdī."

Hārūn's attitude and reply seems to have dispelled Hādī's fears and suspicions, at least for the time being. "Draw nigh, O Abū Jaᶜfar,"[28] he said to his brother, who now approached and kissed his hands, and turned to resume his former distant seat. "Nay, by that illustrious Shaikh and the glorious King, your grandfather Manṣūr, you shall sit nowhere else but here with me!" and seated him accordingly. "O Ḥarrānī," he next called out to Ibrāhīm on his left, "dispatch to my brother a thousand thousand dinars immediately and, when the land tax is in hand, give him the half of it. Put all our treasuries and that which was taken from the accursed

[26] See below, pp. 97–98.

[27] Cf. Mubarrad, *Kāmil*, p. 186.

[28] This was Hārūn's *Kunyah* or surname as Umm Jaᶜfar was that of his young wife, Zubaidah.

Umayyads at his disposal and let him take all that he desires." When Hārūn later rose to leave, Hādī ordered his mount to be brought up for him to the very edge of the royal carpet.[29] That this state of "brotherly love" did not endure was due as much, if indeed not more, to the deeds of Yaḥyā and Khaizurān than to the desires of Hārūn and Hādī.

Just at what point Hādī began to think of replacing Hārūn by his own young son Jaᶜfar cannot be determined with certainty. What is certain is that he at first discussed the idea with Yaḥyā, when he seemed to be receptive to the latter's very logical arguments against such a move. Yaḥyā pointed out the danger of encouraging the foreswearing of allegiance and so establishing a precedent which might be easily followed later to the disadvantage of Jaᶜfar himself. He advised Hādī to leave his brother Hārūn as first heir and to appoint Jaᶜfar as second in line. Hādī commended Yaḥyā on his sound advice and implied that he would consider it.[30]

But Hādī does not seem to have been able to get rid of his initial idea of replacement and so approached Yaḥyā a second time. The latter would not lend himself to the plan. He was, therefore, clapped into jail, whence he sent word to Hādī that he had some advice for him. Hādī had him brought before him and gave him, at his request, a private audience.

"O Commander of the Believers," asked Yaḥyā, "do you think that should that event (Hādī's death) come

[29] Ṭabarī, III, 576–77; Ibn Athīr, VI, 66–67; Masᶜūdī, VI, 283–85.

[30] Ṭabarī, III, 573–74; Ibn Athīr, VI, 65; Ibn ᶜAbdūs, pp. 201–2.

to pass—which, I pray God, I may not live to see—do you (really) think that the people will deliver the caliphate to Jaᶜfar—and he not yet arrived at the age of discretion—and accept him as leader for their prayers, pilgrimages, and military expeditions?"

"Nay, by Allah," answered Hādī, "I do not think they will do that."

"Are you sure that the leading members of your family, like So-and-so and So-and-so and others besides, will not aspire to the caliphate and divert it from the sons of your father?"

"You do, indeed, make me take note of that, O Yaḥyā," said the caliph.

"By Allah," Yaḥyā followed up his advantage, "had not Mahdī appointed your brother as heir, would it not have been necessary for you yourself to do so? How then can you think of removing him from the heirship after Mahdī had appointed him to it? As I see it, O Commander of the Believers, it is by far the best to confirm the matter as it now stands. When Jaᶜfar comes of age, you can then summon Hārūn, who will renounce the caliphate and be the first to swear allegiance to Jaᶜfar and clasp his hand." Hādī soberly accepted both argument and advice and ordered Yaḥyā's release.[31]

But again this happy situation was too good to last. Though the fact is nowhere stated, it is very probable that Rabīᶜ had been already removed from the wazirate and that the open break between Hādī and Khaizurān had likewise taken place before Hādī reverted once

[31] Ṭabarī, III, 574–75; Ibn Athīr, VI, 66; Ibn ᶜAbdūs, p. 202; Masᶜūdī, VI, 281.

more to his idea of removing Hārūn from the succession. It is also quite apparent that Yaḥyā had reason to fear another change of mind on the part of the suspicious and shifty Hādī. He himself, though standing staunchly by Hārūn, kept away from Khaizurān, so as to avoid further complications from that quarter. When Rabīᶜ was no longer wazir, Yaḥyā felt isolated from the administration. He intrigued effectively to have one of his own trusted men appointed as secretary to the new wazir, Ibrāhīm al-Ḥarrānī, so as to keep him, Yaḥyā, informed of new developments. Counterintrigue reported the matter to Hādī, and Yaḥyā, in turn, knew of this move in time enough to have his man, with the cooperation of the wazir himself, transferred to some other post. When Hādī, thinking to test out his wazir and implicate Yaḥyā, asked the former about the secretary involved, Ibrāhīm could truthfully say that the man was not in his service.[32]

Hādī, on the other hand, had not kept this matter of the heirship strictly to himself. He had sounded out several leading generals and notables, who had encouraged him in his plan and promised their support. These men, having thus cast in their lot with Hādī and linked their fate with that of his son Jaᶜfar, trembled for that fate should Hārūn, and with him Yaḥyā, come to power. They did their best, therefore, to keep Hādī's mind on his first plan for his son.[33]

Aside from the natural desire to have one of his own sons as heir, Hādī must have been subjected to some

[32] Ṭabarī, III, 572, 598; Ibn ᶜAbdūs, pp. 199–200.

[33] Ṭabarī, III, 575; Ibn Athīr, VI, 66.

harem pressure in that direction. Though there is some confusion both as to Jaᶜfar's age and as to which of Hādī's several concubines was the young child's mother, there is evidence that Hādī's favorite, Amat al-ᶜAzīz, was in his confidence, that is, if Hādī's physician, ᶜAbd Allah al-Ṭaifūrī, got and told his facts straight.[34]

Over and above these several factors that helped to keep Hādī's mind disturbed and vacillating were still others, superstitious or psychological. These drove him finally into taking action in line with his strong passion and instinct over against the transient hold of his own calm reason. Among these were the rumors associated with his birth and with the nature and length of his reign. Whether these rumors were first in circulation in Mahdī's time or whether, later, the "opposition" looked upon them as good propaganda is not quite clear. Several of these have the earmarks of post-event predictions.[35]

These were the days of horoscopes, and Hādī's had forecast a short reign.[36] Then there was that dream that he warned Hārūn not to dwell on too much.[37] The dream does not seem to have been widely known, since one of Hārūn's special friends asked him later what dream it was that Hādī had referred to. Hārūn then told this story. Mahdī had dreamed that he gave a rod each to Mūsā and to Hārūn. And, behold, Mūsā's rod put forth leaves a little space at the top only, while Hārūn's rod put forth leaves all along its length. Mahdī called for an interpreter of dreams, who told him that, though both

[34] Cf. above, pp. 27–28 and 60–61.

[35] Cf. Masᶜūdī, VI, 435–38.

[36] *Ibid.*, pp. 281–82.

[37] Cf. above, pp. 92–93.

his sons Mūsā and Hārūn would rule, the reign of Mūsā would be short, while that of Hārūn would be long, his days prosperous, and his age the best of ages.[38] Of such stuff are some political prophecies spun!

Hādī is frequently reported as being extremely jealous for the honor and reputation of the royal harem. His attitude toward his mother's "unwomanly" conduct and his line of action and argument with the generals were, in part at least, genuinely motivated by this sentiment. This latter is deeply rooted in most Moslems and highly commended in Moslem societies, particularly with respect to the women of the upper classes. Other specific incidents confirm the general statement made of Hādī in this respect.

Ruqaiyah, like Khaizurān and Raiṭah, outlived the caliph Mahdī, who had married her early in his reign. An ᶜAlid prince married the widow, seemingly at the first opportunity. Hādī summoned him and demanded, "Could you not find women other than the wife of the Commander of the Believers?"

"Allah has forbidden none except the wives of my grandfather (the Prophet)," retorted the ᶜAlid. For this double daring the man was given five hundred strokes, which he endured rather than divorce the former widow of Mahdī.[39]

A still more gruesome story runs as follows. Hādī was with his friends one night when a servant entered and whispered something in his ear. He told the company to

[38] Ṭabarī, III, 577; Ibn Athīr, VI, 67; Masᶜūdī, VI, 285; Ibn Khaldūn, III, 216.

[39] Ṭabarī, III, 483, 587; Ibn Athīr, VI, 71; cf. above, p. 66.

wait, and was gone for quite a while. When he returned, he was breathing very heavily. Silently he threw himself on a couch, and an hour passed before his breathing was calm again. A servant had returned with him, bearing a tray covered with a towel. Hādī now sat up and ordered the servant to uncover the tray. The trembling slave obeyed. The uncovered tray revealed the heads of two of the most beautiful girls. The scent of perfume, jewels, and blood clung to the ghastly sight. "Know ye their offense?" asked Hādī.

"No," they answered briefly.

"I was informed that they were in love," he explained, "and I set my spies to watch them. I caught them in the immoral act and killed them myself." He then resumed his former conversation, as though he had done nothing unusual in the meantime.[40] Thus did Hādī's strong instincts and emotions lead him to settle a case of Lesbian love in his own harem.

Still another harem incident, omitted in the earlier standard histories, but appearing in more than one later source, testifies to Hādī's extremely jealous temperament. It highlights his great passion for a concubine who in all probability was Amat al-ᶜAzīz, involved, as already seen and for reason of the same sort of jealousy, in the death of Rabīᶜ. Early records state the fact that Amat al-ᶜAzīz, slave girl of Rabīᶜ, favorite concubine of Hādī, was later married by Hārūn al-Rashīd and bore him a son named ᶜAlī.[41] The later sources also state that

[40] Ṭabarī, III, 590.

[41] Ibn Ṭaifūr, *Kitāb Baghdād*, ed. H. Keller (Leipzig, 1908), pp. 25–26; Ṭabarī, III, 597–98, 757; Ibn Athīr, IV, 148.

Hārūn married a slave girl of Hādī's but give her name as Ghādir. Unless one is to assume that Hārūn married *two* slave girls of his brother Hādī, this Ghādir of the later sources is to be identified with Amat al-ʿAzīz. It is easy enough to see how the name "Ghādir," which means "Deceiver" or "Betrayer," could come to be applied to the girl in her story as it appears in these later sources themselves, which runs, in brief, somewhat as follows.

Ghādir, the concubine of Hādī, was exceedingly beautiful, and Hādī was passionately enamored of her. One day, while she was singing for him, he became pensive and changed color as the painful thought ran through his mind that he would die and his brother, Hārūn, would marry this beloved. So he sent for Hārūn and made both him and the girl take a most binding oath, even to vowing to make the pilgrimage on foot, that they would never marry each other. In less than a month Hādī was dead and Hārūn asked the girl to marry him.

"What of your oath and mine?" she inquired.

"I will redeem them," answered the royal suitor.

So they were married, and she found more favor with Rashīd than she had found with Hādī. She would go to sleep with her head in his lap, while he would sit motionless so as not to awaken her. One day while thus asleep, she suddenly woke up crying and terrified. She informed Hārūn that she had dreamed of his brother, who recited verses to her, among them, "You did (after all) marry my brother; in truth did they name you 'Ghādir.' Ere morning comes, you shall join and accompany me." Hārūn tried to calm her with, "These are but confused dreams," but she believed otherwise. Her guilty conscience and superstitious terror so completely unnerved her that she was dead within the hour. Hārūn mourned her greatly. It was, according to these records, on account of the oath he had made to Hādī in connection with her that Hārūn made the pilgrimage of 173/790—the year also of her death—on foot, walking, however, on woolen mats all the way.[42]

Convinced of his mother's great resentment, if not indeed, by now, bitter hatred, against him; himself resentful of sustained favoritism shown his younger brother, now all the more the favorite with the disgruntled queen-mother; distracted with ominous rumors and predictions; and stirred to the depths of his passionate and jealous nature when it came to his own harem, Hādī took the wrong road. He finally yielded, against his own better judgment, to the persuasion of his interested advisers and to his own instinctive temptation to place his young son, Jaᶜfar, in line for the succession to the exclusion of Hārūn.

He set about now to accomplish this end with or without Yaḥyā's co-operation.[43] Yaḥyā was, no doubt, faced at this point with one of the most serious steps of his entire career. Most of the Hāshimite leaders and the generals had readily supported Hādī's plan. Khaizurān

[42] Ṭabarī, III, 609; Ibn Athīr, VI, 82; ᶜ*Iqd*, III, 350; Ibn Taghrībirdī, I, 460, 469; Ibn Ḥijjah, II, 2–4; Waṭwāṭ, *Kitāb Ghurar al-Khaṣāʾiṣ al-Wāḍiḥah* (Būlāq, 1384/1867), p. 232; Ferdinand Wüstenfeld, *Die Chroniken der Stadt Mekka* (4 vols.; Leipzig, 1857–61), III, 111; IV, 179–80, where different dates are given.

[43] Ṭabarī, III, 575; Masᶜūdī, VI, 281.

was a liability rather than an asset. Hārūn himself seemed none too eager to put up a genuine struggle for the throne. He anticipated the pleasure of private life in the enjoyable company of his beloved Zubaidah, who was, it must be noted here, at long last with child.[44] Yaḥyā's task of directing and controlling Hārūn was no easy one. For while he held out firmly against the deposition, he advised submission to Hādī on lesser matters. The pleasure-loving and haughty Hārūn would, here, too, reverse that policy. This is clearly brought out in the following incident. Mahdī had given Hārūn a very precious ring which Hādī now desired. Hārūn made no move to part with the ring. Hādī sent for Yaḥyā and threatened him with death should Hārūn fail to return the ring. Yaḥyā sought out Hārūn at the Palace Immortal in Baghdad and pleaded long and earnestly with him to give Hādī the ring. Finally, Hārūn said he would take it to Hādī himself. He left Baghdad for Hādī's court at ᶜĪsābādh, but, in crossing the bridge over the Tigris, he threw the ring in the river saying, "Let him (Hādī) do now whatever he wishes." Hādī, it seems, realized that Yaḥyā was not to blame for this, but he was very wroth with Hārūn.[45]

If Hādī himself did not realize that Yaḥyā was the brain and soul of the opposition, there were those around him who pointed out the fact. Hādī would summon Yaḥyā, accuse him of influencing his brother Hārūn against him, threaten him, and then let him go,

[44] Ṭabarī, III, 573; Ibn Athīr, VI, 65; Ibn ᶜAbdūs, p. 201; cf. below, pp. 137–38 and 141.

[45] Ibn ᶜAbdūs, pp. 207–8; Ṭabarī, III, 602; Ibn Athīr, VI, 74.

so convincing was Yaḥyā's logic and so proper his attitude.[46] Yet, he, more than perhaps anyone else, fully realized the danger to the empire, to Hārūn, and to himself in this now determined move of Hādī's. He was, indeed, between the proverbial frying pan and the fire.

There is a tendency among some to look upon Yaḥyā's logical arguments in the interest of peaceful succession in the event of Hādī's death as political cunning and subterfuge. It is true that Yaḥyā's political hands were not always snow white. But it is to be remembered that some of the dirt they acquired was in the course of service to Manṣūr and Mahdī; and it was Mahdī's will that he was now striving to uphold. Hārūn had been his charge for practically all his life, and it was his interests that he was anxious to safeguard. The realization that his own future interests and those of his entire family would be better served under Hārūn as caliph than under Jaᶜfar or any other aspirant need not detract from his courageous action of holding out against Hādī in the face of threats and worse. For in the months that followed Hārūn's deposition, when Hārūn was ostracized and humiliated, Yaḥyā and his family alone dared to be seen in the young prince's company. As the months passed, Yaḥyā, no doubt, began to fear for his own life and perhaps for that of Hārūn also. It was on his advice that the latter sought and secured permission from his uneasy brother, to put distance between them, for a hunting expedition that proved quite prolonged.[47]

[46] Ṭabarī, III, 572–73; Ibn Athīr, VI, 65–66.

[47] Ṭabarī, III, 572; Ibn Athīr, VI, 281; Masᶜūdī, VI, 281–82.

This situation, by its complex nature and the great issues and interests at stake, was bound to grow worse before it could get any better. Poisoned words and poisoned victuals were rumored to be passing between Hādī and his mother. Death was believed to be lurking in some form or another for Hārūn. Yaḥyā, once more in prison, expected every night or each summons to be his last. Again the stage was being prepared for high tragedy. Some believe it was Khaizurān who gave the cue for the next act. Others, however, place the responsibility for the initial scene definitely on Hādī's shoulders.

Hādī, it seems, had determined on poisoning his mother. He sent her a dish of rice with the message that he had enjoyed it and wished her to share it. For his scheme to work, this must have taken place before the open war between them, unless Hādī hoped that Khaizurān would consider this as a sort of peace gesture on his part. Khaizurān, so the story goes, was warned by her faithful Khāliṣah to test the food first. So it was given to a dog that perished soon after eating it. Hādī, awaiting results, sent to inquire how his mother liked the dish and received the answer that she liked it very well. This was not the answer he had expected. Thwarted of his purpose, he sent back this quite raw reply: "You did not eat it, for, had you eaten it, I would certainly have been well rid of you by now. When did a caliph ever prosper who had a (living) mother?"[48]

Khaizurān now feared not only for her life but also for that of Hārūn. Rumors of plots to murder her favorite son undermined for a while her courage and ambi-

[48] Ṭabarī, III, 570–71; Ibn Athīr, VI, 68–69.

tions. She sent to Yaḥyā a foster-sister of Hārūn who, tearing her clothes and weeping, delivered this message: "The Lady says to you, 'For God's sake save my son! Do not kill him![49] Let him comply with his brother's requests and demands; for his life is dearer to me than this world and all that is in it.' " This was obviously a little too much for Yaḥyā, who cried out sharply, "What do you know of this! If it is as you say (that my advice was leading to Hārūn's death), then I myself, my children, and my family will have to be killed before he is. So, even if I am suspected (by Khaizurān) on his (Hārūn's) account, I cannot be suspected in regard to myself and them."[50]

Hādī's physician, ᶜAbd Allah al-Ṭaifūrī, reports in great detail the scene when Hādī caused his followers to renounce their allegiance to Hārūn and tender it instead to his son Jaᶜfar. Foremost among the generals to comply were Yazīd ibn Mazyad and ᶜAbd Allah ibn Mālik. But the general Harthamah ibn Aᶜyan refused to do so, arguing very much along the lines that Yaḥyā has previously offered. Hādī, according to this account, first scolded and threatened the general and then commended him, in the presence of all the rest of the distinguished men who had taken the oath, for his conscientious objections. When Hādī went home that night he was met by Amat al-ᶜAzīz, who already knew what had happened and who summed up her disappointment and fears thus: "This morning we were full of hopes for this child and this evening we are full of fears for him."

[49] I.e., be the cause of his death by advising him to hold out against Hādī.

[50] Ṭabarī, III, 575.

Hādī then explained to her that policy had forced his hand in dealing with Harthamah. Amat al-ᶜAzīz was, nevertheless, in tears, and Hādī comforted her with, "I have hopes that Allah will gladden you (yet)." And ᶜAbd Allah, the physician, goes on to explain, quite naïvely, that she and all those around her *mis*understood Hādī to mean that he was contemplating poisoning Hārūn. In a few days Hādī himself was dead.[51]

Though the sequence of events is not at all clear, there is no doubt that events moved quite rapidly before the end. Hādī had traveled north to his gardens near Mauṣil, whence he sent out orders, east and west, to all his governors to meet him. But he took seriously ill and returned home to ᶜĪsābādh.[52] In the meantime, Yaḥyā was cast into prison (seemingly at ᶜĪsābād)—being confined in a space so small that he could not stretch his legs—and his life and that of Hārūn were once more threatened.[53] The generals and notables who had declared for Jaᶜfar were again very seriously alarmed lest Yaḥyā escape and Hārūn come to the caliphate in the event of Hādī's death. They first thought of forging an order in Hādī's name for Yaḥyā's immediate execution but, on second thought, gave up the idea for fear of Hādī's recovery.[54] Hādī himself, according to another account, had given the order for

[51] Ibn Abī Uṣabiᶜah, I, 154–55; cf. Ṭabarī, III, 572; Ibn Athīr, VI, 64; Ibn ᶜAbdūs, p. 208.

[52] Ṭabarī, III, 578; Ibn Athīr, VI, 68.

[53] Ṭabarī, III, 599–600, Yaᶜqūbī, II, 490, according to which Hārūn, too, was imprisoned; but cf. Ibn ᶜAbdūs, p. 209.

[54] Ṭabarī, III, 578; Ibn Athīr, VI, 68.

Yaḥyā's execution but was prevailed upon by his wazir, Ibrāhīm al-Ḥarrānī, to grant him a night's delay. Hādī himself died that very night.[55]

Where in all these scenes of fears, plots, death, and worse does Khaizurān fit? Did she just wait passively but hopefully for Hādī's death, or did she once more take the reins in her own hands either in anticipation of his death or in order to hasten it and make it certain?

A messenger brought Khaizurān the first news of Hādī's serious illness, which she received with, "What am I supposed to do about it?" To this, her maid Khāliṣah made reply, "Arise and go unto your son, O Noble Lady. For this is no time for either resentment, reproach, or anger." Khaizurān did now go to ᶜĪsābādh.[56] She seemed all the while to be certain of Hādī's fast-approaching death and so took control of affairs once more, as she had done on hearing of Mahdī's death. She sent word to Yaḥyā, instructing him to have all the state papers that were needed ready to be sent out to the provinces to announce the death of Hādī and the accession of Hārūn. Yaḥyā, from his prison, relayed the order to his son Faḍl, who called the secretaries to his home and prepared the necessary documents.[57]

Hādī, in the meantime, had grown steadily worse. He had summoned his physicians, including Abū Quraish and ᶜAbd Allah, but they were unable to help him. He chided them for accepting his money and gifts and fail-

55 Ibn ᶜAbdūs, pp. 208–9.

56 Ṭabarī, III, 571, 578.

57 *Ibid.*, p. 578; Ibn Athīr, VI, 67.

ing him in his hour of extreme need. Abū Quraish, trying perhaps to calm him, answered that they were trying to do their best but that Allah alone is the bestower of health. This angered Hādī all the more. The chamberlain, Faḍl ibn al-Rabīᶜ, now came forward to suggest a new doctor he knew of, who had a good reputation. Hādī ordered Faḍl to send for him and to put the other doctors to death. Faḍl sent for the physician but did not carry out the rest of the command, since he knew that the severity of the pain had disturbed Hādī's mental balance.

In the meantime, the famous Bakhtīshūᶜ, who had long ago run away from the powerful alliance of Khaizurān and Abū Quraish against him, was also sent for but did not arrive until after Hādī's death. Presently, the new physician, with the half-Arabic, half-Syrian name of ᶜAbd Ishūᶜ ibn Naṣr that the text gives him, arrived and was taken to the sickroom.

"Have you seen the specimen?" asked Hādī.

"Yes, O Commander of the Believers," he answered. "I will now prepare you some medicine to take, and in nine hours you will be free from your pain." But outside he said to the doctors, "Do not trouble your hearts, for today you shall depart to your homes." He set them to pounding some medicines within the caliph's hearing, saying, "Keep on pounding so he will hear you and be reassured and calmed."

About every hour Hādī would send for him and ask for the medicine, and the doctor would draw his attention to the pounding, and that would quiet him. In nine hours, says this account, Hādī was dead and the doctors were safe again.[58] His disease, says another source, was ulcer of the stomach.[59]

As Hādī grew worse, he would have no one about him except the younger servants. He sent some of these to call his mother to him. Khaizurān came and took her position at his bedside. Hādī then said to her, "This night I perish, and my brother Hārūn succeeds me this very same night; for you know the prediction at the time of my birth at Rayy. I had forbidden you to do some things and commanded you to do certain others out of the demands of state policy and not for lack of filial devotion. I was not in opposition to you but sought only to shield you, filially and sincerely." He then reached for her hand and, placing it on his breast, breathed his last.[60]

Khaizurān, it would seem according to one sequence of events, now lost no time in furthering Hārūn's cause. She either went herself[61] or sent her men[62] to release Yaḥyā from prison so that he could come and take a look at Hādī, whom she judged to be dead. When Yaḥyā entered Hādī's room, Amat al-ᶜAzīz sat weeping at Hādī's head. Yaḥyā closed the dead caliph's eyes and hastened to reach Hārūn and give him the news.[63] According to some, Yaḥyā was actually the first to break

[58] Qifṭī, p. 431; Ibn Abī Uṣaibiᶜah, I, 126; for Dāᵓūd cf. *ibid.*, p. 109.

[59] Ṭabarī, III, 569; Ibn Athīr, VI, 68; Suyūṭī, *Taᵓrīkh*, p. 109; Damīrī, *K. al-Ḥayāwān* (2 vols.; Cairo, 1278/1861), I, 105; Ibn Taghrībirdī, I, 458.

[60] Masᶜūdī, VI, 282–83; cf. above, p. 98.

[61] Yaᶜqūbī, II, 490.

[62] Ṭabarī, III, 571; Ibn Athīr VI, 69.

[63] Yaᶜqūbī, II, 490; Ibn ᶜAbdūs, p. 209.

the news to Hārūn;[64] but, according to others, it was the general Harthamah who had that good fortune.[65] The probability is that Khaizurān, at the same time that she released the imprisoned Yaḥyā, sent Harthamah posthaste to Hārūn at Baghdad, where another dramatic scene was enacted. Hārūn was asleep at the Palace Immortal.

"Wake up! O Commander of the Believers!" he heard his trustee cry out.

"How you do frighten me by alluding to my caliphate! What will my standing with Hādī be should he hear of this?"

Then he was told of Hādī's death and was presented with the royal signet ring and with the now-fallen Ḥarrānī. He had barely had time to realize his good fortune when a second messenger came to announce that his slave girl, Marājil, had given birth to a son. Hārūn, there and then, named the newly born ᶜAbd Allah (the future Maʾmūn).[66] Thus, this night of destiny, predicted according to Khaizurān, saw the death of one caliph, the accession of a second, and the birth of a third.[67]

Yet another scene in this dramatic night was the sudden seizure of the sleeping Jaᶜfar, son of Hādī. He was forced at the point of the sword to promise to renounce on the morrow all claims to the caliphate and so release from their sworn obligations all who had taken the oath of allegiance to him. This promise the young and frightened prince could not help but make and keep.

[64] Ṭabarī, III, 601–2; Ibn Athīr, VI, 74; Ibn ᶜAbdūs, p. 209.

[65] Ṭabarī, III, 599–600; Ibn Athīr, VI, 67, 73; Ibn Khaldūn, III, 217.

[66] See preceding note and cf. above, p. 41.

[67] Ṭabarī, III, 578–79; Ibn Athīr, VI, 67, *Fakhrī*, p. 262.

The morrow, therefore, saw the renunciation of Jaᶜfar, the burial of Hādī, and the proclamation of Hārūn as caliph.[68]

Khaizurān, in the harem, herself broke the news to four of the leading princesses, including Raiṭah and Zainab, and all five now awaited further developments. Presently, Khāliṣah entered. Khaizurān asked her what the situation was and received the information that the dead Mūsā (Hādī) was buried. "If Mūsā is dead, (then) Hārūn still lives," said Khaizurān, and called for drinks to be served to her and to the royal princesses. This done, she ordered Khāliṣah to present the princesses with a million dinars each. "What is my son Hārūn doing?" she now asked.

"He has sworn," answered Khāliṣah, "to be in Baghdad for the midday prayer."

"Then saddle the horses," cried out Khaizurān. "What point is there in my staying here when he has departed!" And so she followed Hārūn to Baghdad.[69]

This set of facts gathered from some of the earliest historical sources as well as from others of different dates and pretensions and arranged in the above sequence would seem to offer the most probable march of events connected with the death of the caliph Mūsā al-Hādī. They reveal Khaizurān as having lost all genuine motherly feeling for her firstborn, Hādī. They also show her eagerly awaiting the caliphate of her favorite, Hārūn al-Rashīd, and actively preparing the way for him and for her own return to power. If these were the only incidents recorded in this connection, one would be fairly safe in dismissing the subject at this point. But the

[68] Ṭabarī, III, 602–3; Ibn Athīr, VI, 74.

[69] Ṭabarī, III, 579.

sources offer further complications by the interjection of murder into the scene. The oriental historians,[70] and in their wake a considerable group of more recent Eastern and Western writers,[71] have lent their ears to an alternative rumor that Hādī either was poisoned[72] or, as is more frequently reported, was smothered to death by some of the harem slaves who were acting on Khaizurān's orders. It would seem that these fair instruments of death covered the sick Hādī's face and then sat on it until he ceased to breathe. Dark color is lent to the murder charge by the double motive of revenge and fear, on the one hand, and ambition and love of power, on the other.

Unless some reliable sources earlier than the ones now available bring to light more promising clues, both deductive and detective efforts to unravel the mystery will have to be suspended. In the meantime, let us, in turn, follow Khaizurān as she hastens after Hārūn to the imperial city of Baghdad, where she is to stage a triumphant comeback.

[70] E.g., *ibid.*, p. 571; Ibn Athīr, VI, 69; *Fakhrī*, 261–62; Abū Faraj, *Mukhtaṣar al-Duwal*, p. 222; Ibn Khaldūn, III, 217; Ibn Taghrībirdī, I, 458; Suyūṭī, *Taʾrīkh*, p. 109.

[71] E.g., Zaidan, II, 126; Rifāʿī, I, 109; G. Weil, *Geschichte der islamitischen Völker* (Stuttgart, 1866), p. 152; Carra de Vaux, *Les Penseurs de l'Islam* (4 vols.; Paris, 1921–26), I, 3; William Muir, *The Caliphate . . . .*, ed. Weir (Edinburgh, 1915), pp. 474–75; Edward Henry Palmer, *Haroun Alraschid* (London, 1881), p. 34; Philby, *op. cit.*, p. 35; Reuben Levy, *A Baghdad Chronicle* (Cambridge, 1929), p. 43; for a flighty but unreliable treatment, cf. Audisio, *op. cit.*, pp. 41–42.

[72] E.g., Suyūṭī, *Taʾrīkh*, p. 109, and Ibn Taghrībirdī, I, 458. A few of the later sources introduce an accidental death, which seems to be the least probable, e.g., Suyūṭī, *Taʾrīkh*, p. 109; Quṭb al-Dīn al-Nahrawālī, *Kitāb al-Iʿlām bī Aʿlām Bait al-Ḥarām*, ed. Wüstenfeld, *op. cit.*, III, 110.

IV

Triumph

Th' affrighted sun erewhile had fled,
  And hid his radiant face in night;
A cheerless gloom the world o'erspread—
  But Hārūn came and all was well.

Again the sun shoots forth his rays;
  Nature is decked in beauty's robe:
For mighty Hārūn's sceptre sways,
  And Yaḥyā's arm sustains the globe.[1]

INTO some such verse as the above might one render the couplets with which Ibrāhīm al-Mauṣilī, court poet and musician, received the accession of Hārūn and the latter's appointment of Yaḥyā to the independent wazirate. For, said Hārūn to Yaḥyā, "it is you, dear Father, who have seated me on this throne by your auspicious counsel and excellent direction. I, therefore, invest you with the government of the empire, taking it from off my own shoulders. Govern, then, as you see right. Appoint to office whom you will and remove whom you will. Conduct all affairs as you see fit." And

[1] William A. Clouston (ed.), *Arabian Poetry for English Readers* (Glasgow, 1881), p. 110; the translation is that of J. D. Carlyle. Cf. Ibn Khallikān, IV, 105. For the Arabic verse see Ṭabarī, III, 604.

therewith he handed him the imperial signet ring.[2] Thus did Hārūn reserve himself for his pleasures and put Yaḥyā's shoulder to the wheel of government. Thus did Yaḥyā, in contrast to his own father under Manṣūr, become the grand wazir, or prime burden-bearer and absolute ruler under Hārūn. He and his two sons, Faḍl and Jaᶜfar, who soon came to be known as the lesser wazirs, ruled Hārūn's empire, and ruled it well, for seventeen golden years.

One searches in vain for a specific expression of Hārūn's gratitude to his mother, Khaizurān, for the aggressive part she had played in securing the succession for him. However, since deeds speak louder than words, Hārūn's actions would indicate that he allowed her a free hand and, at times, restrained his own desires out of deference to her expressed wishes. For it was with his consent, tacit perhaps, that Khaizurān shared power with the grand wazir, who, for as long as she lived, consulted her on all state and palace affairs.[3] That Yaḥyā was able to sustain his basic position in this unequal triangle was due, in part, to his ability to estimate correctly and handle tactfully the character and temperament of both royal mother and son. For it is quite obvious that, despite Hārūn's generous words, Yaḥyā had to take both caliph and queen-mother into consideration. He still continued to watch over Hārūn and to steer him into the path he should go. His method, however, was

[2] Ibn ᶜAbdūs, p. 211; Ṭabarī, III, 603–4, 606; Ibn Athīr, VI, 74–75; Masᶜūdī, VI, 288–89; Khaṭīb, XIV, 128–29; Ibn Khallikān, IV, 104; Ibn Taghrībirdī, I, 149.

[3] E.g., Ṭabarī, III, 604; Ibn Athīr, VI, 75; Ibn ᶜAbdūs, p. 211; Ibn Taghrībirdī, I, 460; Ibn Khaldūn, III, 217, 223.

not one of preachment or prohibition but rather one of persuasion and inducement. "Whenever," says the historian, "Yaḥyā saw anything in Hārūn that he disliked, he did not confront him with disapproval; but rather he quoted to him proverbs and related to him stories of kings and caliphs that pointed to the necessity of desisting from whatever it was that he disliked. For, he used to say, 'Prohibition leads to instigation, especially with caliphs, for although you do not intend to incite one to a particular action, if you prohibit it, you do urge it onward.' "[4]

Hārūn inaugurated his reign by a bloodthirsty act of vengeance on one of Hādī's adherents who had been too eager to have Hārūn make way for the newly appointed heir, Jaᶜfar, as he rode by. Hārūn had stepped aside as ordered; but the insult had rankled, and now it cost the unfortunate adherent his head.[5] Khaizurān, even more vengeful, wished to inaugurate her power by a massacre of all the leaders who had forsaken Hārūn and taken the oath of fealty to young Jaᶜfar. Here, again, it was Yaḥyā's master-hand that pointed to a "better way."

"And what is this better way?" asked Khaizurān.

"Let them be exposed to slaughter by the enemy," said the wazir. "If they defend themselves, that defense itself will keep them busy. If the enemy should carry them off, then you will be relieved of them." She approved his plan, and the people involved were thus saved from immediate and direct vengeance.[6]

[4] Ibn ᶜAbdūs, pp. 237–38.

[5] Ṭabarī, III, 602; Ibn Athīr, VI, 74.

[6] Ibn ᶜAbdūs, p. 212.

Time cooled the hot passion of revenge, and statesmanship found ways and means to overlook the past and to utilize able men in the service of empire. Of special interest here is the case of ᶜAbd Allah ibn Mālik, the old captain of police. He was, it will be recalled, among the first to support Hādī's plan and to take the oath of allegiance to Jaᶜfar. Now he sought canon opinion to help release him from his oath and did not shrink from making the prilgrimage on foot, though walking on quilts, in expiation of that oath. He outlived the Barmakids and served both Hārūn and Maᵓmūn with distinction.[7]

Ibrāhīm al-Ḥarrānī, wazir of Hādī and custodian of the imprisoned Yaḥyā, experienced a complete reversal of role when, at Hārūn's command, he found himself Yaḥyā's prisoner. Later he, too, was released and allowed to depart the capital.[8]

Faḍl ibn al-Rabīᶜ, Hādī's chamberlain, who had secretly lent some aid to Yaḥyā and Hārūn, was also taken into the administration.[9] He, however, does not seem to have been in favor with Khaizurān, who prevented Hārūn from bestowing on him the powerful office of keeper of the privy seal. Since the office was held in her lifetime by Yaḥyā's sons, Faḍl and Jaᶜfar, in succession, it is quite probable that her opposition, on this score, to Faḍl was due as much to her recollection of his past position with Hādī as to her definite support of the

[7] Ṭabarī, III, 603, 692, 704, 709, 734, 769, 773; Jāḥiẓ, *K. al-Tāj*, pp. 81 and 92, and references there cited.

[8] Ṭabarī, III, 603; Ibn ᶜAbdūs, p. 212.

[9] Ṭabarī, III, 620; Yaᶜqūbī, II, 520; Ibn ᶜAbdūs, p. 230.

Barmakids and their interests.[10] Retaining the office of chamberlain and grooming his son for the same, Faḍl did, nevertheless, eye the wazirate. Personal ambition and developing circumstances were already providing the wedge that was to split asunder an old association between these two able and powerful wazirate families.

The first pilgrimage of a new caliph is quite an important occasion for favorable propaganda. Mahdī had made the most of this, in personal display and splendor, on the one hand, and public works and charity, on the other.[11] The short and disturbed reign of Hādī did not permit that caliph to make the pilgrimage in person, but he, too, was liberal with the Holy Cities.[12] Hārūn, in his first pilgrimage of 170/787, followed in his father's footsteps.[13] Khaizurān was not to be outdone by either husband or son. Her pilgrimage of 159/776 was made while she was as yet a slave concubine.[14] A dozen years later she made the pilgrimage of 171/788 as the queen-mother whose power had waxed and waned and then waxed again in triumph.

Khaizurān left the capital for Mecca in the month of Ramaḍān (February–March), that is, three months before Dhū al-Ḥijjah, or the month of pilgrimage proper.[15] It is somewhat disappointing to find no mention of her

[10] Ṭabarī, III, 609; Ibn Athīr, VI, 82.

[11] Ṭabarī, III, 187, 483; Yaʿqūbī, II, 476–77.

[12] F. Wüstenfeld, *Die Chroniken der Stadt Mekka* (4 vols.; Leipzig, 1857–61), III, 109.

[13] Ṭabarī, III, 605.

[14] Cf. above, pp. 38–39.

[15] Ṭabarī, III, 606; Ibn Taghrībirdī, I, 464.

companions, of whom she undoubtedly had many; nor is there any detailed account of the journey itself. But this lapse on the part of the historians is somewhat redeemed by the numerous detailed references to her interesting and significant activities during this prolonged stay in the Holy City. For, aside from the usual liberal dispensation of largess and charity, Khaizurān seems to have had the instincts of a natural antiquarian which she now put to good use in the cause of faith and empire. The mosque of the Kaᶜbah at Mecca and that of the Prophet at Medina had early become hallowed ground. With the passage of time they had repeatedly received the liberal and solicitous attention of mighty ruler and humble worshiper alike. But it was left to Khaizurān to think of rescuing and setting apart, as something likewise hallowed, the very birthplace of the Prophet. She wished further to associate her name with it and with the secret meeting-house of Mohammed's earlier years before he had become in any way a national figure.

She was completely successful in her first objective. It was easy enough to locate the birthplace of Mohammed or, at any rate, the house accepted as such by all the Meccans. Mohammed had deeded the place to his cousin, ᶜAqīl ibn Abī Ṭālib. It remained in the possession of his family until Mohammed ibn Yūsuf—brother of the famous governor of the Umayyads, Ḥajjāj ibn Yūsuf—bought it from the family and inclosed it within his own adjoining property, known as the White House residence of Ibn Yūsuf. Khaizurān now purchased the property, set it apart from the original residence of Ibn

Yūsuf, and converted it into the sacred Mosque of the Nativity which now faced the Street of the Nativity.[16]

Khaizurān secured, seemingly for personal use, the property adjoining the house of Arqam, in which Mohammed and his earliest converts met secretly in Mecca. Arqam's house was called "The House of Islam" and had already become a sacred spot associated with Mohammed's revelations. Something of this halo now attached itself to the property acquired by the queen-mother and known thereafter as "Khaizurān's House."[17] Doubtless Khaizurān must have spent thought and money, aside from the initial plan and price of purchase, on these two places which have helped to keep her memory alive through the centuries, though mostly in some dusty pages of history.

Again Khaizurān has to her credit a drinking fountain placed on some Meccan property acquired by Jaᶜfar the Barmakid, who at some time erected a new dwelling on it. Later, when Khaizurān and Jaᶜfar were both dead and the Barmakids fallen, property and fountain passed into the hands of Queen Zubaidah.[18]

Waterworks of one sort or another were everywhere in constant demand in this water-thirsty land except in river regions. These works—fountains, pools, wells,

[16] Wüstenfeld, *op. cit.*, I, 422; IV, 181; Ṭabarī, I, 968; Ibn Athīr, I, 333; Masᶜūdī, IV, 130; Maqdisī, *K. al-Badᵓ wa al-Taᵓrīkh*, ed. and trans. C. Huart (6 vols.; Paris, 1899–1921), IV, 132; Ibn Jubair, *Riḥlah* ("The Travels of Ibn Jubair"), ed. William Wright ("Gibb Memorial Series," Vol. V [Leiden, 1907]), pp. 114, 162.

[17] Ṭabarī, I, 3055; III, 2329–30; Wüstenfeld, *op. cit.*, III, 112–13; IV, 180; Ibn Jubair, *op. cit.*, pp. 115, 167.

[18] Wüstenfeld, *op. cit.*, I, 330.

canals, and aqueducts—demanded constant upkeep and periodic major repairs. Royalty, ministers, and nobles as well as humbler men and women of public-spirited philanthropy turned their attention and their means to this essential service. It is, therefore, but natural to find that Khaizurān had not neglected this outlet for public service and recognition in this world and for forgiveness and reward in the world to come; for the giving of a cup of water to the thirsty is as commendable in Islam as in Christianity. Her efforts along these lines were not limited to her gifts to Mecca. A water pool near Ramlah in Palestine bore her name.[19] Nearer home, in the imperial province of ʿIrāq, she commissioned her agent to dig a river channel to the west of the city of Anbār, and she named it Al-Rayyān, or "The Abounding in Water." The agent partitioned the channel bed into delimited sections and set diggers to work on each—probably with the idea of accomplishing the task as quickly as possible. This, however, gave the channel the more common name of "The Delimited."[20]

Khaizurān was, in all probability, an extensive property owner. There were large sections, in and around the capital itself, that bore her name. There was the Khaizurāniyyah,[21] which later became a favorite section with her grandson, the caliph Amīn, who erected several palaces on it. Whether this was among her personal

[19] Yāqūt, *Geog.*, I, 592.

[20] Balādhurī, *Futūḥ al-Buldān*, ed. de Goeje (Lugduni Batavorum, 1866), p. 274; Yāqūt, *Geog.*, IV, 424.

[21] Ibn Ṭaifūr, p. 2; Ibn Athīr, VI, 193.

holdings or was only named in her honor, as the Khaizurān Cemetery was to be named later, is hard to tell.

That Khaizurān had a great deal of both private and public business to attend to is implied in her position in palace and state. The few incidents of this nature that have survived in the records must be considered as illustrative of some of her interests rather than as exhaustive of her activities. The same comment applies to the few references one finds to her agents. Secretaries, too, she must have had, though only one such figures in the historical records, more so because of his later association with Hārūn than because of his association with Khaizurān herself. This was ᶜUmar ibn Mahrān, a man of extremely unprepossessing appearance, but one of great ability and unusual character. He was Khaizurān's exclusive secretary, serving none besides her, and seems to have had charge of all of her business, her agents, and her other employees. He once sent her a long list of either accounts or requests and received this in answer: "Your letter has arrived with its numerous entries. You shall not be excessive in any of your affairs. Continue with the best that you have, and the best that I have will continue for you. And know that rare is the thing that increases except to decrease again. For decrease destroys the much just as the little grows into the more."[22]

Had Khaizurān applied this valuable knowledge to her own aspirations to excessive power, the tragedy of Hādī might have been avoided. But perhaps it was the very experience with Hādī that taught her this bit of

[22] Ibn ᶜAbdūs, p. 272.

human wisdom. ᶜUmar's reaction is not recorded. Perhaps all he needed was this word to the wise, for wise he seems to have been, judging by the following incident which has perpetuated his name in Islamic history.

Some three years after Khaizurān's death, Hārūn al-Rashīd suspected Mūsā ibn ᶜIsā, governor of Egypt, of planned revolt aimed at making himself master of Egypt. He therefore determined on removing Mūsā from office before his plans had time to mature. Hārūn intended, furthermore, to submit Mūsā to a studied insult in the course of removal. He looked around for the lowliest and homeliest of men, and his choice fell on ᶜUmar. The latter was to act as deputy governor for Jaᶜfar the Barmakid, who was appointed the titular governor of Egypt. Humility and poor looks notwithstanding, ᶜUmar made one condition to his service, namely, that when he had set the province in good order, he should be free to return. The condition was granted.

ᶜUmar departed secretly, poorly attired and sharing his mount with a black slave who rode behind him. He arrived at Fusṭāṭ, Egypt's capital, and for three days went about the city in the guise of a merchant, sizing up the situation and selecting promising men for his assistants in the task ahead. On the fourth night he called these together and, having assigned each his new duty, told them to be ready, on the morrow, to take over the government at the first signs of unrest.

The next day he himself attended the unsuspecting governor's public session and took the most inconspicuous seat at the back. The session broke up and all departed, leaving him alone with Mūsā. He now presented the latter with the caliph's letter. Mūsā's face began to change color as he read. But, not dreaming for one moment that the man before him was the ᶜUmar of the letter, he told him to return to his master and tell him to stay where he was until he could be given a reception befitting his rank. When ᶜUmar at last revealed his identity at this point, the completely surprised, thwarted, and humiliated Mūsā exclaimed, "Cursed be Pharaoh wherever he said, 'Is not the kingdom of Egypt mine. . . . .' "[23] No sooner did the situation become known than ᶜUmar's new appointees took over the government as one man.

ᶜUmar began immediately to put Egypt's finances in order. He aimed to end bribery, corruption, and tax delinquency. He ordered his men not to accept any gifts except cash and small-sized valuables. These he labeled with each donor's name and set them aside for future use. Next he called for the taxes that were due. One taxpayer, thinking to put him off, refused to pay his tax except direct to the capital. ᶜUmar, taking him at his word and by way of making a forceful example of him, required him now to do that very thing, thus putting him to the trouble and expense of the journey in addition to the payment of his tax. Men took note and hastened to clear up tax arrears. They did well enough with the first and second instalments but experienced difficulties in raising the third. Then ᶜUmar brought out the labeled bags and purses and credited each donor with the amount of his past, but not forgotten, gift. This was

[23] Qurʾān, Sūrah 43:50.

honesty with a vengeance! ᶜUmar, everyone realized, was not a man who could be either trifled with or corrupted. By one means or another the taxpayers managed to raise the third and last instalment for the year. Therefore, ᶜUmar closed his tax books with accounts all paid up to date for his year of service—a thing that had never happened before in Moslem Egypt. His task accomplished to his own satisfaction, ᶜUmar returned to Baghdad no richer than he had left it.[24]

This, then, was the man who was Khaizurān's exclusive secretary in her lifetime. Perhaps she deserves some credit for choosing him, looks and appearance notwithstanding. Certainly, a man of his administrative caliber and honesty must have managed well the affairs of the great and exacting queen. The extent of his task, in regard both to her income and to her expenditures, is to be gauged from the known size of her revenue and probable estimate of her legacy.

Khaizurān's annual income, in this her period of triumph and glory, reached the enormous figure of 160,000,000 dirhams. Impressive as this figure is, it takes on added significance when it is seen to be about one-half of the entire land tax—the largest single source of state revenue—for Hārūn's far-flung and prosperous empire.[25] She was undoubtedly, next to her royal son, the richest person in the Moslem world of her day. There seems to be no record of the size of her legacy. Perhaps

[24] Ibn ᶜAbdūs, pp. 267–72; Ṭabarī, III, 926–28; Ibn Athīr, VI, 85–86; Ibn Taghrībirdī, I, 475–78; Suyuṭī, *Ḥusn al-Muḥāḍarah*, II, 10; Ibn Khaldūn, III, 218–19.

[25] Masᶜūdī, VI, 289; Zaidan, II, 126; IV, 178.

she did not indulge in amassing ready cash primarily,[26] as Manṣūr had done and as Hārūn was soon to do. That she probably had a collector's instinct of a sort may be hinted at in the one specific item mentioned in this connection, namely, that there were stored in her palace eighteen thousand brocaded women's dresses or garments.[27] Even allowing for the needs of the queen's personal retinue of palace maids, the figure, at first glance, would seem to be too large for current needs.[28] But perhaps one should not attempt to estimate the "needs" of royalty. That she left, all in all, a large legacy is hardly to be doubted; for Hārūn is on record as "playing ducks and drakes" with her money and property after her death.[29]

Khaizurān did not enjoy her final triumph long, for death claimed her toward the end of the month of Jumada II, 173/November, 789.[30] She could not have been over fifty, if she was indeed that old; for the young girl that Manṣūr recommended to his son, Mahdī, early in the fourth decade of the century was then most probably still in her teens. The sources pass over the cause of her death, which may be assumed, therefore, to have been a natural one. She had been preceded in death by Mahdī's royal widow, Raiṭah.[31]

Her burial took place on a rainy autumn day; for,

[26] Cf., e.g., Ibn Taghrībirdī, I, 468.

[27] Ṭabarī, III, 569.

[28] Cf. Jāḥiẓ, *K. al-Tāj*, p. 149.

[29] Zaidan, II, 126; IV, 178; cf. D. S. Margoliouth, *Umayyads and Abbasids* (Leiden, 1907), p. 230.

[30] Ṭabarī, III, 607_{13} and 609_{11}; Ibn Athīr, VI, 82.

[31] Masʿūdī, VI, 289.

rain or no rain, the funeral must go on for climatic and religious reasons. Hārūn, dressed in the simple and humble garments of mourning—an upper cloak with an old blue belt round the waist—was chief mourner and first pallbearer. Barefooted, he trod in heavy, deep mud from the royal palace to the eastern cemetery north of Ruṣafah, to be known presently as the Khaizurān Cemetery.[32] At the tomb he offered the last prayer for the dead. Then, washing the unclean mud of the streets from his feet, he stepped into the good earth of the freshly dug grave to perform the very last service due the departed at the hands and hearts of their nearest and dearest.[33] Painful duty faithfully performed, Hārūn emerged from the tomb expressing his filial sorrow in the long-famous elegiac verses of Mutammam ibn Nuwairah, quoted by many in days gone by, among them Aishah, the Mother of the Believers, at the tomb of her father, Abū Bakr, first caliph of Islam.[34]

Mourning and sorrow notwithstanding, Hārūn's first state act immediately after the funeral was a negation of his mother's policy and disregard for her expressed wishes. This was the transfer of the royal signet ring from Jaᶜfar the Barmakid to Faḍl ibn al-Rabīᶜ. Hārūn, swearing by his own father Mahdī, now explained to Faḍl that it had been in obedience to his mother's wishes that he had not, ere now, raised him to high office

[32] Cf. Guy Le Strange, *Baghdad during the Abbasid Caliphate* (Oxford, 1900), pp. 192–93, and above, pp. 33 and 121.

[33] Ṭabarī, III, 608–9; Ibn Athīr, VI, 82; Ibn Taghrībirdī, I, 468–69.

[34] Ibn Taghrībirdī, I, 268; Mubarrad, *Kāmil*, pp. 724, 756; *Aghānī*, XIV, 70.

and favor. This was the beginning of Faḍl's rapid climb to power, checked only by the presence of the Barmakids, whose downfall, in which he had a hand, was to bring him, at last, the coveted wazirate.[35]

Hārūn, as already stated, dispensed Khairuzān's property at his will and pleasure, though that seems to have included the distribution of alms in her memory and the provision for her slave girls, retainers, and relatives.[36] Among the latter, her brother, Ghiṭrīf, seems to have been in favor with his nephew-caliph who was also his son-in-law, and who presently appointed him to the governorship of Khurāsān. But Ghiṭrīf was not equal to the government of this the most difficult province of the empire and so was recalled the next year.[37]

There were, no doubt, those among Khaizurān's followers and relatives who regretted her premature death, largely because their own fortunes were linked with hers. Though, doubtless again, there were some who were fairly attached to her, Khaizurān was a woman more to be feared and obeyed than to be loved and mourned. If Yaḥyā, like Hārūn, was glad to be freed from her dominating personality, he was much too wise to give public expression to his feelings. Soon the "Mother of the Caliphs" was to be forgotten in royal palace and governmental circles, except perhaps when there were whispers about the death of Hādī. Her very name,

[35] Ṭabarī, III, 609; Ibn Athīr, VI, 82. The signet ring changed hands at Rashīd's whims (cf., e.g., Ṭabarī, III, 604, 605–6, 644; Ibn Athīr, VI, 104; *Fakhrī*, pp. 281–82).

[36] Ibn Taghrībirdī, I, 469.

[37] Ṭabarī, III, 612, 626, 740; Ibn Athīr, VI, 83–84; Yaqʿūbī, II, 488; Ibn Taghrībirdī, I, 479, 482.

"Khaizurān" or "reed," seems to be avoided by others either as a personal name or in its more common use for that article itself. This was obviously done more out of calculation to please the living caliph than out of any tender memories or respect for the departed queen.[38] Her charities, particularly those at Mecca, helped to keep her name alive for a while with the public. But the public memory is ever and everywhere notoriously short.

It was left, therefore, largely to the Moslem historians to preserve Khaizurān's memory through the centuries. As one, at this great distance of time, marshals the long series of successive historians into an assembled group, each to tell his tale as he received or believed it, several more or less definite conclusions force themselves on one's attention.

First, there is no escaping the fact that, even when all have had their say, the story is still incomplete. The reader, no doubt, will recall references to many a tantalizing omission in connection with even some of the major recorded episodes of Khaizurān's public and private life. Again, there is a steadily growing conviction that the historians, especially the earliest group, wrote under one or more, conscious or unconscious, restraints. To begin with, it was not the proper thing to dwell too much on the affairs of the harem—any harem. Next, from Manṣūr onward, the caliphs demanded that the royal harem in particular be handled with exceptional care and caution.

[38] Masᶜūdī, VI, 353–54; Ibn al-Jauzī, *Akhbār*, p. 42; Ghuzūlī, *Maṭaliᶜ al-Budūr fī Manāzil al-Surūr* (2 vols.; Cairo, 1299/1882), I, 182–83; II, 136.

Over and above these general restraints applicable to the royal harem *in toto*, there developed two others that concerned the affairs of Khaizurān in particular. First, there was Hādī's express command to the court to let the words and deeds of his mother strictly alone. This restriction was relaxed during Khaizurān's brief Indian summer of power in the interval between Hādī's and her own death. Thereafter, Hārūn seems to be tacitly approving his court's cautious avoidance of the very word *khaizurān*. A conspiracy of silence seems to have developed, perhaps with the instinctive desire or the deliberate intention, to drown out rumors, no doubt still lurking in gossip circles, of Khaizurān's own darker conspiracy for the murder of her son Hādī. And, fortunately or unfortunately, Mahdī's Khaizurān, unlike Justinian's Theodora, had not her Procopius among the contemporary court historians.

The succeeding series of ᶜAbbāsid historians, bowing to general usage, on the one hand, and avoiding specific involvement with the reigning caliph, on the other, treated Khaizurān and her story with brevity and caution. Post-ᶜAbbāsid historians, though free from court restraint, lacked the sources of information at the disposal of their professional predecessors, even if they had the inclination—and here or there one or more may have been that curious—to uncover the entire story of this remarkable slave woman and ᶜAbbāsid queen. Therefore, most of the later historical records are, on the whole, echoes—here dimmed, there reinforced, but echoes nevertheless—of the earlier ones extant.

Obviously a modern student, curious enough to delve

into the story of Khaizurān, suffers from the same lack of information that all but the contemporary and near-contemporary historian had to endure. He has, on the other hand, several advantages over all his predecessors. He can, to begin with, bring together all the records and gain therefrom a synoptic view of the whole over against the isolated incidents of the part. Furthermore, he is in a far more advantageous position to achieve that high degree of objectivity so essential to the discovery of historical truth. Thus equipped and conditioned, the modern student can leave the assembled company of past historians—each still clinging to his particular incident and partial view—to meet, as it were, in person, the subject of their common interest. For here, at last, Khaizurān herself seems suddenly to materialize before the mind's eye in a series of pictures that unroll in a progressive and significant tale.

First, there is the lowly slave girl, straight and slender as a reed and gifted richly with feminine charm and beauty. Her dreamy eyes reflect the long thoughts of youth—in her case long enough to bridge the vast distance between the common slave girl and the envied mother of caliphs. In the next picture she holds the center of the stage at a slave market catering to royalty. She summons all her natural gifts and woman's wiles to her aid in this her great moment of opportunity. For she is as eager as any would-be modern prima donna or "star" of the stage, the air, and the screen to insure success and secure a foothold on the ladder to wealth, fame, and glory. If it takes a lie or two—black or white as the occasion may demand—she, like some of these modern aspirants, is willing to risk that. Luck is with her. For her physical charms catch the eye and her well-calculated words win the approval of the caliph Manṣūr.

Her good fortune holds out as, in the very next scene, she captivates the heart of the crown prince Mahdī. Lavish wealth and equally lavish romance are now hers to enjoy. She stops long enough to taste leisurely these fruits of her personal success. She looks around with keen eyes and open mind to observe and learn court etiquette and to allow harem rivals the place due them. Like all women in general and harem women in particular, she has her moments of struggle with the green-eyed monster of jealousy. She emerges, in each instance, with a greater self-confidence in her own power to hold and sway the amiable and indulgent Mahdī. In the meantime her cup of human happiness is rapidly filling to the brim as she gives her loving prince, himself in line for the succession, three sons and a daughter who are the pride and joy of their father's warm heart.

As the white flame of first love tempers to the red heat of passion or dulls into the pale glow of "long-married years," Khaizurān's thoughts dwell more and more on the lure of personal power. The indulgent Mahdī, now himself the caliph, fans the flames of her ambitions by raising her to the enviable status of legal wife and by appointing her two sons successive heirs to his throne. The Khaizurān of this picture is the happy wife and mother, on the one hand, and the completely successful and immensely ambitious woman, on the other. So long as Mahdī goes her way there is little to stem her growing ambition or to jeopardize its eventual fulfilment beyond the harem into the wider and more exciting fields of court politics and the affairs of empire.

But, as the next scene develops, there appears in the distance what seems to be a small cloud on her blue horizon in the person of her firstborn son, Mūsā al-Hādī, first heir to his father's throne. Suffering from odious, if indirect, comparisons with his younger brother, the handsome Hārūn of sunnier temperament, Mūsā is spiritually estranged from his royal parents. As the young heir grows from youth into manhood, he displays a mind of his own linked to a strong sense of ego. The determined and ambitious Khaizurān senses this quicker and resents it more keenly than does the easygoing Mahdī. The small cloud in the distant horizon assumes larger dimensions as it rises overhead. Father and son reach an open break, calculated, from Khaizurān's point of view, to dispel the approaching cloud by discrediting and displacing the wilful son. But here the fates intervened with a thunderbolt out of the blue that struck and carried away no other than Mahdī himself.

As the next scene unrolls, all is quiet on the royal front. The wilful son seems to have had a change of mind and heart. The ambitious mother travels in state on the imperial highway of power. The handsome brother, happy in the arms of his lovely Zubaidah, is content to forego power for love. Suddenly, however, the calm is shattered and a battle royal is in full progress. Khaizurān—the slave become ruler—is both tactless and inordinate in the exercise of unlimited power. Hādī's enormous egotism and strong self-will reassert themselves. And Hārūn's royal fancy toys now with love, now with power. The gentler sentiments of motherly devotion, brotherly love, and filial duty are lost sight of in a tidal wave of the darker human passions—of greed for power born of self-love and of strong hate born of even stronger fear. When the battle subsides, Hādī marches off in triumph, Khaizurān is left to nurse her wounds, and Hārūn seeks distant hunting grounds. There follows an intensive war of nerves to which it is Hādī who finally succumbs, aided by a narrowly superstitious mind and an extensive stomach ulcer. Khaizurān, not yet recovered from her defeat and humiliation, watches the death scene with an unfeeling heart as her mind races forward, impatiently to contrive ways and means to lay her eager hands once more on the reins of power.

Hārūn, who had all but lost his life in this royal family struggle, is now the undisputed caliph. He is, however, content to let his "Father" Yaḥyā and his mother Khaizurān rule his empire. But the experienced and tactful Yaḥyā, though seemingly taking orders, at first, from Khaizurān, manages somehow to restrain her. For some three years she enjoys her public triumph.

Of her private life and thought in this same period nothing at all is known. Did she not, one wonders, dwell on those happier days with Mahdī when she had not yet climbed to such heights of power? Did not remorse seize her as she recalled the tragic life of Hādī? Did an inner loneliness not grip her heart as she realized that Hārūn was drifting away from her, becoming more and more engrossed with his harem and its lovely Zubaidah? Did she not feel some pangs of jealousy, as this same Zubaidah, her own niece though she was, was rapidly coming to the fore? These and other questions that tantalize the mind must be left unanswered.

In the meantime, Zubaidah herself beckons the reader to follow her on the road to royal romance and adventure.

PART II

Zubaidah

V

Royalty and Romance

I

THE young Zubaidah, beloved though she was of her royal cousin and husband Hārūn, had, nevertheless, two major personal problems to contend with—harem rivals and delayed motherhood. Her earliest rival in the legal wife status was probably either her own cousin, ᶜAzīzah, the daughter of Ghiṭrīf, or Ghādir, the slave girl of Hādī, both of whose stories have already been told.[1] After the latter's death in 173/789, Zubaidah was seemingly the sole legal mistress of the harem (nothing more is known of ᶜAzīzah) for some fourteen years. But from 187/803 on she had to share that privileged status with three noble women—Umm Mohammed, ᶜAbbāsah, and an ᶜUthmānid lady from Jurash, all of whom, like Zubaidah, outlived Hārūn.[2] Except for Ghādir, none of these legal wives figured romantically in the harem scene. Zubaidah's real rivals, therefore, were to be found among Hārūn's numerous

[1] Cf. above, pp. 68 and 99–101.

[2] Ṭabarī, III, 757–58; Ibn Athīr, VI, 148; ᶜ*Iqd*, III, 54.

concubines and singing girls. The records speak of Hārūn's two hundred slave girls, list some two dozen concubines who bore him one or more children,[3] and relate many an anecdote of singing girl and palace maid that caught Hārūn's passing fancy.

Hārūn's earliest known concubine was a slave girl of Yaḥyā the Barmakid named Hailānah (Helen). It was she who begged Hārūn, while he was yet a prince, to take her away from the elderly Yaḥyā. Hārūn then approached Yaḥyā, who presented him with the girl. Three years later she died, and Hārūn mourned her deeply with verses that proclaimed joy to have departed forever from his heart.[4] The probabilities are that her death occurred before Hārūn's wedding to Zubaidah in 165/781–82. For the next few years Zubaidah so charmed Hārūn that he was about to renounce his claims to the throne and retire to his harem to enjoy to the full this young wife's company. Yaḥyā prevented the retirement, and fate cast a shadow over the romantic couple, as the passing years brought them no offspring.[5]

In other ways, too, the course of their true love did not run so smoothly. There was, for instance, another slave girl of Yaḥyā's who crossed Zubaidah's royal road of romance. This was the gifted yellow songstress, Danānīr the Barmakid, so called because of her affiliation with that powerful family. She had been educated

[3] Ṭabarī, III, 758–59; Ibn Athīr, VI, 148; ᶜ*Iqd*, III, 54; Yaᶜqūbī, II, 521; Rāghib, *Muḥāḍarāt*, II, 157–58.

[4] Sūlī, *Kitāb al-Awrāq*, ed. Heyworth Dune (Cairo, 1934), pp. 18–19; Khaṭib, I, 97–98; Yāqūt, *Geog.*, II, 362–63; cf. Suyuṭī, *Taʾrīkh*, p. 116, trans. H. S. Jarrett (*History of the Caliphs* [Calcutta, 1881]), pp. 304–5.

[5] Cf. above, p. 102.

at Medina and had studied instrumental and vocal music with the best teachers, both men and women, which that music-loving city had to offer. Yaḥyā's keen ears did not deceive him as to the high quality of her musical talent. He was, however, anxious to have her approved by the famous court musician, Ibrāhīm al-Mauṣilī. One day Danānīr informed him that she had composed a new melody with which she herself seemed to be very well pleased. Yaḥyā put both her ability and her taste to the test by arranging for an audition with Ibrāhīm. The girl sang her song before the master, who was extremely delighted with it. He called for a second and a third performance, listening critically for a possible flaw to detect and correct. Finding none, he pronounced the air perfect and the girl a first-class musician, much to the joy of Yaḥyā, who perhaps had more than an artistic interest in the maid.[6]

It was in Yaḥyā's palace that Hārūn first heard this talented girl. Thereafter, his visits increased as his pleasure mounted, and his gifts to her grew proportionately in both size and frequency. One night he presented her with a necklace that was worth thirty thousand dinars. Zubaidah, alarmed at the trend of affairs, complained of Hārūn's infatuation to his uncles, who took him to task. "I am not interested in the girl herself, said Hārūn, "but only in her singing. Listen to her yourself and see if her singing (alone) does not justify my friendship." So Danānīr came to perform before the ranking ᶜAbbāsid princes, and these, having heard her,

[6] *Aghānī*, XVI, 136–37; V, 43–44; VI, 72; ᶜAlī ibn Ẓāfir al-Azdī, *Badāʾiᶜ al-Bidāʾah*, p. 48; Nuwairī, V, 90.

forgave Hārūn his conduct. They returned to Zubaidah to explain and to advise her not to nag Hārūn over Danānīr. She accepted the situation, and, by way of an apology for her unfounded jealousy, she herself presented Hārūn with ten slave girls, among them the future mothers of three of his sons, two of whom were to succeed, in time, to the ᶜAbbāsid throne.[7]

This method of gaining favor with one's husband, strange and drastic as it seems, is not so uncommon or incomprehensible in a polygamous royal society. The Moslem mind, accepting the assumption that the best gift is that which the recipient desires and which hurts the most to give, rationalizes it thus: "Should a woman of the royal harem possess a slave girl whom she knows the king desires and rejoices in, then it is her duty to present the king with this girl completely equipped and adorned in the best of finery. If she does this, then it is due her that the king should give her preference over all his women and place her in a unique position of increased honor. For he should realize that she has placed his desires over her own and has rendered him a peculiarly unselfish service of which women—except for a few of them—are incapable."[8]

The above episode, which took place while Hārūn was yet prince, is to be placed in 169 or earlier. It most probably occurred after Mahdī's death, since he does not ap-

[7] *Aghānī*, XVI, 137; Nuwairī, V, 90. Cf. L. Bouvat, "Les Barmécides d'après les historiens Arabes et Persians," *Revue du Monde musulman*, XX (1912), 52.

[8] Jāḥiẓ, *K. al-Tāj*, p. 148; cf. Mary Leonora Sheil, *Glimpses of Life and Manners in Persia* (London, 1856), pp. 203–4, for the practice in the Persian royal family.

pear in the story. At any rate, Marājil,[9] one of the ten maids involved, presented Hārūn with his son ᶜAbd Allah—the future Maᵓmūn—on the night of Hārūn's accession to the throne, in Rabīᶜ I, 170/September, 786. She came from distant Bādhaghīs[10] in Persia and is generally referred to as a Persian slave girl. She died at the birth of her son,[11] and Zubaidah claimed that she herself had helped to raise the orphaned ᶜAbd Allah.[12] Some six months later, in the month of Shawwāl, 170/March–April, 787, Zubaidah gave birth to her only child, Mohammed—the future Amīn—who, because of his doubly royal birth and the favored position of Zubaidah, overshadowed the older ᶜAbd Allah and the several sons of Hārūn who were born within the next few years. Among these were ᶜAlī, the son of Ghādir, and Qāsim, the son of Qaṣif, this latter a concubine of whom little else is known, though her son Qāsim was later to figure as an heir to the throne.

Among the ten girls said to have been given to Hārūn by Zubaidah was one named Māridah, daughter of a Sughdian, though she herself was born in Kūfah. She is credited with bearing Hārūn no less than five children. These were Abū Isḥāq—the future Muᶜtaṣim—Abū Ismāᶜīl, Umm Ḥabīb, and two others whose names are

[9] There is another, though highly questionable, version of how Zubaidah forced Marājil, the kitchen maid, on Hārūn's attention (cf. *ᶜIqd*, III, 430; Damīrī, *Ḥayāwān*, I, 108). Masᶜūdī, VI, 424–25 gives yet another version, according to which Hārūn *purchased* Maᵓmūn's mother (unnamed).

[10] E.g., Yaᶜqūbī, II, 538; for the town cf. Yāqūt, *Geog.*, I, 461.

[11] *Fawāt al-Wafāyāt*, I, 306; Ibn Taghrībirdī, I, 482.

[12] Dīnawarī, *Kitāb Akhbār al-Ṭiwāl* (Leiden, 1888), p. 392; cf. below, pp. 213, 221, and 241.

not known.[13] Abū Isḥāq, generally mentioned first in the list, was probably not the oldest of the five, since his birth is placed in 179 or 180,[14] that is, some ten years after his mother was presented to Hārūn.

There are several indications that Hārūn was passionately attached to Māridah and that she used her ready wit to keep him so.[15] But they, too, had their lovers' quarrels. Hārūn, during one of these peeves, departed for Baghdad, leaving Māridah behind at his court in Raqqah. Presently, growing very lonesome for her, he composed four verses to express his mood and asked the court musicians to set them to music. Twenty different tunes were submitted. Selecting the melody that pleased him most, he ordered Ibrāhīm al-Mauṣilī to sing it. When his verses reached Māridah in Raqqah, she called on Abū Ḥafṣ al-Shaṭranjī (Abū Ḥafṣ the chess-player), a poet much in favor with Hārūn's talented sister, ᶜUlaiyah. Abū Ḥafṣ composed eight verses in answer. The burden of these was to marvel at the discrepancy between Hārūn's words and actions and to ask why, if he were indeed the yearning lover, did he leave her at Raqqah while he enjoyed himself with others at Baghdad. No sooner did Hārūn read this gentle rebuke than he sent his man posthaste to bring her to him in Baghdad.[16]

Their estrangement on yet another occasion seems to have been a little more serious. The episode, according to an earlier account, is to be placed in the latter part of

[13] Ṭabarī, III, 758, 1329; Ibn Athīr, VI, 374; ᶜ*Iqd*, III, 54, 433.

[14] Ṭabarī, III, 1324; Ibn Athīr, VI, 373; Khaṭīb, III, 342.

[15] Cf. Ibn Ḥijjah, II, 102.

[16] *Aghānī*, XIX, 70–71; XVII, 77–78.

Hārūn's reign when Faḍl ibn al-Rabīᶜ was his wazir (187–93/803–9).[17] Later accounts place it earlier, substituting Jaᶜfar the Barmakid for Faḍl. Hārūn is described as dying for the love of his Māridah but too proud to make the first move toward a reconciliation. Māridah, too, would not take the first step. Faḍl was alarmed for Hārūn and called on the poet ᶜAbbās ibn al-Aḥnaf to compose appropriate verses, some of which have been literally translated as follows: "Return to the friends you have abandoned; the bondsman of love but seldom shuns (his mistress). If your mutual estrangement long endure, indifference will glide (into your hearts) and (lost affection) will hardly be retrieved."[18] Ibrāhīm was now asked to contrive to sing them before the caliph. This he did with the result that Hārūn immediately hastened to Māridah, and the two were reconciled. There followed the usual liberal gifts to the poet and musician who had been instrumental in bringing about the happy ending.[19]

Several others of Hārūn's concubines must have offered competition to both Zubaidah and Māridah. Hārūn and his poets sang the praises of a trio of them who consisted of Dhāt al-Khāl, Siḥr, and Ḍiyā, that is, "Lady of the Beauty Spot," "Charm," and "Splendor."[20] Ḍiyā passed away, much to Hārūn's sorrow.[21]

[17] Ibn al-Muᶜtazz, *Ṭabaqāt al-Shuᶜarāᵓ*, pp. 120–21.

[18] Ibn Khallikān, I, 21.

[19] See two preceding notes and Zamakhsharī, *Rauḍ al-Akhyār*, pp. 246–47; Ghuzūlī, *Maṭāliᶜ al-Budūr*, pp. 194–96.

[20] *Aghānī*, V, 67; XV, 81–82; Khaṭīb, XIV, 12; Nuwairī, II, 144.

[21] Yāqūt, *Geog.*, II, 363.

Siḥr is evidently to be identified with the mother of Khadījah, daughter of Hārūn.[22] There is a possibility that Dhāt al-Khāl, whose personal name is variously given, is to be identified as the mother of Hārūn's son, Abū al-ᶜAbbās.[23] Be that as it may, she did, for some length of time, disturb the caliph's emotions.

The Lady of the Beauty Spot had a mole on the upper lip or on the cheek, which, as the taste of the day went, enhanced her beauty. She was an accomplished songstress, belonging to a slave-dealer who was himself a freedman of ᶜAbbāsah, the sister of Hārūn. She caught the fancy of Ibrāhīm al-Mauṣilī, whose songs in praise of her soon reached the attention of Hārūn, who bought her for the enormous sum of seventy thousand dinars. Hārūn, alas for his pride and peace of mind, questioned her as to any intimate relations with Ibrāhīm, threatening to check on her answer by questioning the latter also. The girl, thus cornered, told the truth, whereupon Hārūn's love turned into hate. Heaping insults on her head in an effort to wipe out the injury her past revealed, he presented her to one of his slaves named Ḥammawaih. But Hārūn missed the girl and her songs and took the slave to task for keeping her talents all to himself. The slave humbly assured him that the girl was at his command. Hārūn then and there informed him that he would pay her a visit on the morrow.

Ḥammawaih hastened to the jewelers to rent twelve

[22] *Aghānī*, XXI, 159; Ṭabarī, III, 758; ᶜ*Iqd*, III, 54.

[23] The basic written form of the name variously dotted and voweled can account for its different readings (cf. Ṭabarī, III, 758; ᶜ*Iqd*, III, 54; *Aghānī*, V, 61; XV, 81).

thousand dinars' worth of jewelry with which to adorn the girl for the occasion. Hārūn, surprised at the great display of wealth, asked its source. Finding how the matter stood, he sent for the jewelers, paid their price, and presented Dhāt al-Khāl with the jewels. He swore, furthermore, that on that day no request of hers should go unanswered. The happy and grateful girl asked that Ḥammawaih be appointed to a number of high offices in the Persian province of Fars for a period of seven years. This Hārūn did, directing his heir that the period was to run its course, if he himself should die before the seven years were out.[24] The historians report Ḥammawaih as in office in Fars in the last three years of Hārūn's reign,[25] thus helping to date the above episode.

There is yet another anecdote told of Hārūn and Dhāt al-Khāl, with no clue, however, as to its date. The girl once secured a promise from Hārūn to visit her. On the way to her apartment he was tempted by another charmer who persuaded him to visit her instead. This so upset Dhāt al-Khāl that she came as near as possible to literally cutting off her nose to spite her face. For in her jealous rage she cut off her mole to annoy Hārūn, who had a weakness for the beauty spot. When Hārūn heard what had happened, he hastened to appease her with the ever ready verses of the poets and the golden voice of Ibrāhīm.[26]

It would be logical to infer that Māridah and Dhāt al-

[24] *Aghānī*, XV, 79–80; Nuwairī, V, 88–89; cf. H. G. Farmer, *A History of Arabian Music* (London, 1929), p. 135, where it is stated, without authority given, that she *married* the slave and on his *death* returned to Hārūn's harem.

[25] Ṭabarī, III, 712, 764; Ibn Athīr, VI, 152.

[26] *Aghānī*, XV, 81.

Khāl were among the most serious harem rivals from Zubaidah's point of view. The records, however, seem to be silent on their direct relationships. Whether the two were congenial and even friendly, as sometimes does happen with harem inmates, or whether some of Zubaidah's reported but unexplained quarrels with Hārūn were linked with either of them is not known.

It is on record, however, that Zubaidah was alarmed at Hārūn's preoccupation with yet another songstress, ᶜInān, the slave girl of Naṭifī, who is described as "a yellow maid born and brought up in the Yamamah" in central Arabia. Her poetic gifts were considered of the highest order, and she excelled at witty retorts and extempore composition in competition with the ranking poets of the day. She won the approval and affection of that most gifted but reprobate poet of the court, Ḥasan ibn Hānī, better known as Abū Nuwās of *Arabian Nights'* fame. Though she parried words and verses with the poet, she scorned his affection. She lacked not for other admirers but preferred to remain fancy free.

Her verses were brought to Hārūn's attention quite dramatically at a pleasure session when he called on those present to match some verses of Jarīr, the famous poet of the Umayyads. None present was able to measure up to the test. An attendant hastened with Jarīr's verse to the house of Naṭifī, where ᶜInān dictated three verses which surprised and pleased Hārūn so much that he determined on purchasing her that very night, and, according to one version, he did buy her for 30,000 dinars.[27] According to another version, however, her master

[27] ᶜ*Iqd*, III, 258.

would not sell her for less than 100,000 dinars. Hārūn was willing to pay this price at the rate of seven dirhams to the dinar, which rate of exchange Naṭifī refused to accept.[28] Hārūn therefore returned the girl but could not forget her. Seemingly, she, too, did not forget him, to judge by some verses she addressed to him, the effects of which the shrewd courtier and able scholar, Aṣmaʿī, was quick to detect and profit by.[29]

It must have been at this point that Zubaidah, becoming alarmed, sought to enlist Aṣmaʿī's aid, who was to be free to ask what he wished provided he could bring Hārūn to forget the girl. The courtier bided his time. One day Hārūn expressed himself on Naṭifī's attitude in terms of extreme displeasure and added that he had no interest in the girl except for her poetry. With Zubaidah's request and offer in mind, Aṣmaʿī struck while the iron was hot with, "Indeed, by God, poetry is her only gift. Would the Commander of the Believers fall in love with Farazdaq?" referring to that other famous poet of the Umayyads and lifelong rival of Jarīr. Hārūn broke into hearty laughter and was sufficiently cured of his infatuation to forget ʿInān for a while. But, on the death of her master, he sent his trusted servant, Masrūr, to bid for her at public auction. Masrūr was outbid by a Khurāsānian who bought the girl for 250,000 dirhams and took her away with him to Khurāsān, where she died in 226/840–41, long after first Hārūn and then Zubaidah had gone to their rest.[30]

[28] Nuwairī, V, 78; cf. above, p. 37, n. 51.

[29] ʿ*Iqd*, III, 258–59; cf. Khaṭīb, XIV, 9–10; Alī ibn Ẓāfir al-Azdī, *Badāʾiʿ al-Bidāʾah*, p. 117.

[30] Nuwairī, V, 78–79; Ibn Taghrībirdī, I, 670–71.

Hārūn's attempt to purchase a highly priced girl fell through on yet another occasion. This time, too, the owner had vowed he would not part with his slave for less than 100,000 dinars. Hārūn, on seeing the girl, was delighted with her beauty and intelligence as also with her training and manners. He decided to pay the price asked and sent word to Yaḥyā to send him the money. Yaḥyā, alarmed lest this set an evil precedent, claimed that he was unable to meet the demand. Hārūn, greatly angered, questioned his minister's veracity and reiterated his order for the huge sum. The wily Yaḥyā now sent the sum in question, not in gold dinars but in silver dirhams, so that there was involved a veritable hillock of moneybags. He had these placed at a point where the caliph could not fail to see them. Hārūn saw and wished to know what all that money was doing there. "It is the price of the maiden," he was informed. Hārūn stopped and reconsidered, as, indeed, Yaḥyā had hoped he would. He called the sale off and sent the girl back to her master. But he did not return the money to Yaḥyā and the treasury. Instead, it formed the initial capital in a new private treasury which Hārūn named the "Treasury of the Bride."[31]

While physical charm and artistic talent were generally the open-sesame to Hārūn's heart, there were times when learning and culture played the major role on their own merits. Hārūn, while at Raqqah, acquired two slave girls said to be highly educated. He sent to Baghdad for Aṣmaʿī, the ranking scholar of the day, to hasten to him in order to examine them. Aṣmaʿī found himself

[31] Ṭabarī, III, 1332–33.

facing an imposing pair of girls. Turning to the more impressive of the two, he wished to know what branches of learning she had studied. "First," answered the girl, "that which Allah has commanded in his Book. Then, that which engages the people's mind in poetry, language and literature, and historical narration." The scholar then put the girl to an exacting test in the various readings of the Qurʾān, in grammar and prosody, in poetry and history, and found her to excel in one and all. The second girl now took her turn. Aṣmaʿī's verdict was that he had never seen a woman take hold of learning like a man as did this first girl; and that the second girl, though not as yet the equal of the first, would, with proper training, measure up to her. Hārūn then gave orders to have the "perfect" one prepared immediately for his company and pleasure. When Aṣmaʿī departed, he was overtaken by a man and a maidservant who brought him a rich purse of a thousand dinars and said, "Your 'daughter' wishes to share her good fortune with you." "This," concluded Aṣmaʿī, "she continued to do until the civil war of Amīn, when I lost track of her."[32]

Hārūn's harem was thus constantly growing or being replenished by purchase and supplemented by gift and capture. The most spectacular instance of the latter was the captive daughter of a Greek churchman of Hircalah (Heraclea) acquired with the fall of that city in 190/806.[33] Gifts were more numerous. Zubaidah herself once

[32] Khaṭīb, X, 411–13.

[33] Cf., e.g., Ibn Quṭaibah, *Maʿārif*, p. 144; Yāqūt, *Geog.*, IV, 961–62; Ṭabarī, III, 709–10, Zamakhsharī, *Rauḍ al-Akhyār*, p. 238; Nuwairī, II, 163–65. The sources, perhaps confusing Greek ecclesiastic terms, refer to the churchman as a patriarch.

more presented him with one of her personal maids who had caught his fancy, though on another occasion she vowed that she would neither sell nor give him one of her maids whom he very much desired.[34]

Hārūn's half-brother, while governor of Egypt (179–81/795–97),[35] sent the caliph an Egyptian maid who immediately won a place in his large and receptive heart. But she soon took ill, and none of the court physicians could cure her. Hārūn sent for the best physician in Egypt, who came to attend on her and brought with him some Egyptian dainties for the patient. The girl, who was seemingly suffering from homesickness, recovered, and Hārūn saw to it that thereafter she had her Egyptian diet.[36]

But wives, concubines, and songstresses notwithstanding, Zubaidah held a unique position in Hārūn's affections and seemingly enjoyed more of his company than did the rest of the inmates of the harem. He would, on occasion, tease her even to playing tantalizingly on her more dignified name of Umm Jaᶜfar,[37] over against her pet name of Zubaidah. Once, when she thought

[34] *ᶜIqd*, III, 432; Zamakhshari, *Rauḍ al-Akhyār*, pp. 21–22. This second incident, however, would seem to be confused with a similar and early story involving the slave girl, not of Zubaidah herself, but of her brother. Hārūn eventually secured the girl, thanks to the ready accommodation of the courtier judge, Abū Yūsuf (cf. Ibn Khallikān, IV, 280–81; Yāfiᶜī, I, 385–86; Damīrī, *Ḥayāwān*, I, 195–96). For other reported instances of Abū Yūsuf's accommodating decisions see Ibn Khallikān, IV, 275–76; Suyūṭī, *Taʾrīkh*, p. 114; and Qāzwinī, *Athār al-Bilād*, ed. Wüstenfeld (Göttingen, 1848), pp. 211–12.

[35] Kindī, pp. 137–38.

[36] Eutychius, *Annales*, ed. Pocock (Oxford, 1656), II, 409–10.

[37] Al-Sīrāfī, *Akhbār al-Naḥwīyīn al-Baṣrīyīn* ("Biographies des grammariens de l'Ecole de Basra"), ed. F. Krenkow (Paris, 1936), p. 64.

Hārūn was free, she sent word to remind him that she had not seen him for three (long) days. Hārūn sent word in answer that the musician Ibn Jāmiᶜ was with him. Whereupon came her next message: "You know that I never enjoy any entertainment—drinking, musical, or any other kind—unless you share it with me. What would happen if I were to share with you what you now have!"

Hārūn decided to do just that, that is, share his company with her. He sent word back that he was on his way to visit her, and, taking Ibn Jāmiᶜ by the hand, he led him to her quarters. This unexpected presence of a "stranger" in the secluded harem caused some initial commotion and excitement. But presently the singer was led to a spot where he could be heard but not seen. Then Zubaidah came forth to greet her royal husband, who embraced her affectionately and, having seated her by his side, ordered the hidden musician to sing. His four verses in the background of this happy surprise party so pleased Zubaidah that she rewarded him most liberally. Hārūn commented, perhaps half in approval and half in gentle rebuke, on the speed and generosity with which she rewarded one who was his own guest and companion. The entertainment over, Hārūn sent Zubaidah a dinar for each dirham it had cost her, a golden way of insisting on his prior right to liberality as royal host and husband.[38]

Another incident, involving the transfer of hundreds of thousands of dinars, is thus told. Hārūn one day came out of Zubaidah's apartment laughing. He was asked

[38] *Aghānī*, VI, 77.

the cause of his laughter by some courtier. His answer was that he had recently received 300,000 dinars from Egypt which he presented to Zubaidah, who, nevertheless, scolded him and disclaimed that she had ever received any benefit at his hand.[39] There must have been more to this incident than either Hārūn or the record told. That Hārūn was a generous husband at all times is to be inferred from Zubaidah's luxurious way of private life and her spectacular public expenditures.

The mettlesome Zubaidah did on occasion match Hārūn's impetuous wrath with her own sustained disdain, as is seen from the following incident. Hārūn had, for some unspecified reason, lost his temper with her. He must, on second thought, have regretted the incident, since he took steps to reconcile her. But she refused to be reconciled. One night, unable to sleep, he watched the rising waters of the Tigris flow by. Presently, he heard a song in the air—the song of a river winding its way to the valley of the beloved, the song of the romantic Tigris. Hārūn located the house whence came the singing and sent for the singer. The latter informed him that the verses were the composition of ᶜAbbās ibn al-Aḥnaf, who was next sent for. Poet and musician entertained the caliph, repeating the song over and over again, until the break of dawn. Then dismissing his company, he swallowed his pride and went the whole way to visit and make his peace with his estranged but beloved Zubaidah.[40]

[39] Zamakhsharī, *Rauḍ al-Akhyār*, p. 183. See above, pp. 45–46, for Mahdī's experience with Khaizurān.

[40] *Aghānī*, XVIII, 77.

There seem to have been one or perhaps two occasions when a stormy scene between the royal couple almost broke up their union. Zubaidah, so one story goes, once consigned her cousin and husband to hell-fire. Hārūn, no doubt burning with rage, pronounced the dreaded triple formula of final divorce. Then, as he cooled off and realized the seriousness of the situation, he regretted his words. He therefore called on his jurisconsults to help him out of his difficulty by finding a way to nullify the divorce. Accommodating service was rendered, among others, by Abū Yūsuf.[41]

Under more normal conditions, Zubaidah, no doubt, considered her husband's moods and kept herself informed as to his whims and comforts. Once she learned that Hārūn had presented one of the court poets with a valuable ring that she knew Hārūn himself fancied. She therefore redeemed the ring. Hārūn, however, let the poet keep ring and price rather than be considered an "Indian giver."[42] When Hārūn was known to be indisposed, Zubaidah's messengers were among the first of those who waited at the royal entrance to deliver her greetings and make solicitous inquiries about his health. One shrewd doorkeeper, on such an occasion, made himself a large fortune by ranking the numerous inquirers and giving the first entry to the royal chamber to Zubaidah's messenger.[43]

There were times, however, when Zubaidah felt unequal to holding her own with Hārūn, against some new

[41] Qazwīnī, *Athār al-Bilād*, pp. 211–12; cf. E. H. Palmer, *Haroun Alraschid* (London, 1881), pp. 157–58.

[42] Ibn Taghrībirdī, I, 464.

[43] Ṭabarī, III, 746.

glamorous rival, without the aid of some of her in-laws. She seems to have been on particularly good terms with her young sister-in-law, ᶜUlaiyah. Spirit, talent, beauty, and courage were the weapons that this gay and sophisticated princess employed to bend her half-brother, Hārūn, and his court to her pleasure. The occasion that led Zubaidah to seek her aid was the gift to Hārūn of a new maid, "perfect in beauty." Hārūn staged, in her honor, a big entertainment at which were present hundreds of the palace personnel in colorful and gay costumes. The jealous Zubaidah could not endure this in silence. She complained to ᶜUlaiyah, who comforted her with, "Don't let the incident alarm you. For, by Allah, I shall bring him back to you." Then she explained her plan. "I shall compose a new verse and set it to a new melody and teach it to all my maids. Let all your maids, too, learn it along with mine."

When evening came and Hārūn was taking the fresh air in his palace courtyard, ᶜUlaiyah and Zubaidah, each at the head of her train of maids, all splendidly and colorfully attired, rushed into his presence singing, as though with one voice, the new melody and song that began with, "Departed from me, though my heart will not part from him. . . . ." Hārūn was flattered and overjoyed. He rose to meet the ladies and remained to enjoy their company, declaring he had never before had such a happy day. Neither had the rest of the gathering seen anything like that day which ended with a heavy shower of thousands upon thousands of dirhams scattered in their midst.[44]

[44] *Aghānī*, IX, 88.

Apart from her personal affairs of the heart, Zubaidah's attention must have been, at times, engaged with other court romances, legitimate or clandestine. There was, for instance, the infatuation of ᶜUlaiyah herself for two of Hārūn's page boys to whom she addressed a goodly number of her short lyrics that told of burning passion. Hārūn sent away the first of these boys and at one time forbade ᶜUlaiyah even to mention the other. But, later, he relented and presented her with the boy in question.[45] Perhaps it was in connection with these love affairs that Hārūn was once so severely angered with her that she called on the blind poet Abū Ḥafṣ to produce some verses which would soften his heart. She herself then set them to music and taught them to a group of Hārūn's maids. Hārūn was touched on hearing the song and its story. He sent immediately for his sister, greeted her affectionately, accepted her apology, and asked her to sing the song herself. This she did so effectively that she brought tears to his eyes and the voluntary promise that he would never again be wroth with her.[46]

The gay-spirited, gayly attired ᶜUlaiyah with the magnificent head ornament, which she herself had designed so as to cover a blemish on her forehead, was the talk of the court. Her excellent taste and passionate love for music brought her into competition with leading musicians of the day, including her half-brother, Ibrāhīm ibn al-Mahdī, and that master-musician, Isḥāq al-

[45] *Ibid.*, pp. 83–84; *Fawāt*, II, 125; Ḥuṣrī, I, 11–12.

[46] *Aghānī*, XIX, 71.

Mauṣilī. She easily surpassed the former but had to resort to ruses and threats to keep pace with the latter.[47]

Hārūn had yet another half-sister whose beauty and wit brought her a dramatic court career that Zubaidah must have watched with interest if not indeed with some envy. This was his oldest sister, ᶜAbbāsah, thrice married and thrice widowed[48] while still comparatively young, if not in years then certainly in mind and spirit. Hārūn enjoyed her wit and sought her company as he did that of Jaᶜfar the Barmakid. But time spent in the company of his sister was time robbed from the company of Jaᶜfar and vice versa. For ᶜAbbāsah's high birth and consequent seclusion made it improper for her to appear before her brother in Jaᶜfar's presence. So Hārūn, thinking he had a brilliant idea that would enable him to enjoy the company of these two at one and the same time, arranged for a legal formal marriage—that and no more—between them. Had this been a true marriage, it might have helped to ease the racial and social tension between the conquering Arab and the conquered Persian. As it was, the very restriction placed on the marriage, that is, there was to be no thought of its consummation, and that Jaᶜfar and ᶜAbbāsah were never to meet except in Hārūn's presence,[49] emphasized the gap between the Arab ᶜAbbāsah's royal station and the Per-

[47] *Ibid.*, IX, 83; *Fawāt*, II, 125.

[48] Cf. above, p. 21; Yāqūt, *Geog.*, III, 200; Ibn Quṭaibah, *Maᶜārif*, p. 193; Zamakhsharī, *Rauḍ al-Akhyār*, p. 264; Ibn Taghrībirdī, I, 465, 469; cf. Horovitz in *Encyclopaedia of Islam*, I, 13.

[49] Ṭabarī, III, 676–77; Ibn Athīr, VI, 118–19; Masᶜūdī, VI, 387–88; *Fakhrī*, p. 288; Ibn Taghrībirdī, I, 516.

sian Jaᶜfar's subject status. This bizarre arrangement functioned well enough for a while when Hārūn enjoyed to the full the joint company of these two at delightful sessions from which, by the nature of Moslem society in general and Harūn's honor in particular, Zubaidah herself was excluded. But propinquity is ofttimes the handmaid of romance. At any rate, nature, with the couple in question, rebelled at the fantastic arrangement and found means to circumvent it. Unfortunately, however, Jaᶜfar's political interest lay athwart Zubaidah's path. This dual development gave Zubaidah reason for resentment and opportunity for impetuous revenge, as will be told elsewhere in this story.[50]

The affairs not only of Hārūn's sisters but also of his daughters must have occupied some of Zubaidah's thoughts, though here conventional marriages rather than sophisticated romances were the rule. Here, too, Jaᶜfar the Barmakid once played a part when he, on his own authority, promised the hand of ᶜĀliyah[51] to a distant royal cousin, which promise was presently approved and carried out by an amused caliph.[52] Hārūn himself kept his word given to his brother, Mūsā al-Hādī, when he arranged for the marriage of two of his several daughters, Fāṭimah and Ḥamdūnah, to Hādī's sons, Ismāᶜīl and Jaᶜfar, respectively.[53] There were also

[50] Cf. below, pp. 191–200 and 262.

[51] Ṭabarī, III, 759, mentions a daughter named Ghāliyah, but none named ᶜĀliyah; the two are no doubt identical, since the different names can readily be understood as a slight scribal error.

[52] Ibn ᶜAbdūs, p. 262–63; Ibn Khallikān, I, 303–5.

[53] Ṭabarī, III, 576–78; Masᶜūdī, VI, 284–85; cf. above, p. 93.

the marriages of the young heirs. Though no definite date is given for the marriage of either heir, the two events were probably not far apart and seem to have involved two of Hādī's daughters.[54] Maʾmūn's marriage to his cousin, Umm ʿĪsā, could not have taken place either much before or much after Hārūn's death in 193/809, since the pair is credited with two young sons by 196.[55]

But Islamic royalty, democratic in its social contacts with the large personnel of its numerous establishments, does frequently take an interest in—or even lend a hand to—the progress of the love affairs of the humbler members of the royal harem. The case of ʿUtbah and the poet Abū al-ʿAtāhiyah in the time of Mahdī and Khaizurān is one in point. That particular case came to light again in Hārūn's reign, for Hārūn enjoyed the poet's love verses and would not hear of his giving them up for an ascetic mode of life and turn of thought.[56] Eventually, the poet, weary of his long unrequited love, longing for peace of heart and mind, and preoccupied with otherworldly thoughts as age advanced upon him, renounced his passion for ʿUtbah.[57] Later, in the reign of Maʾmūn, the poet was ushered into the presence of Faḍl ibn al-Rabīʿ, who was talking to some woman. Turning to the poet, Faḍl asked, "Does ʿUtbah still hold a place in your heart?"

54 Yaʿqūbī, II, 529; Mubarrad, *Kāmil*, p. 773; but cf. below, p. 222.

55 Ṭabarī, III, 836; *ʿIqd*, III, 55.

56 Cf. *Aghānī*, III, 140–41, 151; VIII, 24–25; cf. Palmer, *op. cit.*, pp. 189–91.

57 Cf. Masʿūdī, VII, 84; Khaṭīb, VI, 258.

"That is all gone and departed," answered Abū al-ᶜAtāhiyah.

"There still remains something of it though," said Faḍl.

"No, by Allah," insisted the poet.

"This, by Allah, is ᶜUtbah," said Faḍl, indicating the woman before him. The poet took one glance at her and rushed out running, leaving, in his haste and confusion, his sandals behind him.[58] Though Zubaidah is not linked specifically with these anecdotes, her partiality to the poet and her frequent use of his talents in her service would lead one to suspect that she was interested in the ups and downs of his romance with ᶜUtbah.

Zubaidah herself had a maid whose love affair recalls the case of ᶜUtbah. This time the unrequited lover was the court jester, Ḥusain ibn al-Ḍaḥḥāk. He enlisted the services of a nobleman in favor with Zubaidah. The nobleman pleaded with the queen, but Zubaidah would not part with her maid.[59]

Sometimes Zubaidah was called upon to help in love affairs that did not involve her own palace personnel. There was, for instance, the case of the Kūfan merchant, ᶜAlī ibn Ādam, who fell in love with a maid named Minhalah. The girl was sold to a member of the imperial family and taken away from Kūfah, presumably to Baghdad. The unhappy lover went to the capital to enlist Zubaidah's aid only to be told that between him and his love were insurmountable obstacles. He returned to Kūfah and died, on arrival, of a broken

[58] Ibn Ṭaifūr, *Kitāb Baghdād*, ed. H. Keller (Leipzig, 1908), p. 21.

[59] *Aghānī*, VI, 203.

heart. When the girl heard of her lover's sad end, she too, alas, lay down and died.[60]

Royal and palace romances aside, Zubaidah devoted attentive care to the training of her own large retinue of palace boys (eunuchs) and girls. She bid high for those of reputed talents and guarded jealously her own accomplished group.[61] Among her many slave girls there were said to be a hundred who were expert at chanting the Qur'ān in successive relays of tens so that the hum of their voices issued from her palace all the day long.[62] She was the first to organize units of girls and page boys, the uniformed and mounted *shākirīyah*, to do her bidding and run her errands.[63]

Large numbers of her girls were, no doubt, occupied with entertaining her guests at the numerous harem functions. Examples have already been given of the use she made of some of them to win and retain Hārūn's favor. As the years passed, and her only son, Mohammed al-Amīn, grew to manhood, Zubaidah found, in connection with him, yet another use for some of her most elegant and charming maids.[64]

II

There was for Zubaidah in Hārūn's time yet another type of romance—the thrill of political intrigue and personal power. Her major political interest centered round

60 *Ibid.*, XIV, 51–52.

61 *Ibid.*, IX, 99; VII, 34.

62 Ibn Khallikān, I, 533.

63 Mas'ūdī, VIII, 298. The word is arabicized from the Persian *chākir*, a hired man or maid.

64 See below, p. 212.

the succession to the throne and will be detailed elsewhere in this study. For the rest, the urge for personal power found outlet mainly in her contact with this or that poet whose talents were at her disposal or with here and there a judge who could be bribed or intimidated into doing her bidding. There were times, too, when she did not hesitate to order Hārūn's chief of police about or to poke fun at one of his ranking generals.

Poets of varying ability and rank sought this queen in the hope of profiting by her influence or generosity or both. Seldom did she disappoint even the least gifted of these. When once a mere novice of a poet blundered in his verses in praise of her liberality, her attendants handled him roughly. But Zubaidah came to his rescue, explaining that he meant well but went astray, and added that she preferred such to those who mean ill and achieve it. She closed the incident with, "Give him what he had hoped for and explain to him his error."[65]

Once a group of poets and singers had congregated in her palace. Presently, in came one of Zubaidah's slave girls with her sleeve full of silver coins and asked to know who the author was of the verse, "Who dares reproach you for a weeping eye? Saw you ever a weeping eye to be reproached?" It turned out that ᶜAbbās ibn al-Aḥnaf was the lucky author, into whose lap, therefore, the girl emptied her sleeveful of coins. ᶜAbbās, himself no miser, scattered them around for the attendants to pick up. The girl, having no doubt reported the scene to Zubaidah, returned presently, followed by three serv-

[65] Ḥuṣrī, I, 317; Rāgib, *Muḥāḍarāt*, I, 54–55; Waṭwaṭ, p. 227.

ants each carrying a bag of silver coins to be delivered at the poet's house.[66]

Among the poets whom Zubaidah openly favored was Abū al-ᶜAtāhiyah, whose verses in praise of Amīn, along with similar verses of other courts poets, will be met with later. At one time this poet incurred, through his sharp lines, the displeasure of Prince Qāsim,[67] who ordered him to be flogged and then locked up in his residence. The poet appealed to Zubaidah, who brought the incident to Hārūn's attention and secured his release. Hārūn himself insisted that the young prince exonerate the poet and render him an apology.[68]

Zubaidah had recourse to the poets when Hārūn, weary of Baghdad and its climate, decided in 180/796 to move his court to Raqqah,[69] the port of the Syrian Desert on the Upper Euphrates. He used to say that there were but four cities in this whole world—Damascus, Raqqah, Rayy, and Samarqand—and that he had been privileged to dwell in the first three.[70] He took an active interest in the further development of the city, with its new canals and palaces and other surrounding estates, some of which were to come, in time, into the possession of Zubaidah herself.[71] He had with him at

66 *Aghānī*, VIII, 23–24.

67 See above, p. 141.

68 *Aghānī*, III, 159.

69 Ṭabarī, III, 644–46; *Fakhrī*, p. 319. For Raqqah see Yāqūt, *Geog.*, II, 802–4; *BGA*, II, 225–26; III, 141, 145; VI, 98; 216–18; *EI*, art. "Rakkah"; K. A. C. Creswell, *Early Muslim Architecture* (2 vols.; Oxford, 1932 and 1940), II, 39–49.

70 Ibn al-Faqīh al-Hamadhānī, *K. al-Buldān*, ed. de Goeje (*BGA*, Vol. V [Lugduni Batavorum, 1885]), p. 273.

71 Yāqūt, *Geog.*, IV, 112, 862, 889, 994; Balādhurī, *Futūḥ*, pp. 179–80.

this northern capital not only that burden-bearer, Yaḥyā the Barmakid, and his retinue of administrative personnel, but also some of his boon companions, including Isḥāq al-Mauṣilī. The latter could not quite overcome his homesickness for Baghdad, and his nostalgic longings proved, on occasion, contagious for Hārūn himself.[72] Eager poets, keeping up with the caliph's move, sang the praises of the city of his choice and won favor for themselves, as did in particular the new court poets Ashjaᶜ[73] and Mohammed al-ᶜUmānī.[74] Zubaidah now called on the poets to compete in producing a poem in praise of Baghdad, promising a rich prize for the winner whose verses would cause Hārūn to long for the city of her own choice. The prize—a gem valued at 800,000 dirhams—went to Manṣūr al-Namrī, whose nostalgic verses led Hārūn to visit Baghdad.[75]

Zubaidah's luxurious mode of life matched that of Hārūn. Her agents, like those of Khaizurān, were everywhere seeking to procure the best for the queen, while her secretaries at the capital administered her vast estates. It was in connection with such matters that Zubaidah's personal power was, at times, felt outside the palace, as the following incidents reveal. Agents and secretaries were, by their very position, men of power. They were sought after by persons in high office who hoped for help or favor from Zubaidah;[76] or they were

[72] *Aghānī*, XVII, 75; cf. *ibid.*, p. 77–78.

[73] *Ibid.*, pp. 30–31, 48; Ibn al-Muᶜtazz, *Ṭabaqāt*, pp. 117–18; Khaṭīb, VII, 45; Yāqūt, *Geog.*, IV, 961–62.

[74] *Aghānī*, XVII, 80–81.

[75] Ibn al-Muᶜtazz, *Ṭabaqāt*, p. 115; cf. Khaṭīb, I, 51–52, 68.

[76] Kindī, *Governors and Judges of Egypt*, ed. Guest, p. 392.

envied and denounced by others less fortunately placed. Her secretary Saᶜdān was once denounced in verse for his bribery and partiality. Hārūn remonstrated with Zubaidah, who asked him to repeat the verse in question. Rising to the defense of Saᶜdān, she replied with an even more damaging verse—suspected of being her own extemporizing—concerning Hārūn's minister of the tax bureau. "These are lies," said Hārūn, "about both your secretary and mine," and therewith dismissed the matter.[77]

Whatever their public sins, Zubaidah's secretaries guarded her interests, which clashed at times with those of her agents. Once her secretary Dāʾūd saw fit to imprison an agent in charge of some of the queen's estate for a shortage of 100,000 dirhams. The agent appealed to two of his friends, who decided to put in a word for him with Dāʾūd. On their way to see the latter, they met Mahdī's old wazir, Faiḍ ibn Ṣāliḥ (d. 173/789–90), who joined them on their friendly mission. But the secretary stated he could take no action in the case without Zubaidah's permission. He informed her of their request for the agent's release and received her note of refusal which he showed to his guests. Faiḍ now suggested that they meet the payment out of their own funds. They signed a security note to that effect. Dāʾūd informed Zubaidah of this move, too. Quickly came back her answer: "It is not for Faiḍ to be more generous than we. Return his note and release the man."[78] The episode leaves the strong impression that Zubaidah's secretaries

[77] Ibn ᶜAbdūs, pp. 323–24.

[78] *Ibid.*, pp. 194–95; cf. *Fakhrī*, pp. 256.

took no major step without her knowledge and that she herself was quick at jotting down her instructions, brief and to the point, in their correspondence.[79]

But it was not always on such a generous note that the queen's claims and legal cases were resolved. One of her agents once bought goods from a Khurāsānian and withheld the payment for a long time. The merchant sought the advice of the judge, Ḥafṣ ibn Ghaiyāth, an honest man who had refused the Baghdad judgeship until dire poverty had compelled him to accept it. He took office in 177/793 and served the capital for two years. He advised the merchant to bring the case to trial. Having secured an admission of the debt, he ordered the agent to pay it. But the latter sought refuge in the repeated phrase, "It is the queen's debt." "Fool," said Ḥafṣ, "you acknowledge the debt and then place the responsibility on the queen!" He then sent him to the debtor's prison.

When Zubaidah heard of what had happened, she sent word to Hārūn's chief of armed police[80] to release her man, which he did immediately. It was Ḥafṣ' turn now to be indignant. The judge refused to sit on the bench until the agent was returned to prison. The alarmed chief of police prevailed on Zubaidah to yield up her agent. But, far from yielding the case, she turned to other tactics. "O Hārūn," she said to her royal husband, "your judge is indeed a fool. He belittled and im-

[79] Cf. Jāḥiẓ, *Al-Bayān wa al-Tabyīn* (Cairo, 1332/1913–14), I, 59, where the lady in question is far more likely to be Queen Zubaidah than Zubaidah, the mother of Jaᶜfar ibn Yaḥyā.

[80] Ṭabarī, III, 681–83; Ibn Khallikān, 310–11, 318.

prisoned my agent. Command him not to try the case; but let it be brought instead before (Chief Justice) Abū Yūsuf." Hārūn was willing to oblige her and sent word to Ḥafṣ to transfer the case. The caliph's messenger arrived with the letter which Ḥafṣ refused to take until after he has rushed through the case and passed judgment. The messenger, who realized full well the significance of Ḥafṣ's refusal and haste, threatened to inform Hārūn. "Tell him what you please," said the judge. When Hārūn was told of the scene, he was greatly amused and himself sent Ḥafṣ the sum owed by Zubaidah's agent.

Hārūn's wazir, Yaḥyā, rejoiced and praised Allah that a just judge had come to sit in judgment. But not so Zubaidah, who informed Hārūn that she would have nothing to do with him until and unless he expelled Ḥafṣ from office. Hārūn refused to comply at the time. But Zubaidah, whose pride had been doubly wounded in this skirmish, soon returned to the fight and prevailed on her husband to transfer the good judge to Kūfah.[81]

The reader will have gathered from the above incident that the chief justice, Abū Yūsuf, who solved many of Hārūn's legal perplexities,[82] was willing, on occasion, to do as much for Zubaidah. The record of one such instance has survived, though the nature of the case involved is not specified. Zubaidah rewarded the judge handsomely and elegantly, for her gift consisted not only of silver and gold but also of exquisite perfumes and fine raiments and two young slaves with their mounts. When the royal gift arrived, those present

[81] Khaṭīb, VIII, 189–94.

[82] See above, pp. 150 and 153.

hinted that the Prophet Mohammed had said that, when a man receives a gift, he should share it with those of his companions who are present with him. To this Abū Yūsuf replied that that was when the usual presents consisted of dates and figs and not of silver and gold and other precious things. He ended up with the Qurʾānic verse. "That is the bounty of Allah. He bestows it upon whomsoever he pleases. Allah is of infinite bounty."[83]

One suspects that Zubaidah possessed a sense of humor that enabled her to enjoy a joke even at her own expense. The poet Abū Nuwās may or may not have put her to the test in this respect. But it took a madman's courage to claim her for his kind. There was the crazed Bahlūl the Possessed, who certainly had method in his madness and who was a sort of celebrity. Hārūn was once visiting with Zubaidah and her brother ʿĪsā, when Bahlūl was brought in to amuse them. The caliph asked the madman to enumerate for him the insane.

"I am the first," said Bahlūl.

"Right," said the caliph.

"And this one here is the second," he added, pointing to Zubaidah. It was not the latter but her indignant brother ʿĪsā who shouted:

"Why you son of a vile mother, how dare you say that of my sister!"

[83] Sūrah 57:21; Masʿūdī, VI, 294–95; Khaṭīb, XIV, 252; Ibn Khallikān, IV, 282; Yāfiʿī, *Mirʾāt al-Janān* (4 vols.; Hyderabad, 1337–40), I, 387. It is this same judge who, though he gave Islam, at the specific request of Hārūn, its first book on taxation, robbed Allah and the state of his own contribution by writing his property in his wife's name in order to avoid paying taxes on it. Cf. Abū Yūsuf, *Kitāb al-Kharāj* (Būlāq, 1302/1884); Ghazālī, *Iḥyā Ulūm al Dīn* (4 vols.; Būlāq, 1289/1872), I, 17.

"And you yourself are the third, you ill-natured one," said Bahlūl undaunted. Hārūn, thinking, no doubt, that the "joke" had gone far enough, ordered Bahlūl out of the room.

"And you are the fourth," shot back this madman at the caliph as he made his exit.[84]

Zubaidah had certainly developed a craze for her pet monkey, whom she had named Abū Khalaf.[85] Girt with girdle and sword, Abū Khalaf had thirty men to wait on him and take him on his outings. Zubaidah herself took the attitude of "Love me, love my monkey," for she required all who came to court to pay homage to her to show respect also to her pet by kissing the creature's hand. This homage she demanded from no less a personage than one of Hārūn's ranking generals, Yazīd ibn Mazyad (d. 185/801), a man not to be trifled with.[86] Outraged at the demand, he drew his sword and cut the monkey in two and turned away in anger. The tenor of Zubaidah's complaint to Hārūn can be well imagined. The caliph summoned the seasoned general and demanded an explanation.

"O Commander of the Believers, shall I then serve apes after having served caliphs? No, by Allah, never!" Hārūn saw the point and forgave his general.[87] Meanwhile, Zubaidah's great grief over the loss of her spoiled

[84] Rāghib, *Muḥāḍarāt*, II, 425.

[85] Yāqūt *Irshād* ("Dictionary of Learned Men") (Gibb Memorial Series" [7 vols.; Leyden, 1907–27]), VI, 75, and following note.

[86] Ṭabarī, III, 597, 650.

[87] Ibn Isfandiyār, *History of Ṭabaristān*, trans. Edward G. Browne ("Gibb Memorial Series," Vol. II [London, 1905]), p. 45. Cf. Abū al-ᶜAlāʾ al-Maᶜarrī, *Risālat al-Ghifrān*, ed. Kāmil Kīlānī (Cairo, 1925), II, 51–52.

pet was known to all in her service, big or small. Some went so far as to send her a letter of condolence which was graciously acknowledge and amply rewarded.[88]

But sumptuous living and royal romance, poets, judges, generals, and monkeys were not enough to absorb completely the Lady Zubaidah. She had, concurrent with one or more of these, two major interests of far-reaching significance for the welfare and future of the empire. These were spectacular philanthropy, on the one hand, and the imperial succession, on the other. We turn first to the latter of the two.

[88] Ḥuṣrī, III, 281–82.

VI

Heirs to Hārūn's Empire

KHAIZURĀN, it will be recalled, came to be associated with a prophetic comment on that night of destiny in which a caliph (Hādī) passed away, a second (Hārūn) ascended his throne, and a third (Maʾmūn) was born.[1] Whatever halo surrounded the infant ʿAbd Allah, the future Maʾmūn, through his birth at this auspicious time began slowly to fade with the birth of his half-brother Mohammed, the future Amīn, some six months later. For ʿAbd Allah's mother was a Persian slave girl who, as already stated, died in childbirth, while Mohammed's mother was the royal Hāshimite Arab Zubaidah and a very live favorite of Hārūn. But in this short interval ʿAbd Allah, as the firstborn male child, touched off in Hārūn's heart nature's responsive chord of fatherhood and, as a motherless babe, seems to have crept quite naturally into the expectant Zubaidah's tender arms. Other sons—and daughters, too—came to join the royal nursery, but none seem to have claimed as much of Hārūn's affections as his first two darlings, whom he loved to have around and whom

[1] Cf. above, pp. 41 and 110.

he proudly displayed before some especially privileged courtier or some passing visitor from afar. In physical appearance both princes were strong, tall, and handsome, but, while Mohammed was fair, ᶜAbd Allah inherited some of his mother's darker color.[2]

There is a touching scene reported, according to an early source, by the famous scholar Aṣmaᶜī,[3] but, according to a somewhat later account, by Kisāʾī,[4] tutor in turn to Hārūn and the two princes. The probabilities are in favor of the earlier and briefer source, which is followed here. The time is early in the princes' childhood. The scholar in question, along with others, was paying the caliph a formal visit. When he rose to depart, Hārūn detained him until all the rest had taken their leave. Then, turning to the scholar, he asked if he would not like to see Mohammed and ᶜAbd Allah and received, as was to be expected, an enthusiastic answer in the affirmative. Hārūn sent for the princes, who entered together and with eyes cast down approached and saluted their father as caliph. Hārūn, having seated Mohammed on his right and ᶜAbd Allah on his left, called on the scholar to examine them in the various branches of learning. They answered all the questions put to them readily and to the point. The scholar marveled at the extent of their understanding and the excellence of their memory. He prayed Allah to grant them long life and to bless the na-

[2] Ṭabarī, III, 938, 1140–41; Ibn Athīr, VI, 202, 305; Khaṭīb, III, 337; X, 184.

[3] Dīnawarī, p. 384.

[4] Masᶜūdī, VI, 317–20; Yāqūt, *Irshād*, V, 185–86; cf. E. H. Palmer, *Haroun Alraschid* (London, 1881), pp. 116–17.

tion through their mercy and benevolence. Hārūn, overcome by his emotions of pride and joy which brought tears to his eyes, clasped the young princes to his heart in a tender embrace before he dismissed them.[5]

But a royal prince born of a royal Arab mother was a rarity in early Islam. Poets and politicians, frequently combined in one and the same person, were not to be expected to overlook such a prince's doubly noble birth. Add to that the fact that Hārūn's attachment to Zubaidah was no secret, and one has the setting for the numerous verses that soon began to make their appearance, capitalizing on Mohammed's full royal descent and winning thereby Zubaidah's special favor.[6] When in 175/791–92, Mohammed, at the age of five, was nominated heir to his father's throne (while the older ᶜAbd Allah was passed by), the occasion called for a number of such verses.[7] Some long-established court poets mentioned Zubaidah herself by name. There was, for instance, Salm al-Khāṣir—whose talents with words surpassed that of his teacher, Bashshār ibn Burd. He wove Zubaidah's name in the last line of his verse in return for which she filled his mouth literally with pearls—so highly did she value the literary gems at the tip of his tongue.[8] Marwān ibn Abī Ḥafṣah received a similar reward for a verse of his that was addressed to Zubaidah

[5] Cf. *ᶜIqd*, I, 118; Ḥuṣrī, III, 345–46; and Ṭabarī, III, 762–63, for other touching incidents.

[6] *Aghānī*, XVII, 37; cf. Masᶜūdī, VI, 436; *Fawāt*, II, 336.

[7] E.g., Ṭabarī, III, 611; *Aghānī*, XVII, 78–80; Khaṭīb, III, 338–39; IX, 412; and nn. 8 and 10 below.

[8] Ṭabarī, III, 610; Khaṭīb, IX, 138–39.

herself either on this occasion or perhaps at some earlier time in anticipation of this much-desired event.[9]

The records detail some of the intrigue on the part of Zubaidah's family in connection with this early nomination of the child Mohammed. A number of the senior ᶜAbbāsid princes were "stretching their necks toward the caliphate," that is, they were reaching out for the throne, after Hārūn. So Zubaidah's brother, ᶜĪsā, approached the powerful Faḍl the Barmakid and enlisted his help on behalf of Mohammed, saying, "My sister's son is like a child of yours; his rule will be your rule." Faḍl promised to try to secure the child's succession and, no doubt, had a hand in the initial step, when Mohammed's nomination was first announced at Baghdad. Much as Hārūn and his supporters tried to counteract the unfavorable factor of the prince's youth, yet there were those who refused to accept so young an heir to the throne. It was here that Faḍl played his decisive role, by securing allegiance to the new heir in the key province of Khurāsān, to which he himself had been recently appointed governor. The rest of the provinces readily followed suit. Thus was firmly established the heirship of Zubaidah's son, who was to be known henceforth as Mohammed al-Amīn, "Mohammed the Trustworthy."[10]

The education of the princes was one of Hārūn's major concerns in the years that followed. These were

[9] *ᶜIqd*, I, 119; cf. *Aghānī*, XX, 31–32, where the poet Nuṣaib refers to her, probably on her pilgrimage of 176/793, as "mother of the heir to the throne."

[10] Ibn ᶜAbdūs, p. 234; Ṭabarī, III, 610–11; Ḥuṣrī, II, 149; cf. Yaᶜqūbī, II, 493.

years in which the boys' intellectual gifts and inherent character were rapidly unfolding. Manṣūr and Mahdī had both exercised great care in the selection of tutors for their children.[11] It was Mahdī himself who had selected the Kūfan scholar, Kisā'ī,[12] as tutor to Hārūn. The pupil-teacher relationship between Hārūn and Kisā'ī ripened into one of genuine respect and friendship so that Kisā'ī came to have the enviable distinction of being promoted from the rank of tutor to that of courtier and boon companion to the caliph.[13] Hārūn, however, instructed him as to the nature of the friendly and scholarly service he was to render him in their more intimate contacts. "Recite for us," said he, "the purest of classical poetry and relate to us such traditions as reflect the most ethical conduct. Discourse with us upon the polite learning of the Persians and of India. Hasten not to contradict us in public, but do not refrain from correcting us in private."[14]

Hārūn's great respect for Kisā'ī as a teacher led him, in turn, to appoint the latter as tutor to his two sons,[15] probably quite early in their young lives, since Moham-

[11] Cf. above, pp. 7 and 62; Rifā'ī, *'Aṣr al-Ma'mūn*, I, 174.

[12] Khaṭīb, XI, 403–15; Ibn Khallikān, II, 237–39 (Arabic I, 336–37); Yāqūt, *Irshād*, V, 108–11, 183–200; Gustav Flügel, "Die grammatischen Schulen der Araber," *Abhandlungen für die Kunde des Morganlandes*, II, No. 4 (Leipzig, 1862), 121–29.

[13] Khaṭīb, XI, 403, 406; Yāqūt, *Irshād*, V, 183.

[14] Aḥmad Amīn, *Ḍuḥā al-Islām* (Cairo, 1933), p. 172. Hārūn abided by his own rules, for he himself corrected Kisā'ī in private (cf. Khaṭīb, XI, 408). For a comparable set of instructions given to Aṣma'ī see Zamakhsharī, *Rauḍ al-Akhyār*, p. 32.

[15] Dīnawarī, p. 383; Yāqūt, *Irshād*, V, 183, 185–86; Rāghib, *Muḥāḍarāt*, I, 29.

med is reported as receiving formal instruction in letters when but four years old.[16] Later, Kisāʾī had a colleague in the person of Yaḥyā ibn al-Mubārak al-Yazīdī,[17] who was to teach ʿAbd Allah the reading of the Qurʾān, while Kisāʾī did the same for Mohammed.[18] Kisāʾī was very jealous of his position, which he guarded sometimes at the expense of his finer qualities.[19] Numerous are the anecdotes in which Kisāʾī emerged the victor in contests with representatives from the different schools. Closer home, he had his scholarly bouts with colleagues in the palace school, including the judge Abū Yūsuf, who was jealous and resentful of him and who was, for some time, tutor to Amīn.[20] Of more interest is the contest reported between him and Yazīdī, tutor to ʿAbd Allah. The event took place in the presence of Hārūn and his wazir, Yaḥyā the Barmakid. Kisāʾī, for once, lost the contest. Yazīdī, flushed with victory, flung his turban on the floor and gloated over his defeated rival—conduct unbecoming the dignity of a tutor in the presence of the caliph. Hārūn, therefore, reproved the excited scholar with, "By Allah, Kisāʾī's mistake, joined to his good breeding, is better than your right answer joined to your

[16] Cf. *Aghānī*, XVII, 37.

[17] *Ibid.*, XVIII, 72–94; Khaṭīb, XIV, 146–48; Ibn Khallikān, IV, 69–78; Flügel, *op. cit.*, p. 61.

[18] Sīrāfī, pp. 40, 45; Khaṭīb, XIV, 147; Ibn Khallikān, IV, 71.

[19] Cf. Yāqūt, *Irshād*, V, 188–89. The story is discounted by Yāqūt himself and seems to be transferred from the reign of Mahdī to that of Hārūn (cf. *Aghānī*, XIII, 78, and Rifāʿī, I, 197, this last further confusing the two versions by impossible combinations).

[20] Khaṭīb, XI, 406; Yāqūt, *Irshād*, VI, 187–88, 190–91; *EI*, I, 490.

bad manners." To this, Yazīdī pleaded, "The sweetness of my triumph put me off my guard."[21]

As Kisāʾī grew older, he developed leucoderma and, thereafter, Hārūn disliked having him around Mohammed. Yet, so greatly did he esteem the scholar that, instead of replacing him, he offered to retire him on full pay and asked him to find as his successor one whose qualifications met with his approval. Kisāʾī took his time and pleaded that he could not find a man good enough for the position. His real reason, says the record, was that he did not wish to relinquish his influential post. But the caliph's patience wore out, and Kisāʾī was informed that if he did not soon find one in his own circle, they would look elsewhere for his successor. Kisāʾī was now seriously alarmed, especially as rumor had it that Sībawaih,[22] of the rival Baṣran school, was expected in the capital. To avoid, as his successor, one who would and could challenge either his reputation or his influence, Kisāʾī hastened to appoint to the office a comparatively unknown man.

ʿAlī ibn al-Ḥasan (or Ibn Mubārak) better known as al-Aḥmar,[23] was a soldier by training and profession and a member of the caliph's bodyguard. He had, however, a thirst for knowledge and had discovered a pleasant way of satisfying it at Kisāʾī's font of scholarship. He would watch for the royal tutor, greet and escort him to his

[21] Zamakhsharī, *Rauḍ al-Akhyār*, p. 220; Ibn Khallikān, IV, 73; Yāqūt, *Irshād*, V, 188; cf. *Aghānī*, XVIII, 73–74, 76–77.

[22] Khaṭīb, XII, 195–99; Ibn Khallikān, II, 396–99; Yāqūt, *Irshād*, VI, 80–88; Flügel, *op. cit.*, pp. 42–45.

[23] Khaṭīb, XII, 104–5; Ibn Khallikān, IV, 69; Yāqūt, *Irshād*, V, 108–11; Flügel, *op. cit.*, p. 129.

palace destination, plying him the while with questions on points of grammar and other branches of learning. When Kisāʾī's duties at the palace were done, there would be the young bodyguard ready again to serve and be informed. The man was intelligent and made a favorable impression on the scholar, who was perhaps flattered by his attentions.

It was on this soldier-student that Kisāʾī's choice fell. To the objections that the man was a soldier and not a scholar, Kisāʾī replied that he knew no one in his circle who was more intelligent and modest. The unassuming Aḥmar had his own doubts about his fitness for the new task. But Kisāʾī hastened to reassure him. The children's daily needs at his hands were but two problems in grammar and two in poetry, and Kisāʾī intended to tutor his lieutenant in these a day ahead so that he could teach them to the princes. Aḥmar was willing. Kisāʾī himself visited the palace school once or twice a month, when, in the presence of Hārūn, he would test the princes on the subjects taught them by Aḥmar.[24] These, so far as Mohammed al-Amīn was concerned—he was Aḥmar's particular charge—went much beyond Kisāʾī's initial program of grammar and poetry. Hārūn's instructions to Aḥmar at the time of his appointment give a better idea of their nature and extent:

"O Aḥmar, the Commander of the Believers has intrusted to you his very soul and the fruit of his heart. He has given you a free hand with him and made obedience to you his bounden duty. Therefore, fill well, in regard to him, the position in which the Commander of

[24] Yāqūt, *Irshād*, V, 109–10.

the Believers has placed you. Teach him the reading of the Qurʾān, instruct him well in the traditions, enrich his memory with the recitation of classic poetry, and instruct him as to the accepted manners. Let him perceive the proper moment for speech and the correct manner of beginning it. Restrain him from laughter except when the occasion demands it. Teach him to receive with great respect the senior Hāshimites when they call upon him and with due consideration the generals that are present at his receptions. Let not one single hour escape you in which you do not seize some opportunity for his improvement without, however, being so severe with him as to deaden his intellect. Do not be so lenient in excusing him as to make him find idleness sweet and, therefore, seek it. Correct him, as much as you can, through friendliness and gentleness; but should he fail to respond to these, then be sharp and severe."[25]

That either Kisāʾī, or Aḥmar, or more likely both, had reason to exercise, at times, severity with the young Mohammed is indicated by the fact that Zubaidah felt the need to plead for leniency on his behalf. She sent Khāliṣah—the old palace woman from the days of Khaizurān—to the tutor to make the plea for her son, "the flower of her heart and the apple of her eye for whom she had much compassion." The tutor replied, in effect, that as Mohammed was heir to his father's throne, it was his bounden duty not to fall short in educating and disciplining him.[26]

[25] Masʿūdī, VI, 321–22.

[26] Dīnawarī, p. 383; Damīrī, *Ḥayāwān*, I, 106; cf. Rifāʿī, *ʿAṣr al-Maʾmūn*, I, 195.

ᶜAbd Allah, too, needed, on occasion, some disciplinary measures. But seemingly there were none to plead for him. The youth, moreover, took his punishment like a man, as the following story, told by his tutor, Yazīdī, indicates. The prince's offense was tardiness in reporting for his lesson and his punishment seven strokes of the whip. The strokes were quite severe, since the boy struggled in vain to force back his tears. Jaᶜfar the Barmakid was announced while the punishment was in progress. The stoic young ᶜAbd Allah brushed away his tears, pulled himself together, and admitted the distinguished visitor to his presence, with whom he talked and joked quite naturally. When Jaᶜfar departed, this paragon of a student prince presented himself before his tutor ready to take the rest of his punishment which had been so suddenly interrupted. It was Yazīdī who now broke down, called down Allah's blessings on his royal pupil, and confessed that he had feared the prince would complain of his treatment to Jaᶜfar.

"Do you think," asked ᶜAbd Allah, "that I would want even the caliph to know of this? How then could I ever think of letting Jaᶜfar know that I stood in need of discipline. Continue with your affair. That which passed through your mind you will never see come to pass, not even if you were to repeat the punishment a hundred times daily."[27]

Hārūn was quick to perceive that ᶜAbd Allah was a youth of great intellectual promise. Once he came upon him reading a book and wished to know its theme.

[27] Khaṭīb, X, 184–85; cf. Suyūṭī, *Taʾrīkh*, p. 124, and translation, p. 328.

"It is a book that stimulates the mind and improves one's social manners," answered the boy.

"Praise be to Allah," said Hārūn, "who has blessed me with a son who sees with the mind's eye even more than he sees with his physical one."[28]

An incident is told of the poet ᶜUmānī, who was eager in his praises of Amīn and who urged Hārūn to reaffirm his succession. Hārūn, much to the poet's joy, assured him of that but asked for his opinion of ᶜAbd Allah. The poet replied in a desert idiom that implied mild praise in contrast with his extravagant eulogy of Amīn. Hārūn smiled as he, having first discounted the poet's opinion, exclaimed: "As for me, by Allah, I perceive in ᶜAbd Allah the resolution of Manṣūr, the piety of Mahdī, the self-respect of Hādī, and, did Allah permit me, I would compare him even to the fourth (that is, the Prophet Mohammed himself)."[29]

Aṣmaᵓī describes some of Hārūn's struggle in coming to the decision to nominate ᶜAbd Allah as his second heir. Agitated and in tears, the caliph murmured to himself:

Let him alone o'er nations rule
  Whose mind is firm, whose heart is pure;
Avoid the vacillating fool
  Whose thoughts and speech are never sure.

He then dispatched his trusted servant, Masrūr, to summon the wazir Yaḥyā to his presence. After a brief survey of Islam's succession troubles from the time of the Prophet on, Hārūn revealed his own problem.

[28] Ḥuṣrī, I, 131.

[29] Masᶜūdī, VI, 322–23; cf. *Aghānī*, XVII, 80, where the implied date of 170 is obviously too early.

"I desire to see," said the calph to the wazir, "that my succession is assured to one whose conduct I approve, and whose ways I can praise, whose good statesmanship I can trust, and whose folly and weakness I need not fear—and that one is ᶜAbd Allah. But the Hāshimites incline with their favor toward Mohammed, although he is led by his passions and whims, is extravagant, and much given to the influence of women and slaves in his affairs. On the other hand, ᶜAbd Allah is pleasing in his ways, basically sound in his judgments, and is fit to be intrusted with great matters. Now, should I incline to ᶜAbd Allah, I will displease the Hāshimites; and should I leave Mohammed as my sole heir I fear he will cause disturbances in the state. Advise me, then, in this affair." When the wazir left at last, they had decided that ᶜAbd Allah was to be second heir.[30]

It was, therefore, largely the young ᶜAbd Allah's obviously superior gifts of intellect and character that recommended him to Hārūn as second heir to the throne. The historic step was taken in 182–83/798–99, first at Raqqah and then at Baghdad.[31] Among those who accompanied the young prince to Baghdad for the ceremony of the oath of allegiance was Zubaidah's father. ᶜAbd Allah was now given the title of al-Maʾmūn, "The Trusted," and was officially delivered to the care

[30] Masᶜūdī, VI, 323–25; cf. Palmer, *op. cit.*, pp. 118–19.

[31] Ṭabarī, III, 647, 652; Ibn Athīr, VI, 110; Ḥuṣrī II, 149; Yaᶜqūbī, II, 500–501; Ibn Taghrībirdī, I, 516; cf. F. Gabrieli, "La Successione di Hārūn ar-Rašīd," *Rivista degli studi orientali*, XI (1926–28), 344.

of Jaᶜfar the Barmakid.[32] Thus came Faḍl and Jaᶜfar, the sons of Yaḥyā, to be the political mentors and guardians of Amīn and Maʾmūn, respectively. Thus also came Hārūn's empire to be divided even in his own day, ᶜIrāq and the west to go to Amīn and Khurāsān and the east to Maʾmūn. Thus, too, came Zubaidah to be known as the "Mother" of the heirs to the throne.[33]

This occasion, which called also for the renewal of the oath to Amīn as first heir, touched off the poets' fancy so that there were a number of eulogies all in praise of Amīn, the prince of doubly noble birth. Hārūn took note of the almost complete silence regarding Maʾmūn and determined to end it. He therefore approached one of his numerous uncles to find him a gifted poet who would sing Maʾmūn's praises. The uncle's choice fell on Ashjaᶜ, whose verses met with Hārūn's approval.[34] More spontaneous praise for Maʾmūn came from his devoted tutor Yazīdī.[35]

Several incidents are recorded which indicate that Hārūn continued, through the years which followed, to take a hand in Maʾmūn's education. The following anecdotes, significant enough in the young prince's training, reflect also the prevailing court concept of politeness, morality, and youthful manliness. Hārūn did not spare the rod when the welfare of the princes demanded it.

[32] Ṭabarī, III, 647; Ibn ᶜAbdūs, pp. 234 and 258; Masᶜūdī, VI, 367; cf. Yāqūt, *Geog.*, I, 807. To avoid confusion in names, Mohammed al-Amīn and ᶜAbd Allah al-Maʾmūn will be hereafter referred to as Amīn and Maʾmūn, respectively.

[33] Cf. above, p. 170, and below, pp. 185 and 241. [34] *Aghānī*, XVII, 38–39.

[35] *Ibid.*, XVIII, 82–83; cf. Rifāᶜī, I, 214–15.

Maʾmūn once entered Hārūn's presence while a singing girl was amusing him. She spoke incorrectly, and Maʾmūn frowned at her error. The girl changed color. Hārūn took note and wondered why. Then, turning to Maʾmūn, he asked if the prince had reproved her.

"No, my Lord," said Maʾmūn.

"Not even with a sign?" insisted Hārūn.

"That is just what did happen," confessed the youth.

"Stay within sight and hearing," said Hārūn. "When you receive my order, carry it out." Then he took pen and papyrus and wrote some verses which first took the prince severely to task for his rudeness and then instructed him to see to it himself that he receive twenty strokes of the whip. The boy called on the gatekeepers to flog him, but they refused. He insisted, and so they obliged him. The incident was used by an unfriendly poet to cast reflection on Maʾmūn and his plebeian mother.[36]

On another occasion Maʾmūn had taken a fancy to one of Hārūn's palace maids. She was once pouring water for Hārūn when Maʾmūn entered. The prince signaled her a kiss. She reproved him with her eyebrows and ceased for the moment to pour the water.

"What is the matter?" cried Hārūn. The girl faltered in her answer, whereupon Hārūn made her tell the story on pain of death. Then, glancing at his son, he saw that fear and shame had so overcome him that he took pity on the youth.

"Do you love her?" asked the father.

[36] *ʿIqd*, III, 55; Ibn Qutaibah, *Maʿārif*, p. 196; Maqdisī, VI, 113; ***Fakhrī***, pp. 291–92; Rifāʿī, I, 212.

"Yes," confessed the son. Ma'mūn was presented with the girl for his immediate pleasure but was asked to compose some lines on the incident. He produced the following:

> A Gazelle, I hinted with my glance
> As to my feelings to her.
> I kissed her from afar,
> But she made excuses with her lips,
> And returned the best of answers
> By the contraction of her eyebrows.
> But I did not quit my place
> Before I obtained possession of her.[37]

At still another time, a Greek captive was brought before Hārūn, who commanded one of his men to strike off the captive's head. The Moslem's sword glanced off, and a second man was next ordered to the task. But he, too, was no more successful than the first. Then Hārūn, turning to the youthful Ma'mūn, enjoined him to finish the ghastly affair. The young prince severed the unfortunate unbeliever's head with one stroke. Hārūn called in another captive, and the prince repeated the performance. Proud of his accomplishment, Ma'mūn gave his tutor, Yazīdī, an eloquent glance, whereupon, the latter burst into verse that contrasted the prince's effective strokes with the ineffectual ones of the two men who had tried their swords before him.[38]

As the years passed, Hārūn felt increasingly the need and the urge to protect Ma'mūn against the jealousy and antagonism of Amīn, backed as this was by Zu-

[37] Khaṭīb, X, 185; Suyūṭī, *Ta'rīkh*, p. 127, and Jarrett's translation, pp. 337–38.

[38] *Aghānī*, XVIII, 73.

baidah and the Hāshimites. It is very likely that the rivalry between the half-brothers, so opposed in natural gifts and character and so close to Hārūn's heart from the start, began to be felt quite early in the young princes' lives. Kisāʾī, no doubt, was in a position to note this rivalry, and Hārūn may have confided his fears and suspicions of it to so trusted and honored a tutor and companion. This may have been the basis for the obviously embellished account of Hārūn's very ominous "prophecy" of the wars and tribulations that were to overtake his two sons.[39]

That later in the princes' lives there came a time when Hārūn feared his plans for them might not go through is indicated in various ways. When once Hārūn introduced the young heir Amīn to a visitor and the latter expressed a fervent wish for the success of Hārūn's plans for the boy, Hārūn received the wish with contemplative silence.[40] Watching the two boys, Hārūn sensed Amīn's antagonism and warned him, in verse, not to hate his brother or wrong him, since hatred and wrong return, like a boomerang, to their source.[41]

Zubaidah, as was perhaps to be expected, came to be more and more involved in the growing rivalry of the princes. There is little reason to doubt that she who had mothered the orphaned Maʾmūn, son of her own slave and gift to Hārūn, had, to begin with, anything but a kindly feeling for the child. There is as little reason to assume that, in these early years, she had any occasion to fear serious competition from this source—except

[39] Masʿūdī, VI, 320–22.

[40] Yāqūt, *Irshād*, II, 378–79.

[41] *Fawāt*, II, 336.

perhaps in the exercises of the palace school. For here, Maʾmūn's keener intellect—not that Prince Amīn himself was a dunce or even below average[42]—and his quicker and more retentive memory,[43] with the almost all-important role assigned to that function, reflected to her son's disadvantage. In the matter of self-discipline, absent by contrast with Maʾmūn's stoic attitude, young Amīn may have had his mother to blame, in part at least, for this weakness. For, as her one and only son, he was probably much too pampered in the royal nursery for his own later good, his tutors' efforts at correction notwithstanding.[44]

The seven or eight years that passed between Amīn's early nomination as first heir and the nomination of Maʾmūn as second heir must have given Zubaidah some food for serious thought on the succession of her son. For she was much too intelligent to miss the significance of the trend of events as reflected in Hārūn's avowed pleasure in the gifted Maʾmūn. Still, there was, in this period, no specific move on her part to discredit the latter. Her position, as also that of the Hāshimites, seems to have been not so much a stand against Maʾmūn as one for their Amīn. Therefore, outwardly at least, the nomination of the former as second heir does not seem to have met with any expressed opposition on the part of Zubaidah and the royal family. This seemingly happy situation could not

[42] Cf. Suyūṭī, *Taʾrīkh*, pp. 119–20, and translation, pp. 315, 317.

[43] Yaʿqūbī, II, 501; Ḥuṣrī, III, 147; Suyūṭī, *Taʾrīkh*, p. 130, and translation, p. 342.

[44] Cf. above, p. 178.

be expected to last long, especially if and when it became known or suspected that Hārūn had conceived and entertained the idea of making Maʾmūn his sole heir. Hārūn's contemplated plans were supposedly a state secret between the caliph and his minister, but one known to the eavesdropping Aṣmaʿī[45] and very likely early suspected by more than one Hāshimite, if not by Zubaidah herself.

There is considerable evidence that after Maʾmūn's nomination, Zubaidah doubled her efforts on behalf of her son. ʿAbd Allah al-Maʾmūn received the province of Khurāsān, which was, on the whole, a turbulent province to control. Hārūn, therefore, allotted him a large force for that purpose. Zubaidah saw danger to her son's interests in this move and protested to Hārūn himself. The latter, quite evidently losing patience, rebuked her severely for meddling in the affairs of his empire, though not without pointing out to her Maʾmūn's greater need for military force than was the case with Amīn. He dismissed her unwelcome complaint with, "We fear for ʿAbd Allah at the hands of your son, and fear not for your son at the hands of ʿAbd Allah."[46]

Once she was annoyed when Hārūn praised Maʾmūn to the exclusion of Amīn. Hārūn, therefore, undertook to prove to her the former's superiority over the latter. He sent a messenger to each of his heirs to ask, "What will you do when you are caliph?" Amīn replied that he would reward the messenger richly. Maʾmūn, on the

[45] Masʿūdī, VI, 323–25.

[46] *Ibid.*, pp. 325–26; Gabrieli, *op. cit.*, p. 347; cf. Palmer, *op. cit.*, pp. 119–20.

other hand, hurled an inkwell that happened to be at hand at the messenger as he exclaimed, "Dare you, indeed, ask me what I shall do on the day that the Commander of the Believers dies? Verily, I hope that Allah may make all of us a ransom for him!" Both answers were reported to the royal parents.

"Now, what do you think?" asked Hārūn of Zubaidah, who remained silent.[47]

The few years following Maʾmūn's nomination were tense ones for all concerned. This was also the period in which yet a third son came into the succession picture—Prince Qāsim, younger than either of the first two heirs by some three or four years.[48] The poets, as usual, had a word to say. The most effective verse came from ʿUmānī and is of special interest in that it addresses Hārūn as one guided by his mother.[49] But Khaizurān had been dead for a decade or more. ʿUmānī, it will be recalled, was not overenthusiastic concerning Maʾmūn. He probably meant to imply here that Hārūn's own preference for Maʾmūn was influenced by a tradition transmitted by Khaizurān regarding that night of destiny which saw the death of Hādī, the accession of Hārūn, and the birth of ʿAbd Allah al-Maʾmūn. Qāsim won third place in the succession by 186/802. Among the poets who sang in praise of the occasion was Abū al-ʿAtāhiyah. He lauded Hārūn for safeguarding the security of Islam in

[47] Rifāʿī, I, 212; Ibrāhīm Zaidān, *Nawādir al-ʿUdabāʾ* (Cairo, 1922), pp. 29–30; cf. Yāfiʿī, II, 78–79, for another incident with same purpose.

[48] Cf. above, p. 141. He was born about 173/789–90 (cf. Khaṭīb, XII, 402; Ṭabarī, III, 652–53).

[49] Ṭabarī, III, 760; *Aghānī*, XVII, 80.

these three heirs, whom he described as angels possessed of the soft eyes of the gazelle and the brave heart of the lion.[50] But there were others who saw in this double and triple division of the empire quite the opposite of angelic peace and lionhearted strength.[51] Hārūn himself, even if convinced of the wisdom of his plans, was none too sure of their eventual execution, as the dramatic events of the pilgrimage of 186 (December, 802) clearly show.

Leaving his last and youngest heir behind in his own northern territories, Hārūn started on the journey, accompanied, among others, by Yaḥyā (and Zubaidah?) as also by Amīn and Maʾmūn traveling in the company and in care of Faḍl and Jaʿfar, respectively. Medina was long to remember the blessing of triple largess showered on it first from the bounty of the caliph himself, then by the hand of Amīn and Faḍl, and, finally, from Maʾmūn and Jaʿfar.[52] Mecca, too, was not forgotten in this respect. But here an even more unusual drama was soon to take place.

Hārūn had previously caused each of his two sons to write out, in their own hand, their complete agreement to the succession plans and their most solemn oath to abide by them. The oath involved the severest penalties, short of death, conceivable within the law and practice of Islam. These penalties included, over and above the forfeiture of all claims on Allah, his Apostle, and on the community of Islam, the making of many a pilgrimage on foot to Mecca, the distribution of all

[50] *Aghānī*, III, 178–79.

[51] Ṭabarī, III, 652–53.

[52] Ibn ʿAbdūs, p. 273; Ṭabarī, III, 651; Yaʿqūbī, II, 501.

their wealth to the poor, the setting-free of all their slaves, and the divorcing of all their wives.[53]

Still Hārūn felt that that in itself was not enough. These agreements on oath must be published and the public itself made witness and party to them. This was now done in the most solemn and dramatic manner. The scene was within the sacred mosque before an assembled host of the high and the low in the state and in Islam. The documents in question were hung on the very walls of the sacred Kaᶜbah. Official letters of notification were started on their way to the far-flung provinces of the empire, while the returning pilgrims were to broadcast the news by word of mouth to every corner of the realm.[54] Thus did Hārūn call on Allah and all the Believers to bear witness to the vows on the observance of which rested his hopes for the future peace of his vast empire. But fate, it seemed to the omen-minded crowd, was against these plans, for the documents slipped to the ground in the process of posting them. And though they were in the end firmly secured to the wall, yet the rank and file of the superstitious crowd stood in awe of the fearsome omen which to them meant the speedy negation of the planned successions.[55]

Among those who still had fears for the miscarriage of these plans was Jaᶜfar the Barmakid. As Amīn was about to leave the scene, Jaᶜfar accosted him for further assurance of his honest intentions as regards his own

[53] Ṭabarī, III, 659, 662; Yaᶜqūbī, II, 505, 509.

[54] Ṭabarī, III, 654–67; Yaᶜqūbī, II, 509–10.

[55] Ṭabarī, III, 654; Masᶜūdī, VI, 326–27. It is not clear if Zubaidah was there in person or heard of this later.

ward, Maʾmūn. He asked that Amīn repeat thrice, "May Allah forsake me should I forsake him (Maʾmūn)." Amīn complied, but the incident increased Zubaidah's wrath against Jaᶜfar.[56]

The Barmakids, father and sons, came to be deeply involved in the succession in a series of events that progressively alienated the queen from them, until her resentment of Yaḥyā and her enmity for Jaᶜfar in particular were no longer secrets. Zubaidah, it will be recalled, had more than one good reason to be grateful to this family. She could not have failed to realize Yaḥyā's all-important role in placing Hārūn himself on the throne and of relieving that monarch of the burdens of administration so that he could be all the freer to enjoy her company. It was Yaḥyā's son, Faḍl, who had brought about the first nomination of her son to the heirship. Again, it was Yaḥyā's restraining hand that prevented Hārūn from placing Maʾmūn ahead of Amīn. But, from Zubaidah's point of view, these services came, in time, to be overshadowed by a series of events that centered, primarily, round Jaᶜfar, the third and youngest member of the family.

The Barmakids were, undoubtedly, the most gifted and able wazirate family in the history of the early ᶜAbbāsids. The sons, born of different mothers and both richly endowed with intellect, were, in a sense, as different in temperament and personality as Hārūn's two heirs. Faḍl, the more reserved and serious-minded, came closer to being a chip off the old state rock that was Yaḥyā. He was, therefore, a son after Yaḥyā's own

[56] Ibn ᶜAbdūs, p. 273; Masᶜūdī, VI, 327–28.

heart, in which he was tenderly cherished to the end. Jaᶜfar, on the other hand, was of a more amiable and sunnier temperament, with an extraordinary capacity for fun and pleasure.[57] He, furthermore, displayed a lightning speed in the effective execution of heavy administrative duties.[58] It is not surprising, therefore, that the pleasure-loving Hārūn found in Jaᶜfar a man much to his taste. In vain did the experienced Yaḥyā warn his young son to attend more to the public business of state and less to the private royal pleasure. He even went so far as to solicit no less than Hārūn's aid to this end, only to be told that he, Yaḥyā, was plainly partial to Faḍl.[59]

The young Jaᶜfar progressed rapidly from being the life of royal parties to becoming the boon companion of the caliph, whose very shirt he shared,[60] and ended up, in time, as the husband of Hārūn's talented sister ᶜAbbāsah. This progressive degree of private familiarity and favor was reflected in a series of public offices and honors: Jaᶜfar, a simple minister subordinate to Faḍl; Jaᶜfar given Faḍl's office of the keeper of the privy seal; Jaᶜfar, along with Faḍl, known as the "little wazir"; and Jaᶜfar the political mentor and guardian of the favored Maʾmūn, whose half of the empire he was to administer. In the meantime, Faḍl had fallen out of favor though in a measure still associated with Amīn.[61]

[57] Masᶜūdī, VI, 361; Khaṭīb, XII, 334, 336; *Fakhrī*, pp. 281–82.

[58] E.g., Ibn ᶜAbdūs, p. 249.

[59] Ṭabarī, III, 676; Ibn ᶜAbdūs, pp. 228, 312–13.

[60] Ibn ᶜAbdūs, p. 249; Ibn Khallikān, I, 306; Yāfiᶜī, I, 408.

[61] Ibn ᶜAbdūs, p. 281.

This, then, was the general background for Zubaidah's changing attitude toward the Barmakids. Faḍl's influence was no longer a powerful factor in the succession question; Yaḥyā as grand wazir was suspect, and Jaᶜfar as Maᵓmūn's able and ardent supporter was first feared and finally hated. But had not Hārūn's own relationships changed toward the Barmakids in general and Jaᶜfar in particular, Zubaidah's fear and hate would have been disregarded. The following succession of incidents is illuminating in this respect.

Yaḥyā, among his other duties, had charge of Zubaidah's royal palace. It was he who controlled the gates and watched over the personnel who linked the palace with the outer world. Zubaidah came to resent his strict supervision and complained of it, more than once, to Hārūn. The latter questioned "Father" Yaḥyā as to why Zubaidah was dissatisfied with him.

"Do you, then, doubt my loyalty to your harem and palace?" ashed Yaḥyā.

"Nay, by Allah," answered Hārūn.

"Then pay no attention to her complaints against me." Hārūn promised not to mention the matter again. Yaḥyā increased his vigilance, and Zubaidah's resentment grew in proportion but availed her nothing.[62]

The court physician, Jabrāᵓīl, son of Bakhtīshūᶜ, who owed his success at court to the Barmakids, tells this next tale. He was once summoned by Hārūn to the palace to attend on Zubaidah herself. Suddenly there was heard a great shout of acclaim from the street below. On inquiry, Hārūn was informed that it was in

[62] Masᶜūdī, VI, 391–92.

honor of Yaḥyā, who was hearing the public's petitions and appeals.

"May Allah bless and reward him," said Hārūn spontaneously, "for he has lightened my burden and has himself shouldered the weight of my empire." He continued to praise Yaḥyā highly. Zubaidah, says the physician, echoed every praise uttered by the caliph and others present in honor of the wazir. Jabrāʾīl hastened to report the happy event to his patron, Yaḥyā, and together they rejoiced over it.

Years passed, and, as chance would have it, Jabrāʾīl was called once more to the very same palace to attend the Lady Zubaidah. Again was heard the cry of acclaim, and again, on inquiry, Hārūn was informed that it was in honor of Yaḥyā, who was receiving the public's petitions.

"May Allah do unto him according to his deeds," said Hārūn and proceeded to accuse and condemn Yaḥyā thus: "He has taken hold of affairs to my exclusion and has conducted them without reference to me. He has done what he pleased and has disregarded my pleasure." Again Zubaidah seconded his words. She, indeed, accused and censured Yaḥyā more than did any of the others. Then Hārūn, turning to the physician, said: "No one except you and Faḍl (ibn al Rabīʿ) has heard these my words; and Faḍl is certainly not the man to repeat any of them. I swear it, and again I swear, that should you divulge what just took place, you shall perish." The astonished and troubled Jabrāʾīl promised to hold his tongue and departed. But his loyalty to, and trust in, Yaḥyā led him, even at the risk of his life, to inform the latter of the extremely disturbing incident.[63]

This is not the place to go into the complicated question of the fall of the Barmakids. Suffice it to point out here that Hārūn's grievances, actual and imagined, were many and varied;[64] that his growing displeasure with the family stretched over a long period of years;[65] and that the Barmakids themselves were not unaware of the danger threatening them.[66] But accumulated causes of long standing do frequently wait upon some specific occasion to direct them into corrective or retributive channels. That, at any rate, was the case in the downfall of the Barmakids.

It is precisely at this point that Zubaidah's contribution to the fall is of great interest. According to one set of accounts, it was Zubaidah, who, taking advantage of Hārūn's growing displeasure, smarting under Yaḥyā's strict control of the palace, and fearing Jaᶜfar's support of Maʾmūn, revealed to Hārūn the secret love of Jaᶜfar and ᶜAbbāsah and its fruit of one or more children sent, in the interest of secrecy and safety, to live in Mecca. Hārūn was shocked to the core of his royal being at the great dishonor Jaᶜfar had inflicted on the ᶜAbbāsid blood and name. He determined, then and there, to destroy Jaᶜfar but delayed the execution until he had seen

63 Ibn ᶜAbdūs, pp. 278–80; cf. *Fakhrī*, p. 287.

64 Ṭabarī, III, 667–77, 1332–34; Ibn Athīr, VI, 118–22; Ibn ᶜAbdūs, pp. 304–5, 331; Masᶜūdī, VI, 362, 386–87.

65 Jāḥiẓ, *K. al-Tāj*, p. 66, and *ᶜIqd*, III, 30, for a period varying from five to seven years; Yaᶜqūbī, II, 510–11.

66 E.g., Ṭabarī, III, 667–68; Ibn ᶜAbdūs, pp. 265, 280–81, 312–13; *Aghānī*, V, 113; Rāghib, *Muḥāḍarāt*, I, 279.

the children for himself. Having satisfied himself on that point on that fateful pilgrimage of 186/802, Hārūn lost no time, on his return, in wreaking his vengeance on Jaᶜfar in particular and on the Barmakids in general. But that in itself did not blot out the royal dishonor. To accomplish this, Hārūn wiped off the face of this earth his beloved sister ᶜAbbāsah and her innocent children—whose sex and number vary in the different accounts.[67]

But to return to Zubaidah's role in this tragedy. Some of the historians who mention the Jaᶜfar-ᶜAbbāsah story either as one of many causes or as the main reason for the fall of Jaᶜfar, leave Zubaidah entirely out of the picture.[68] But perhaps more eloquent than this omission is yet another set of reports that make not the ᶜAbbāsah story but the escape of the ᶜAlid Yaḥyā ibn ᶜAbd Allah the immediate determining factor in the Barmakid downfall. Briefly told, this point of view is as follows: All

[67] Masᶜūdī, VI, 392–94; Ibn Khallikān, I, 306–8; Yāfiᶜī, I, 408–9; Ibn Taghrībirdī, I, 516; *Fakhrī*, p. 288; Maqdisī, *K. al-Badʾ wa al-Taʾrīkh*, VI, 104–5; F. Wüstenfeld, *Die Chroniken der Stadt Mekka* (4 vols.; Leipzig, 1857–61), IV, 183–84; cf. Palmer, *op. cit.*, pp. 91–98; L. Bouvat, "Les Barmécids d'après les historiens Arabes et Persians," *Revue du monde musulman*, XX (1912), 117–18. The nucleus for this version of the tragic story of Jaᶜfar and ᶜAbbāsah is found in some of the earliest as in some of the most authoritative histories of Islam. It was not long, however, before the major tragedy had caught the imagination of men of literary fancy, who enlarged upon it, embellishing it here and there until, alas for the royal honor of the ᶜAbbāsids, it soon came to be one of the most widely known tales in Moslem lands. No less a historian than the famous Ibn Khaldūn (*Taʾrīkh*, I, 126) tried to kill the story by removing it, in its entirety, from the realm of authentic history into the pale of questionable fiction. But he failed. The tale continued to grow and thrive and still promises to be as immortal as the very name of Barmak, on the one hand, and Hārūn al-Rashīd, on the other.

[68] Ṭabarī, III, 677; Ibn Athīr, VI, 119.

the ᶜAlids were constantly more or less suspect to the early ᶜAbbāsids. Hārūn, like his predecessor, was on his guard when any of them gave the slightest indication of dynastic pride and claims. The ᶜAlid Yaḥyā had had the misfortune to rouse Hārūn's suspicions. The latter, though he had given Yaḥyā promise of safety of life, did, nevertheless, order Jaᶜfar to put him away. Jaᶜfar could not bring himself to carry out the order, since he believed the ᶜAlid to be innocent and harmless. He therefore made possible Yaḥyā's escape. The fact was soon discovered and made known to Hārūn, with Faḍl ibn al-Rabīᶜ taking a hand in this move. Hārūn questioned Jaᶜfar, who broke down and confessed. Hārūn hid his displeasure and commended Jaᶜfar to his face but swore behind his back to have his head for this deed.[69]

Some accounts insist that this and this only was the ultimate cause of the fall of Jaᶜfar. These accounts are traced back to key figures in the palace. Maʾmūn's tutor, Yazīdī, is reported as saying: "Whoever says that Hārūn killed Jaᶜfar for any other reason than Yaḥyā ibn ᶜAbd Allah, do not believe him."[70] ᶜAṣmaᶜī has preserved the following. Faḍl ibn al-Rabīᶜ was asked in the caliphate of Maʾmūn, "Was this matter of ᶜAbbāsah the only cause of the slaughter of the Barmakids, or had they committed some other offense?" Faḍl smiled as he replied, "You have indeed come to the very one who is best acquainted with the matter," meaning, of course, himself. He next proceeded to tell the story of Jaᶜfar and the ᶜAlid, and how it was actually then that Hārūn de-

[69] Ṭabarī, III, 669–70.

[70] *Ibid.*, p. 669.

termined to avenge himself on Jaᶜfar, and said to Faḍl, "I am going to tell you a secret which you must on no account divulge. I am going to destroy Jaᶜfar."[71]

Faḍl ibn al-Rabīᶜ no doubt received this confidence with inward satisfaction, for his professional rivalry and ambition as well as his personal differences with the Barmakids had led him, from the beginning of the reign of Hārūn, to envy and hate them, particularly Jaᶜfar. As chamberlain to Hārūn he was in an excellent position to sense which way the wind of royal favor or disfavor was blowing. He, more than any other in Hārūn's service, stood to gain the most by the fall of the wazir and his sons. For even before that event actually took place, there was talk of it in the capital coupled with the prediction of Faḍl's wazirate. Faḍl was indeed made the wazir and, as such, lifted not a finger to aid the aged and hopelessly fallen Yaḥyā, who in the past had rendered him and his father numerous favors.[72]

Zubaidah, on the other hand, is credited with a serious effort on behalf of the imprisoned Yaḥyā. The latter appealed to Amīn on the strength of the foster-relationship between him and a son of Jaᶜfar's, let alone Faḍl's services to that heir. Amīn took the matter to Zubaidah, who watched for a favorable opportunity to present Yaḥyā's written appeal to Hārūn in person. Having read the pathetic verses, Hārūn jotted below them, "The enormity of your guilt has hardened all feelings of forgiveness for you," and threw back the slip to

[71] Ibn Isfandiyār, pp. 136–39; cf. Ibn ᶜAbdūs, p. 265, for another example of such confidence.

[72] Ibn ᶜAbdūs, pp. 265, 314–18; Ibn Khallikān, II, 468–69; Yāfiᶜī, II, 42.

Zubaidah. When she read the royal comment, she realized that there was indeed no hope for Yaḥyā and his son Faḍl.[73]

Jaᶜfar's sudden doom had overtaken him with the swift stroke of the executioner's sword. His head and split body hung at the different bridgeheads of the capital and were a grim warning of the wretchedness of "that poor man who hangs on prince's favors." Yaḥyā and Faḍl, on the other hand, were exposed to torture of mind and body and left to languish behind prison bars.[74] Well might each, with Wolsey, have exclaimed:

> Had I but serv'd my God with half the zeal
> I serv'd my king, he would not in mine age
> Have left me naked to mine enemies.

Indeed, the Barmakids had fallen "like Lucifer, never to hope again."[75] Father and son found some consolation in the recollection of verses pertinent to their fallen state.[76] Tenderly they sought to comfort each other, the son being anxious to retain his father's approval and blessings to the end.[77] Yaḥyā passed away quietly in the prison at Raqqah in 190/805.[78] The unhappy Faḍl,

[73] ᶜ*Iqd*, III, 28–29; cf. Yaᶜqūbī, II, 509–10.

[74] E.g., Ibn ᶜAbdūs, pp. 306–12; Masᶜūdī, VI, 408–10.

[75] Not even the women were spared, some of whom, including Hārūn's foster-mother, made pathetic and futile appeals on behalf of the two prisoners. Danānīr the songstress, who in her earlier years had so charmed Hārūn, fell with the rest, faithful to the last (cf. ᶜ*Iqd*, III, 28–29; Ibn ᶜAbdūs, p. 302).

[76] Masᶜūdī, VI, 504–5.

[77] Ṭabarī, III, 693; Ibn Athīr, VI, 119–20; Ibn Khallikān, II, 464, 467; IV, 112.

[78] Ibn ᶜAbdūs, pp. 329–30; Khaṭīb, XIV, 132; Ibn Khallikān, IV, 112; Ibn Athīr, VI, 135; cf. Masᶜūdī, VI, 413.

whose one desire now was to outlive Hārūn, died, nevertheless, several months before the latter.[79]

In the years that followed, Hārūn had cause to repent the fall of this gifted family.[80] But to the end he refused to assign any specific reason for his act, particularly in regard to the swift and barbaric end of Jaᶜfar. One day his sister ᶜUlaiyah spoke to him thus, "I have not seen you enjoy a day of perfect happiness since you put Jaᶜfar to death. Why did you do it?" She received in answer. "If I thought that even my inmost garment knew the reason, I should tear it in pieces."[81] Others report him as saying that if he thought that his own right hand knew the reason for Jaᶜfar's murder, he would cut it off.[82]

There is no definite evidence that Zubaidah and Faḍl ibn al-Rabīᶜ worked together before the downfall of the Barmakids. They were, in all probability, thrown closer together after that event. Faḍl, as wazir, was expected to support Hārūn's plans for the succession, but his long political experience warned him of troubles to come and his antagonism to Jaᶜfar led him away from the departed Jaᶜfar's political ward, Maʾmūn. All in all, the weaker Amīn, with Zubaidah and the Hāshimites behind him, promised better prospects for Faḍl's own cause. What Faḍl the wazir does not seem to have taken

79 Ṭabarī, III, 733; Ibn Athīr, IV, 143–44; Ibn ᶜAbdūs, p. 330; Khaṭīb, XII, 339; Ibn Khallikān, II, 467; cf. Bouvat, *op. cit.*, p. 100, according to which Amīn, Zubaidah, and the notables of Baghdad attended the funeral.

80 Ibn ᶜAbdūs, p. 325; Ibn Khallikān, IV, 112–13.

81 Ibn Khallikān, I, 310; Yāfiᶜī, I, 411; cf. Rāghib, *Muḥāḍarāt*, I, 285.

82 Yaᶜqūbī, II, 510; cf. Masᶜūdī, VI, 363.

into account was the coming to the fore of Faḍl ibn Sahl, who was, for all practical purposes, to replace Jaᶜfar so far as Maʾmūn was concerned.

The Persian Magian family of Sahl and his two sons, Faḍl and Ḥasan, came to Baghdad to seek redress at the hands of Yaḥyā the Barmakid. The latter took them into his service. Faḍl was a young man of exceptional ability and advanced rapidly. As secretary to Jaᶜfar the Barmakid, he came in close contact with Maʾmūn. With Jaᶜfar's downfall, Faḍl fell heir to his post. When, in 190/806, Faḍl took the step of public conversion to Islam, it meant that he had become Maʾmūn's most trusted adviser and a serious aspirant to the wazirate.[83] Thereafter, first under cover for the rest of Hārūn's reign, and then in the open in the reign of Amīn, the struggle for the throne between Amīn and Maʾmūn was also the struggle for the wazirate between the two Faḍls. And through these latter more than through the two royal brothers, the contest was to take on increasingly a racial color of Arab versus Persian and a religious trend of Sunnite versus Shīᶜite. Not that the discordant notes of race and creed were absent before this multiple conflict took shape, but that the clash of personalities was more to the fore. It was around this clash of personalities as a focus that the different racial and religious elements finally arrayed themselves.[84]

The party lines were already forming in Hārūn's later years. The caliph had felt the need to reaffirm his succes-

[83] Ibn ᶜAbdūs, pp. 285–88; Ṭabarī, III, 709; Khaṭīb, XII, 304; Ibn Khallikān, II, 472; *Fakhrī*, pp. 305–6.

[84] Cf. Gabrieli, *op. cit.*, pp. 385–86.

sion plans in 189/805.[85] As Faḍl ibn Sahl and Maʾmūn drew closer together, Faḍl ibn al-Rabīᶜ depended more and more upon Zubaidah and Amīn. The queen was accumulating a fortune for her son's expected needs.[86] Amīn, for his part, struck his mother's name on his coins minted in 191/806 at Bājunais.[87]

When in 192/808 Hārūn determined to go to Khurāsān on a punitive expedition against the rebel, Rāfiᶜ ibn Laith,[88] he intended to take Faḍl the wazir along with him and leave his three heirs behind. It was Faḍl ibn Sahl who advised Maʾmūn to find a way to accompany his ailing father and the large army that was to go with him to the very provinces that formed Maʾmūn's share of the divided empire. Should death overtake Hārūn and Amīn prove faithless, Maʾmūn, argued Faḍl, would be at a safe distance and in a much better position to assert, by force of arms if need be, his claims to his portion of Hārūn's empire. Hārūn would not, at first, consent to Maʾmūn's request. But the latter expressed such great concern over his father's health and disavowed any other motive for his eagerness to accompany him that Hārūn finally yielded. He departed with Maʾmūn and the two Faḍls, leaving Qāsim at Raqqah and Amīn at Baghdad.[89]

Hārūn took seriously ill at Ṭūs, and his condition

[85] Ṭabarī, III, 704; Yaᶜqūbī, II, 514.

[86] Ṭabarī, III, 730.

[87] *Catalogue des monnaies de la Bibliothèque Nationale* (Paris, 1887), I, 199, No. 848.

[88] Ṭabarī, III, 707–8, 730–35.

[89] *Ibid.*, pp. 730–31; Ibd Athīr, VI, 141–42; Ibn ᶜAbdūs, p. 337.

grew rapidly worse. He was conscious, to the end, of his heirs' rivalries and realized full well that each had an agent to watch and report every move the caliph made. Masrūr, he felt sure, was in touch with Ma᾿mūn—who had pushed ahead farther west to Merv[90]—and the physician Jabrā᾿īl was guarding Amīn's interests, while the name of Qāsim's agent has escaped the record.[91] In his last days Hārūn lost confidence in this same Jabrā᾿īl, who had served him for practically a lifetime and whom he had honored above all his professional class. Realizing his own end was at hand, he gave the order to have the doctor cut into pieces. Faḍl the wazir rescued the doctor from this terrible fate until, in a day or two, Hārūn himself breathed his last.[92] In his final, bitter days it was not comfort that Hārūn found in recalling the verses of Abū al-ᶜAtāhiyah on the futility of this world, even for kings.[93]

Thus passed away, on the third of Jumadā II, 193/ March 24, 809, the mighty Hārūn al-Rashīd, disillusioned and all but deserted, but active and vengeful to the end. His son Ṣāliḥ prayed over the body, which was laid to rest in a garden tomb dug and consecrated on Hārūn's all but final command.[94] We will return later to his tomb at Ṭūs in far-off Khurāsān.

[90] Ṭabarī, III, 734; Ibn Athīr, VI, 145.

[91] Ṭabarī, III, 731; Ibn Athīr, VI, 142.

[92] Ṭabarī, III, 737; Ibn Abī Usaibiᶜah, I, 128–30; Rāghib, *Muḥāḍarāt*, I, 273–74. His death was due to a fever brought on by a stomach ailment, the nature of which is not specified.

[93] Māwardī, *Kitāb Adab al-Dunyā wa al-Dīn* (Cairo, 1925), p. 99; cf. *Fakhrī*, pp. 264–65; Palmer, *op. cit.*, p. 31.

[94] Tabarī, III, 736–39; Ibn Athīr, VI, 144–45.

VII

War and Peace

AMĪN at Baghdad had prepared, some seven to eight months before Hārūn's death, letters of instructions to Maʾmūn, Faḍl ibn al-Rabīʿ, and the key men with his sick father. He intrusted these to a secret agent who was to deliver them in the event of Hārūn's death. These letters, as preserved, indicate that Amīn intended, at that time, to abide by Hārūn's succession plans. They, however, contained instructions that ordered Maʾmūn, Faḍl, the generals, and the armies that were with them to return immediately to Baghdad. But Hārūn, before death overtook him, had instructed Faḍl and the generals to turn over the armies in question to Maʾmūn, who was to continue the as yet unsuccessful expedition against the rebel Rāfiʿ. When, therefore, Amīn's letters were read at Ṭūs, Faḍl and the rest had to choose between carrying out Hārūn's recent orders or obeying Amīn's commands of several months' standing. Faḍl settled the matter when he publicly preferred to cast his lot with "a reigning sovereign (Amīn) rather than with one (Maʾmūn) whose future (reign) was uncertain" and then gave the order for the return march. The generals and their armies, eager to get back to home and family, readily obeyed the command, thus repudiating their word to Hārūn to support Maʾmūn and help him reduce the rebellion in Khurāsān.[1]

In the meantime, news of Hārūn's death had been dispatched by rapid post to Amīn at Baghdad and to Maʾmūn at Merv. Both heirs publicly mourned the departed Hārūn and indicated, by word and deed, their intentions to abide by the succession. For Amīn on this occasion declared Maʾmūn and Qāsim al-Muʾtamin as his successive heirs, while Maʾmūn himself took the oath of allegiance to Amīn and administered it to the generals and the soldiery that were with him.[2]

When the news of Hārūn's death reached Zubaidah at Raqqah, she gathered, that night, the daughters of the caliphs and all the Hāshimite women for a session of public mourning at her palace. She sent for Isḥāq al-Mausilī and asked him to compose an elegy on Hārūn for her own use on that occasion. The poet-musician could think of nothing original on the spur of the moment; but his memory came to his aid with the words and melody of a dirge he had long ago heard sung in Medina—Sallāmah's choice of a mourning song for the Umayyad caliph Yazid II (101–5/720–24). He now taught the words and melody to one of Zubaidah's singing maids, who in turn taught it to the bereaved queen:

[1] Ṭabarī, III, 765–72; Ibn Athīr, VI, 152–53.

[2] Ṭabarī, III, 771–72; Dīnawarī, p. 388.

Blame us not if we grow silent or are overcome with
sorrowful emotion;
For, by my life, we have come to keep close company
with a painful malady.
Whenever we behold an empty place, our tears gush forth;
For it is a place void of a master who was never negligent
of us.[3]

Perhaps none of the royal princesses mourned Hārūn more sincerely than did his sister ᶜUlaiyah, whose company he had sought and enjoyed.[4] She, in her great sorrow, forsook both wine cup and lyric song until Amīn later compelled her to resume them for his own amusement.[5]

Abū Nuwās, on the other hand, who had a weakness for Amīn, with whom he was a favorite, tried to kill two birds with one stone in a verse that was meant both to console and to congratulate the new caliph:

The ascending Amīn makes us smile, and the death
Yesterday of the Imān makes us weep.
They are two moons. One hath appeared at Baghdad
In Al-Khuld, and a moon at Ṭūs hath sunk in the grave.[6]

But if Hārūn's star had set at Ṭūs, the sun shone once more for several of his political prisoners in the jails of Baghdad and Raqqah. Zubaidah, now queen-mother, seems to have influenced Amīn's move in this direction. Faḍl ibn Yaḥyā, however, did not live long enough to

[3] *Aghānī*, VIII, 12–14; for Yazīd and his slave girls see Nabia Abbott, "Women and the State in Early Islam," *Journal of Near Eastern Studies*, I (1942), 358.

[4] *Fawāt*, II, 125; Ghuzūlī, II, 296; cf. above, pp. 154–56.

[5] *Aghānī*, IX, 94.

[6] See preceding note. Al-Khuld is the Palace Immortal of Manṣūr.

profit by it. But his brothers and other imprisoned members of the Barmakid family now regained their freedom.[7]

Some three months after Hārūn's death, Zubaidah, who had secured his vast treasures at Raqqah, traveled with this great wealth to join her caliph-son at Baghdad. Amīn and the nobles of his court came out as far north as Anbār to meet and escort her back to the capital in regal style. In these months and the few more that followed, the relationship between the major royal characters was, to all appearances, quite satisfactory. Mother and son worked together. Maʾmūn and Qāsim were confirmed in their holdings, and the former sent friendly letters and liberal gifts from his province of Khurāsān to his brother at Baghdad.[8]

Once more, however, appearances were to prove deceptive. The wrong step had been taken when Faḍl ibn al-Rabīʿ turned his back on Maʾmūn in Khurāsān. Amīn received him at Baghdad with great joy and retained him in the wazirate.[9] The new caliph then laid the burden of government on his wazir's shoulders and himself lost no time in giving uncontrolled rein to his own pleasures.[10] The wazir, anxious to preserve power in his own hands and fearing Maʾmūn's vengeance, should he come to the throne, began to persuade Amīn to remove

[7] Ibn ʿAbdūs, p. 376; Ibn Qutaibah, *Maʿārif*, p. 195; Khaṭīb, IX, 141–42.

[8] Ṭabarī, III, 775; Ibn Athīr, VI, 155.

[9] Ṭabarī, III, 7718, 1068; Ibn Ṭaifūr, pp. 141–42; *Fakhrī*, p. 292–93; Ibn Manẓūr, *Akhbār Abī Nuwās* (Cairo, 1924), I, 86, 114.

[10] Ṭabarī, III, 774, 950–52; Khaṭīb, XII, 343–44.

Maʾmūn and Qāsim from the succession in favor of Amīn's own sons, Mūsā and ʿAbd Allah.[11]

Maʾmūn and his right-hand man, Faḍl ibn Sahl, sized up the situation. It is at this point that Faḍl made excellent use of Maʾmūn's part-Persian blood to build up for him a strong Persian party among his "maternal uncles," as the Persians soon came to be referred to. Faḍl, the Persian, was willing, if only for appearance' sake, to have some of the foremost Arab generals, such as the experienced ʿAbd Allah ibn Mālik, take the lead in securing the caliphate for Maʾmūn. But these Arabs showed great distaste at first for any such bold and treacherous move. Faḍl, therefore, undertook to accomplish the feat himself.[12]

The next year, 194/809–10, saw a steadily growing deterioration in the relationship of the two brothers. The climax was reached with the public nomination of Mūsā as first heir and the expulsion of Maʾmūn and Qāsim from the heirship. The documents that Hārūn had so ceremoniously publicized and hung on the walls of the Kaʿbah were, on Faḍl ibn al-Rabīʿ's orders, brought to Baghdad and there torn to pieces by Amīn himself.[13] He eased his conscience and counteracted sounder advice by claiming that Maʾmūn's nomination was, to begin with, nothing but the magic influence on Hārūn of that wizard, Jaʿfar ibn Barmak.[14]

[11] Ṭabarī, III, 776; Ibn Athīr, VI, 156, Ibn ʿAbdūs, pp. 368–70; Yaʿqūbī, II, 529; Ibn Khallikān, II, 469–70; *Fakhrī*, pp. 292–93.

[12] Ṭabarī, III, 773; Ibn Athīr, VI, 154–55, 158; *Fakhrī*, pp. 293–94.

[13] Ṭabarī, III, 776–80, 796; Ibn Athīr, VI, 156–60, 164–65; Yaʿqūbī, II, 529; Ibn ʿAbdūs, p. 369.

[14] Ṭabarī, III, 790–91; Ibn Athīr, VI, 161–62; Ibn ʿAbdūs, p. 370.

The year 195/810–11 started, therefore, with both parties preparing for the inevitable outbreak of that major curse of the Islamic state—fraternal civil war. Maʾmūn's family, consisting of his royal cousin and wife, Umm ʿĪsā, the daughter of the caliph Hādī, and her two sons, Mohammed the Younger and ʿUbaid Allah, had remained behind in Baghdad when Maʾmūn himself had accompanied Hārūn. When Maʾmūn decided to remain in Khurāsān, he wrote Amīn to send him this family unit along with the large cash inheritance that Hārūn had left him in the treasury of Raqqah. Amīn's answer had then been that the cash was needed for the general welfare of the empire and that he would send Maʾmūn his family, in time, when it was safe to do so. But, as matters developed, Zubaidah secured all of Hārūn's treasuries for herself and Amīn, while the latter, as civil war loomed nearer and nearer, demanded from Umm ʿĪsā the valuable jewels left with her by Maʾmūn. Umm ʿĪsā refused to hand these over. Amīn, therefore, had her palace stormed and the jewels taken by force. When Maʾmūn learned of this outrage, there was heard in his camp open talk of war and the deposition of Amīn if need be.[15]

What, it is time to ask, was Zubaidah's relationship with her son as the dark clouds of war were fast gathering? There is, for this period, no reference to Zubaidah in connection with public and state affairs. But she is mentioned, both directly and indirectly, in connection with the private life of Amīn. Sometime early in this period Amīn lost his favorite concubine Faṭm, the

[15] Ṭabarī, III, 787–88; Yaʿqūbī, II, 529, 574; Ibn ʿAbdūs, pp. 366–67.

mother of his chosen heir Mūsā. The caliph grieved over her, and Zubaidah, being informed of his grief, came to comfort him, quoting, as usual, some apt verses of the poets.[16]

Amīn's sorrow was soon forgotten in the extravagant and novel pleasures that he indulged in, be it at his several palaces or on his unique river barges. He had five of these latter—in the form of a lion, elephant, eagle, snake, and horse—that sailed the river Tigris on their mission of pleasure.[17] The records have also preserved a picture of this caliph prancing around in a merry-go-round on a wooden hobby horse in the midst of a great crowd of singers and entertainers. He, on this occasion, ordered his musically gifted uncle, Ibrāhīm ibn al-Mahdī, among others, to sing in repetition the whole night long a popular love song on the songstress Danānīr.[18] On another occasion Amīn had no less than a hundred girls ready to amuse him with their song in relays of tens. These, however, because they referred to disaster and hinted broadly at the women's grievance at his hands, failed to please him.[19]

And well might the women complain. For Amīn soon separated himself from the company and influence of his family, both men and women, and gave himself over

[16] Ṭabarī, III, 958; Masᶜūdī, VI, 430; *ᶜIqd*, III, 54.

[17] Ṭabarī, III, 951; Ibn Athīr, VI, 206; Suyūṭī, *Taʾrīkh*, p. 119, and Jarrett's translation, p. 313.

[18] Ṭabarī, III, 971; *Aghānī*, XVI, 138–39; cf. Reuben Levy, *A Baghdad Chronicle* (Cambridge, 1929), pp. 70–71, for translation of passage and correcting Levy's "half-brother" to read "uncle" and "gold coins" to read "Danānīr (the songstress)."

[19] Ṭabarī, III, 956–57; Ibn Athīr, VI, 206–7.

wholly to dissipated pleasure in the company of his eunuchs. He dressed some of these latter as girls and organized them into a group of blacks whom he named "The Ravens," and another group of whites who were called "The Grasshoppers."[20] His personal relationship to these eunuchs became a major scandal, first in the capital city and later throughout the empire. Particularly obnoxious was his infatuation for the eunuch Kauthar.[21] Bold poets watching the wazir Faḍl ibn al-Rabīᶜ run the government while Amīn, on the one hand, lost himself in his pleasures and, on the other hand, sought to impose his little son on them as heir, called a spade a spade and denounced alike the scheming wazir, the homosexual caliph, and the infant heir.[22] But Abū Nuwās, who for the most time was in great favor with Amīn, used his great poetic talents and originality to write brazen verses of the caliph's extravagant and unnatural pleasures.[23]

Maʾmūn and Faḍl ibn Sahl did not fail to take note of these factors and to make good propagandistic use out of them. The further Amīn went in the way of pleasure and dissipation, the more Maʾmūn took, on Faḍl's advice, the path of piety and morality.[24] They made public denouncement of Amīn and his favorite poet, Abū

[20] Ṭabarī, III, 950–51; Ibn Athīr, VI, 205; Yaᶜqūbī, II, 530.

[21] *Aghānī*, XVIII, 117; Khaṭīb, III, 339; *Fawāt*, II, 336–37; Suyūṭī, *Taʾrīkh*, p. 119, and translation, pp. 313–14; cf. below, p. 215.

[22] Ṭabarī, III, 804–5, 950–51; Yaᶜqūbī, II, 530; Masᶜūdī, VI, 438–39; Suyūṭī, *Taʾrīkh*, p. 117, and translation, p. 308.

[23] Ṭabarī, III, 952–53, 965; Ibn Manẓūr, I, 100–101.

[24] Ibn ᶜAbdūs, p. 378; *Fakhrī*, p. 292; Ibn Manẓūr, I, 147–48.

Nuwās. Amīn made an effort to restrain the latter at the same time that he taunted Maʾmūn with his mother's humble origin.[25]

Zubaidah could not have failed to know of her son's weakness and the public's reaction to his conduct, but she does not seem to have felt equal to reforming him by either protest or preachment. She sought, instead, to wean him from his young eunuchs by a novel counter-attraction. She selected some of her most gifted and attractive maidens with beauty of form and of face and dressed them up in the current elegant costume of page boys. She then displayed these, in large numbers, before her son in the hope of winning him away from his unnatural life. Amīn was quite amused with the sight. Some of these girls did indeed touch a normal spring in his heart, which they now shared with his eunuchs. Hence Zubaidah's aim was but partially accomplished. Thereafter, society, high and low, made these boy-attired page girls the popular fad of the day.[26]

It was probably in this period of Amīn's reign that he took steps to secure the coveted songstress ᶜUraib (or ᶜArīb).[27] She was believed to be the daughter of none other than Jaᶜfar the Barmakid by a marriage of mis-alliance. The mother died before the fall of the Barmakids, and with this latter event ᶜUraib was sold by her nursemaid into slavery.[28] Being richly gifted, she re-

[25] Yaᶜqūbī, II, 529–30; Ibn ᶜAbdūs, pp. 370–71; Ḥuṣrī, II, 13–14, 18; Suyūṭī, *Taʾrīkh*, p. 120, and translation, p. 315; cf. Rifāᶜī, III, 239.

[26] Masᶜūdī, VIII, 299.

[27] *Aghānī*, XVIII, 175–91, and Index; Nuwairī, V, 92–108; cf. Farmer, *A History of Arabian Music* (London, 1929), pp. 132–33.

[28] *Aghānī*, XVIII, 178; Nuwairī, V, 93–94.

ceived a liberal education and excelled in calligraphy, grammar, poetry, and music.[29] Amīn, while yet prince, had heard of this promising child and had made an effort to acquire her but had failed. Now he had this young girl in her early teens brought before him and tested by his own musically gifted uncle, Ibrāhīm ibn al-Mahdī, whose enthusiastic verdict led to her purchase.[30]

Zubaidah's patience must have been sorely tried during these months not only on account of Amīn's private life but also because of his antagonistic policy toward Maʾmūn. This is to be inferred from her words and deeds at the outbreak, finally, of the fraternal civil war. The occasion which brought forth a forceful statement on her part was the departure of the expedition against Maʾmūn under the leadership of ʿAlī ibn ʿĪsā, who had come to take leave of the queen-mother.

"O ʿAlī!" said Zubaidah to her son's general, "though the Commander of the Believers is my own son, my pity for him has reached its limits and my cautiousness on his behalf is ended. Indeed, I am favorably inclined toward ʿAbd Allah (Maʾmūn)—for it was I who brought him up[31]—who has my sympathy for the disagreeable and injurious events that befall him. For my son is a monarch that has contested his brother's (legitimate) authority and envied him his possessions. The better sort (among his followers) devour his (worldly) sub-

[29] *Aghānī*, XVIII, 178; Nuwairī, V, 92–93.

[30] *Aghānī*, XVIII, 181; Nuwairī, V, 96–97. ʿUraib was lost track of after the death of Amīn, much to Zubaidah's regret. Later she was acquired by Maʾmūn.

[31] This detail is found only in Dīnawarī, pp. 391–92; cf. above, p. 141.

stance and the rest would be the death of him. Render, therefore, to ᶜAbd Allah the recognition due the dignity of his father and brothers. Do not speak haughtily to him, for you are not his equal. Compel him not as slaves are compelled, nor hamper him by fetter or handcuff. Withhold not from him either maidservant or manservant. Do not subject him to harsh treatment on the journey and travel not on an equal footing with him. Do not ride ahead of him and take not your seat on your mount ere you have seen to it that he is first mounted. Should he abuse you, bear with him, and should he revile you, do not retaliate." The general's answer can be effectively rendered by: "I hear your commands and shall endeavor to obey them."[32]

Several of the records add that Zubaidah, at that time, gave ᶜAlī a silver chain to be used on the captured Maʾmūn. This detail, being in contradiction to her instructions at the time and not in keeping with her later conciliatory approach to Maʾmūn, is open to question. Amīn and not Zubaidah may have been responsible for this chain, for he, too, as will be seen presently, had a keen sense of honor for the royal dignity and blood.[33]

ᶜAlī's expedition left ᶜIrāq in Jumadā II, 195/March, 811, and met with disaster two months later when ᶜAlī himself lost his head to Maʾmūn's general Ṭāhir. The news of this catastrophe reached Amīn when he was

[32] Ṭabarī, III, 817–18; cf. pp. 797–98; Ibn Athīr, VI, 165; *Fakhrī*, pp. 295–96; Ibn Khaldūn, III, 233.

[33] Cf. Yaᶜqūbī, II, 530, and Ibn Abī Usaibiᶜah, I, 134, where Amīn is said to have given the chain to ᶜAlī; Ṭabarī, III, 797–98, and Ibn Taghrībirdī, II, 553, where the chain, though mentioned, is not credited to either. Maʾmūn himself credited the chain incident to Faḍl (cf. Ibn Ṭaifūr, p. 14).

fishing in the company of Kauthar. He brushed aside the informant with: "Woe to you! Leave me alone. Kauthar has hooked two fishes and I have caught none as yet."[34] It was left to Faḍl the wazir to organize and dispatch a second army against the enemy.

In the meantime, Zubaidah had had occasion to step in, in an effort to prevent another sort of catastrophe. Amīn had retained an escaped slave who belonged to the Hāshimite ʿAbbās ibn ʿAbd Allah, great-grandson of the caliph Manṣūr. ʿAbbās managed to lay hands on the fugitive when the latter, feeling secure in royal patronage, came to display his finery before his former associates. Amīn, hearing of this, determined on punishing ʿAbbās in public. The news reached Zubaidah, who hastened to plead with Amīn. But the latter swore, by his ties to the Prophet himself, to kill ʿAbbās. Zubaidah persisted with her pleadings only to be told by her son that he had a mind, by Allah, to overthrow her, too. Whereupon the unhappy mother uncovered her head—a sign of great distress—and asked to know who would want or dare to enter her presence while she was thus bareheaded. The news of ʿAlī's death caused the affair of ʿAbbās to be forgotten for the time being, though a few days later he was cast into prison.[35]

Maʾmūn, after ʿAlī's death, claimed the caliphate and declared Amīn deposed. Amīn, at Baghdad, confiscated all of Maʾmūn's funds and holdings that were being ad-

[34] Ṭabarī, III, 797–803; Ibn Athīr, VI, 169; *Fakhrī*, pp. 295–96; *Fawāt*, II, 336; cf. Masʿūdī, VI, 431–32; F. Wüstenfeld, *Die Chroniken der Stadt Mekka* (4 vols.; Leipzig, 1857–61), III, 119–20.

[35] Ṭabarī, III, 953–55.

ministered by his agent and took Maʾmūn's family of wife and two sons as hostages.[36]

The second expedition against Maʾmūn also met with failure and disaster at the hands of Ṭāhir. Even this does not seem to have impressed Amīn forcefully enough to rouse him into effective action. Faḍl the wazir realized only too late that little indeed was to be expected from the weak caliph. But knowing also that his own life and fortune hung in the balance, Faḍl sought out likely generals for yet a third expedition. His choice fell on the Arab Asad ibn Yazīd (son of the Bedouin general who had struck down Zubaidah's pet monkey), whom he took for an interview with Amīn. Asad asked that Amīn deliver to him Maʾmūn's two sons and give him power of life and death over them. This power he hoped to use as an effective threat to bring Maʾmūn back to obedience; for he was bent on sacrificing the princes should Maʾmūn fail to respond as expected. Let it be noted here to Amīn's credit that he was so outraged at the suggestion that he clapped into prison the "mad Bedouin who dared to think of shedding royal blood." He had, however, to fall back on Asad's uncle, Aḥmad, for the next leader of the Arab troops, while ʿAbd Allah ibn Ḥamīd led the troops of Persian extraction.[37]

The new forces were ordered to Ḥulwān northeast of Baghdad to meet and turn back the enemy. But news of disunity and poor morale in the capital led to a difference of opinion and to disputes among them. They soon

[36] *Ibid.*, pp. 802–4, 825, 836; Ibn Athīr, VI, 169–70.

[37] Ṭabarī, III, 833–36, 840; Ibn Athīr, VI, 174–76; Ḥuṣrī, II, 149–51; Ibn ʿAbdūs, pp. 372–73.

fell to fighting among themselves and turned back before engaging the enemy. Ṭāhir, therefore, in these early months of 196 took Ḥulwān without opposition. He was soon replaced there by the Arab general, Harthamah, while he himself was ordered to Ahwāz.[38]

These developments reflected, in their turn, on the situation in the imperial province of ʿIrāq, with disturbances leading to major revolts first at Raqqah and then at Baghdad. The rebels seized the caliph and the royal family including Zubaidah and Amīn's two young sons. The climax was reached when in Rajab, 196/April, 812, they deposed Amīn and declared for Maʾmūn. Zubaidah herself was subjected to threats and public humiliation. The rebels, however, were unable to control the situation for more than a few days. This led to the fall of their leader, followed by the restoration of Amīn. Faḍl the wazir had, in the meantime, taken to flight, rightly judging that Amīn's cause was a lost one.[39]

The beginning of the next year, 197/812–13, saw Ṭāhir before Baghdad itself ready to begin the first siege of the Round City that was to run its course well into the following year. Sometime early in the siege Amīn sent out a peace feeler toward Faḍl and Maʾmūn but met with no response.[40] His cause weakened progressively. His adherents fought among themselves or deserted. The merchants of the city, facing inflation and famine, went over to Ṭāhir. "Amīn the Deposed" him-

[38] Ṭabarī, III, 840–41.

[39] *Ibid.*, pp. 846–51, 932, 955; Ibn ʿAbdūs, pp. 382–83; Thaʿālibī, pp. 80–81; *Fakhrī*, p. 296.

[40] Ibn ʿAbdūs, p. 377.

self ran out of equipment and funds. And, finally, the rabble took over the capital.[41] The distraught caliph came to curse both those who were for and those who were against him.[42]

Zubaidah's anxiety must have mounted rapidly during the siege. Her superstitious fears went so far that she had some fine old verses cast into the river because they referred to some disaster.[43] Once at least she made her fears known to her son as she came weeping into his presence, perhaps to urge him to a new course and endeavor. Amīn, however, repelled her with, "Silence! Crowns are not to be firmly secured through women's frets and fears. The caliphate demands statesmanship beyond the ability of women, whose function is to nurse children. Away! Be gone!"[44]

The hard-pressed Amīn and his family, including Zubaidah and her old mother,[45] were in the *Khuld* or Immortal Palace and Zubaidah's adjoining *Qarār* or the Palace That Abideth, just without the Round City.[46] As early as Jumadā II, 197/February, 813, Amīn had realized the hopelessness of his cause. He resigned himself to his fate by taking refuge in his mother's quarters

[41] Ṭabarī, III, 868 ff., 890, 899; Masʿūdī, VI, 447 ff.; Ibn Athīr, VI, 189 ff.

[42] Zamakhsharī, *Rauḍ al-Akhyār*, p. 232.

[43] *Aghānī*, XIV, 65. [44] Masʿūdī, VI, 435. [45] *Ibid.*, p. 444.

[46] Ṭabarī, III, 848, 906; Ibn Athīr, VI, 180, 195. Guy Le Strange (*Baghdad during the Abbasid Caliphate* [Oxford, 1900], pp. 102–3) translates *Qarār* as "Stagnant pool!" If this palace did, indeed, get its name from its large pool, a more appropriate translation would be "Tranquil pool." There can be little doubt, however, that permanency is meant here as in the case of the *Khuld* palace. For *dār al-qarār* as applied to the next and eternal world see *Qurʾān*, Sūrah 40:39.

to await further developments but reverted, in the meantime, to his pleasures.[47] He did, nevertheless, have his serious moments of despair and met them with philosophic verses of his own composing:

O soul! now must thou beware
For where is there a refuge from fate?
Every man, of what he feareth
And hopeth, is in peril.
He who sippeth the sweets of life
Shall one day be choked by affliction.[48]

Toward the end of the siege, Ṭāhir and Harthamah concentrated on the royal palaces. Amīn, being rapidly deserted by friend and foe, offered to surrender on condition of safety for himself, his family, and his followers. He, however, wished to surrender not to the Persian Ṭāhir but to the Arab Harthamah. Rivalry between these two generals of Maʾmūn complicated an already difficult situation. Amīn, along with Kauthar and a few others, embarked in a boat in an initial step to reach Harthamah. The generally accepted story is that the boat capsized, and Amīn swam ashore and was discovered and killed. The fallen caliph's head was severed and displayed on a spear at the city gate. It was next sent on to Maʾmūn in Khurāsān, there to keep company with the severed head of ʿAlī ibn ʿĪsā. So died the son of Zubaidah on the twenty-fifth of Muḥarram 198/September 25, 813.[49]

[47] Ṭabarī, III, 881–82; Masʿūdī, VI, 421–22; cf. Wüstenfeld, *op. cit.*, III, 119–20, from which it would seem that Amīn fished while Baghdad fell.

[48] Suyūṭī, *Taʾrīkh*, p. 120, and translation, p. 316.

[49] Ṭabarī, III, 911 ff., 924–25, 938; Ibn Athīr, VI, 194–201; Yaʿqūbī, II, 536; Masʿūdī, VI, 474–84; *Fakhrī*, pp. 296–97.

Anarchy, chaos, and vandalism took temporary hold of the city of the caliphs before Maʾmūn's generals could restore order. It was during this period that Zubaidah was urged to follow in the footsteps of Aishah, the Mother of the Believers, to avenge blood of Amīn as Aishah had avenged the blood of the caliph ʿUthmān in the very first civil war of Islam. But this step Zubaidah refused to take, saying to her advisers: "What have the women to do with avenging blood and taking the field against warriors?" She went, instead, into deep mourning, wearing garments of black cloth of hair.[50] She consoled herself with verses, mostly composed expressly for her, bewailing the tragic fate of her son and her own misfortunes.[51] One long poem was addressed from her to Maʾmūn as *imám* and caliph. It painted a pathetic picture of her unhappy state and, playing on the name Ṭāhir—which means "pure"—complained bitterly of that general's misdeeds in lines that ran:

> Ṭāhir came, may Allah not purify Ṭāhir from sin,
> For Ṭāhir was impure in the purpose for which he came.
> He turned me forth with uncovered head and unveiled,
> And plundered my goods and destroyed my dwellings.
> What I have suffered will afflict Hārūn!
>
> Oh, what hath befallen me from the basest of mankind!
> If he has acted under orders from thee
> Then must I indeed endure a fate ordained.
> Remember, O Commander of the Believers, my kinship.
> May I be a ransom for thee who art revered and remembered.[52]

[50] Masʿūdī, VI, 485–86.

[51] E.g., *ibid.*, pp. 484–86; *Aghānī*, XXI, 18; Ibn Ṭaifūr, pp. 21–22; cf. also Wüstenfeld, *op. cit.*, III, 121.

[52] Ṭabarī, III, 956–57; Ibn Athīr, VI, 203–4; Masʿūdī, VI, 486; cf. Suyūṭī,

When Maʾmūn read this and other conciliatory verses that she sent him, his heart was touched so that he, too, sent back friendly letters, addressed her as "Mother," and promised to fill a real son's place for her. He ordered the return of her properties and sent her an additional gift from Khurāsān.[53] He declared, furthermore, quoting the words of the caliph ʿAlī when he was accused of the murder of the caliph ʿUthmān, "I have not taken part in, nor given the order for, nor even approved his (in this case, Amīn's) murder." Thus, Maʾmūn placed the full immediate responsibility for the evil deed on Ṭāhir's shoulders,[54] though he held Faḍl ibn al-Rabīʿ and his chief accomplices responsible for the real cause of Amīn's misfortunes and death to the exculpation of both Ṭāhir and himself.[55]

In the meantime, while these letters and sentiments were being exchanged between Zubaidah and her victorious stepson, the latter's general, Ṭāhir, had kept her and her two grandsons under strict guard in the palace. When some two months had passed, he transferred the

Taʾrīkh, p. 118, and translation, p. 312. There is some confusion as to authorship and time of composition of this poem (cf. *ʿIqd*, II, 20; *Aghānī*, XXI, 18; Ibn Ṭaifūr, p. 21).

53 Ibn Ṭaifūr, pp. 21–22; *ʿIqd*, II, 20; cf. Ibn Taghrībirdī, I, 632; Rifāʿī, III, 38. Zubaidah could not have recovered the treasure looted from her palace. Some of her fabulous jewelry found its way into distant Spain, where, like the modern Hope diamond, it is said to have brought misfortune to its successive possessors.

54 Masʿūdī, VI, 487; Ibn Ṭaifūr, pp. 30–32; Ibn ʿAbdūs, p. 384; Ṭabarī, III, 1041–42; Ibn Athīr, VI, 255; Wüstenfeld, *op. cit.*, III, 121, but cf. Ibn Khallikān, I, 650.

55 Ibn Ṭaifūr, p. 27.

three, whether or not on Maʾmun's order is not clear, from Baghdad to the northeastern town of Humainiyā on the Upper Zāb River. Later still he sent the child princes to their uncle in Khurāsān. Some state that Maʾmūn wished to have Zubaidah also join him at Merv but that she preferred not to go.[56] It was, most probably, about this time that Maʾmūn's own wife, Umm ʿĪsā, and her two young sons joined him in Khurāsān.[57]

Among those who mourned Amīn was his royal cousin and still-virgin wife, Lubābah. Her verses for the occasion became a type for the use of noble ladies who lost their husbands before the marriage was consummated.[58] His talented uncle, Ibrāhīm ibn al-Mahdī, who had contributed to his pleasure gatherings, bewailed the sad fate of the young caliph at the hands of Ṭāhir.[59] Abū Nuwās, too, grieved for his royal patron.[60] There were, on the other hand, those who not only refused to mourn for Amīn but would not even refrain from speaking evil of the dead. These, with the tribulations of the civil war, which they blamed on Amīn, not yet all behind them, listed in verse all that departed caliph's shortcomings.[61]

The center of imperial affairs now shifted to Merv and

[56] Ṭabarī, III, 934; Ibn Athīr, VI, 207; ʿ*Iqd*, II, 20; cf. Guy Le Strange, *The Lands of the Eastern Caliphate* (Cambridge, 1905), p. 37, where this is confused with a place of similar name, but south of Baghdad.

[57] Ṭabarī, III, 836; cf. above, pp. 158 and 209.

[58] Ṭabarī, III, 941–42; Masʿūdī, VI, 485; Mubarrad, *Kāmil*, p. 773.

[59] Ṭabarī, III, 952–53; Ibn Athīr, VI, 201–2.

[60] Ḥuṣrī, III, 102; cf. Rifāʿī, III, 323; Abū Nuwās, *Dīwān* (Cairo, 1322/1904), pp. 108–9. The poet died before Maʾmūn's return to Baghdad (cf. Ṭabarī, III, 965).

[61] Ṭabarī, III, 939; Ibn Athīr, VI, 205.

Khurāsān, where, contrary to expectations, Maʾmūn continued to reside and to hold his court. Faḍl ibn Sahl had, in these short years, made good his promise of establishing Maʾmūn as sole caliph of the vast Islamic Empire. For this service he had been honored by the grateful Maʾmūn with the distinguished function and title of Dhū al-Riyāsatain, "He of the Two Headships." He was presented with, among other distinctive insignia, an official sword inscribed on the one side, "Headship of War," and on the other side, "Headship of the Administration." Faḍl thus became both commander-in-chief and prime minister for Maʾmūn.[62] Maʾmūn, it seems, was willing, nay eager, to go further in honoring Faḍl. For he tried his very best, so says the record, to persuade the latter to marry one of his royal daughters. Faḍl refused the honor. Perhaps the memory of Jaᶜfar the Barmakid and the royal ᶜAbbāsah had something to do with his refusal.[63]

The military victory won, Faḍl turned his attention to the politico-religious questions. The Persians had been, from early Umayyad days, associated with the Shīᶜah, or party of ᶜAlī. Therefore, Faḍl the Persian now used his tremendous influence to secure the political leadership for the ᶜAlid party, so as to give Persia and the Persians the central role in the empire. Religious convictions and implications apart, Faḍl succeeded in convincing Maʾmūn that this could be done and that it would be to the general interest of the empire. Keymen

[62] Ibn ᶜAbdūs, pp. 387–88; Ṭabarī, III, 841; Ibn Athīr, VI, 177; cf. Waṭwāṭ, p. 142, where two swords are mentioned.

[63] Ibn ᶜAbdūs, pp. 388–89.

in this situation in ᶜIrāq were to be Faḍl's own brother, Ḥasan, who was appointed governor of the province with his seat at Baghdad, and Ṭāhir, who was transferred north to Raqqah.

The next two years saw a number of revolts in ᶜIrāq and the Ḥijāz, with both ᶜAlid and ᶜAbbāsid counter-caliphal movements. The ᶜAlids were put down by military force, while the ᶜAbbāsids were not any too sure of their next move. But Maʾmūn, in Ramadhān, 201/March, 817, appointed as his heir the Shīᶜite ᶜAlī al-Riḍā, eighth *imām* of that party and at least some seventeen years Maʾmūn's senior. He furthermore accompanied the nomination by striking ᶜAlī's name on the coin of the realm and by changing the dynastic colors from the ᶜAbbāsid black to the ᶜAlid green. The ᶜAbbāsids were, by now, thoroughly outraged. They renounced Maʾmūn and looked to their membership for a new caliph. Their choice narrowed down to Maʾmūn's uncle Ibrāhīm, the son of Mahdī, who thus found himself caliph under the title of Al-Mubārak, "The Blessed," at the end of 201/July, 817. He reigned but hardly ruled, first at Madāʾin and then at Baghdad, opposed by Ḥasan and troubled by further rebellions.[64]

Faḍl ibn Sahl had, in the meantime, withheld from Maʾmūn knowledge of the true state of affairs at Baghdad. The unsuspecting caliph had taken the further step, seemingly early in 202, of reinforcing ᶜAlī al-Riḍā's nomination by marriage alliances. Two of Maʾmūn's own daughters were involved—Umm Ḥabīb, who was married to ᶜAlī, and Umm al-Faḍl, who was betrothed

[64] Ṭabarī, III, 976–98; Yaᶜqūbī, II, 539–40, 542–46; *Fakhrī*, pp. 303–4.

to ᶜAlī's young son, Mohammed.[65] It was left, therefore, to the heir himself to inform Maʾmūn of the serious situation at Baghdad and elsewhere and to point out that the people in these provinces considered him, Ma'mūn, as bewitched and insane, being utterly under the influence of Faḍl and Ḥasan, the sons of Sahl. Maʾmūn now took immediate steps to ascertain the truth from others. He was presently informed of the false charges against the Arab Harthamah (who had been imprisoned and killed), of Ḥasan's weakness at Baghdad, of Ibrāhīm's caliphate, of Ṭāhir's growing power at Raqqah, and of the general disapproval of Maʾmūn's succession plan. He was, furthermore, advised to return to Baghdad himself if he wished to restore order and win back his empire.[66]

Maʾmūn lost no time in starting on his way back to ᶜIrāq. But strange things, indeed, began to take place on that long and memorable journey. First, in Shaᶜbān, 200/ March, 816, Faḍl was murdered at Sarakhs in his bath, with the murderers claiming they acted on Maʾmūn's orders. They were, nevertheless, put to death, while Maʾmūn himself publicly mourned his wazir and comforted the bereaved mother in tender words. Furthermore, he replaced Faḍl in office by his brother Ḥasan and contracted for his own future marriage with Ḥasan's eight-year-old daughter, Būrān.[67]

[65] Ṭabarī, III, 1029, 1102–3; Ibn Athīr, VI, 248, 294; Maqdisī, VI, 110; Masᶜūdī, VII, 61–62; Yaᶜqūbī, II, 552–53; Ḥuṣrī, II, 29–30; Yāfiᶜī, II, 80–81.

[66] Ṭabarī, III, 1025–26; Ibn Athīr, VI, 245–46; *Fakhrī*, pp. 301–2.

[67] Ṭabarī, III, 1027, 1029; Ibn Athīr, VI, 246; Masᶜūdī, VII, 35–36; Yaᶜqūbī, II, 549; Ḥuṣrī, I, 274; Ibn Khallikān, I, 270; II, 474–75; *Fakhrī*, pp. 300–301, 306.

The royal caravan and armies moved on to arrive at Ṭūs, in Safar, 203/August–September, 818, where Maʾmūn stopped to pay his respects at the tomb of his father. Suddenly ᶜAlī al-Riḍā took ill and died—from overeating grapes, the report had it, but poisoned grapes no doubt. Maʾmūn himself prayed over the body and saw to its burial near the tomb of Hārūn al Rashīd. He then sent word of the death to Baghdad and at the same time called on the ᶜAbbāsid family—which had numbered in the census of the year 200/815–16 some 33,000 souls, both male and female[68]—to return to their allegiance. The response was not encouraging at first.[69] But as Maʾmūn drew nearer and nearer to ᶜIrāq, Ibrāhīm's hold grew weaker and weaker, until he was deposed toward the end of 203/June, 819, in favor of the approaching Maʾmūn.[70] Faḍl ibn al-Rabīᶜ had, during this brief period, come out of his hiding but was now again forced to take cover.[71] Ibrāhīm himself fled in disguise and entered incognito on a long period of *Arabian Nights'* adventure.[72]

Maʾmūn at last reached Nahrawān, where Ṭāhir had been ordered to meet him. Here, too, came the generals and the notables from Baghdad to meet the returning

[68] Ṭabarī, III, 1000.

[69] *Ibid.*, pp. 1029–30; Yaᶜqūbī, II, 550–51; *Fakhri*, p. 301.

[70] Ibn ᶜAbdūs, pp. 395–97; Ibn Athīr, VI, 225–28, 229–30, 241, 250–52; Yaᶜqūbī, II, 544–45; *Fakhrī*, pp. 299–300; Wüstenfeld, *op. cit.*, III, 121–22.

[71] Ibn ᶜAbdūs, pp. 372–73; Yaᶜqūbī, II, 247–48, 252; Ṭabarī, III, 1011, 1035; Ibn Athīr, VI, 226, 251; Ibn Khallikān, II, 470.

[72] Ṭabarī, III, 1075; Ibn Athīr, VI, 250–51; Masᶜūdī, VII, 60; Ibn Khallikān, I, 16–18; Ibn Ḥijjah, I, 233–41; Abū Faraj, pp. 283–84; Ghuzūlī, I, 197–207; *Islamic Culture*, III (1929), 263.

caliph and accompany him back to the city of his ancestors. The ᶜAbbāsid Maʾmūn entered the capital on a Saturday in Ṣafar, 204/August, 819, but dressed in the ᶜAlid uniform of green and with the green ᶜAlid banners floating before him. In less than a month he was persuaded to cast these, too, aside and return to the black uniform and standards of the ᶜAbbāsids.[73] Among the Hāshimites who urged this last step was the aged but much revered ᶜAbbāsid Princess Zainab, who later crossed words with the caliph for his ᶜAlid partiality.[74]

Thus passed an imperial crisis that had all but ended in the transfer of the caliphate from the sons of ᶜAbbās to the descendants of ᶜAlī.

It is to Maʾmūn's credit that he did not celebrate his victory by shedding the blood of his former enemies.[75] Amīn, Faḍl ibn Sahl, and ᶜAlī al-Riḍā fell in the interests of a restored and united empire. That won, the victor could afford to be generous, even to the scheming Faḍl ibn al-Rabīᶜ, who was so largely responsible for the outbreak of the civil war. He was forgiven on the plea of Ṭāhir and was allowed to live in peaceful, but pointedly humble, retirement until his death four years later.[76] On the other hand, Ṭāhir himself, the conqueror of Baghdad, fell a victim in 207/822 to Maʾmūn's growing suspicions that his able and powerful general was

[73] Ṭabarī, III, 1036–38; Ibn Ṭaifūr, pp. 2–4; Ibn Athīr, VI, 253.

[74] Masᶜūdī, VIII, 333–35; *Fakhrī*, pp. 302–3; Suyūṭī, *Taʾrīkh*, p. 121, and translation, p. 320.

[75] Cf. Ibn Ṭaifūr, p. 28.

[76] Ṭabarī, III, 1067; Ibn Ṭaifūr, pp. 8–9, 11–20; Yaᶜqūbī, II, 552; Isfandiyār, p. 136; Ibn Khallikān, II, 470.

harboring dynastic ambitions. There are those, however, who would explain Maʾmūn's growing dislike of Ṭāhir by the persistent memory of the part played by the latter in the death of Amīn.

But to return to Zubaidah. The time of Zubaidah's return to the capital, from which Ṭāhir had removed her, is nowhere specified. But since Maʾmūn restored her properties and did not insist on her joining him, she probably returned to Baghdad early in this period. The tenor of her private life at the time must be inferred from the general custom of the society of her day. This latter called for an extended period of mourning and greatly curtailed social activities. The records are silent on her political attitude and actions in the critical period of some six years between the death of her son early in 198/813 and the entry of Maʾmūn into Baghdad early in 204/819. The probabilities are that she who had refused to take any steps to avenge the blood of her son and had followed that up with a successful reconciliation with Maʾmūn was not likely to lend herself in any way to the support of the countercaliphate of Ibrāhīm ibn al-Mahdī.[77]

When Maʾmūn arrived at Baghdad, Zubaidah greeted him with the following congratulatory speech: "I congratulate you on a caliphate for which I have already congratulated myself ere I saw you. Though I have lost a son who was a caliph, I have been recompensed with a caliph son whom I did not bear. He is no loser whose

[77] It is interesting to note that it was a relative or a freedman of Ibrāhīm's who was said to have recognized Amīn after the capsized boat incident and to have made his identity and whereabouts known to Ṭāhir and his men (cf. Ṭabarī, III, 917; Yaʿqūbī, II, 536).

compensation is one like you and no mother is bereft who holds you by the hand. So, I pray Allah for a substitute for that which he has taken and for the long enjoyment of that which he has provided in return."[78] She presented him also with some quite conciliatory and flattering verses, calling on Abū al-ᶜAtāhiyah's talents for the supply of poetry. It was probably at this, their first meeting after Maʾmūn's return, that the latter again disclaimed any responsibility for the murder of his half-brother, to which Zubaidah replied, "There is a day on which you two will meet again, and I pray Allah that he will forgive both of you."[79]

Once, when Zubaidah entertained Maʾmūn, one of Amīn's former slave girls dared to refer to his murder in the course of her singing. This disturbed Maʾmūn and roused his wrath, but Zubaidah hastened to assure him that she had had nothing to do with the choice or sentiment of the song. Maʾmūn accepted her statement but took his departure.[80] Yet another reference tells of Zubaidah's visit to Maʾmūn and her comment on his kindness and patience with his personal attendants.[81] The two continued in all probability to exchange their friendly visits, though these have either not come to light as yet or have altogether escaped the early records.

Perhaps the real test of the cordial relationship that existed between this stepmother and son is Maʾmūn's practice of sending her annually newly minted coin of

[78] Khaṭīb, III, 433–34.

[79] ᶜ*Iqd*, II, 20.

[80] Ibn Ḥijjah, I, 187; cf. Ṭabarī, III, 958, for the verse in question.

[81] Ibn Ṭaifūr, p. 95; cf. Zamakhsharī, *Rauḍ al-Akhyār*, pp. 109, 265–66.

the realm in the generous sums of 100,000 gold dinars and 1,000,000 silver dirhams. She in turn made a habit of presenting Abū al-ᶜAtāhiyah annually with 100 dinars and 1,000 dirhams of these same newly minted coins, no doubt in recognition of the good service his verses had rendered her with Maᵓmūn. Once, when she overlooked this gift to the poet, the latter used his talents to remind her of her practice and promptly received the regular allotment, which, most likely, continued to arrive regularly until his death several years later.[82]

There are, furthermore, one or two incidents of this period that would seem to indicate that property, too, exchanged hands between Maᵓmūn and Zubaidah. For, on the one hand, Maᵓmūn is recorded as passing some of Zubaidah's holdings in Baghdad on to his general, Ṭāhir, and, on the other hand, Zubaidah herself is the recipient of a former holding of hers—the entire village estate of Ṣilḥ in the district of Wāsiṭ al-ᶜIrāq—that had been acquired by Maᵓmūn's governor and wazir, Ḥasan ibn Sahl.[83]

One seeks in vain for any reference to Zubaidah in relation to her two grandsons, from whom she was parted by Ṭāhir. The princes and Maᵓmūn's own son, ᶜAbbās, did not accompany that caliph back to Baghdad. But the three joined him later in Shaᶜbān, 205/ January, 821. Zubaidah probably saw quite a little of them thereafter. Mūsā, Amīn's choice of first heir, died while still a youth in Sahᶜbān, 208/December, 823—

[82] Ṭabarī, III, 1098; Ibn Khallikān I, 205; see also *Aghānī*, XXI, 17–18; Ibn Ṭaifūr, p. 298.

[83] Khaṭīb, I, 93; Ibn Ṭaifūr, p. 211.

January, 824. His younger brother, ᶜAbd Allah, moved for long in the court of the succeeding caliphs and was the only one to carry on the royal line of Hārūn and Zubaidah.[84]

Time passed with Zubaidah coming once more to the fore at the celebration of the wedding of Maʾmūn to the decade-long-bretothed Būrān—or Khadījah as she is called by some[85]—the daughter of Ḥasan ibn Sahl. The historic event took place at Fam al-Ṣilḥ in Ramadhān, 210/December, 824—January, 825, and has gone down in Islamic history as the most magnificent of its kind in an age of extravagant weddings.[86] Numerous are the references to it and copious are the growing passages in praise of the liberality and splendor of the happy event. The festivities lasted seventeen days, and the occasion served for a double wedding in the Sahl family.[87]

The entire expenses of the groom's royal guests and his large military camp were met by the bride's father. This item alone ran into some 50,000,000 dirhams.[88] But it was Ḥasan ibn Sahl's unique and amazing gifts to the guests that have caught the imagination. Balls of musk the size of mellons were scattered among the special guests of honor, who included members of the royal Hāshimite family, the army generals, the state secretaries, and others of high rank at court. The surprise

[84] Ibn Ṭaifūr, p. 25; Ṭabarī, III, 1067; *Aghānī*, IX, 103; XV, 145.

[85] *ᶜIqd*, I, 119; Ibn Khallikān, I, 268 (Arabic, I, 93); Masᶜūdī, VII, 65.

[86] Cf. Ibn Ḥijjah, II, 159–64, for a Barmakid wedding.

[87] Ibn Ṭaifūr, pp. 207–8; Ṭabarī, III, 1081–82; for Fam al-Ṣilḥ cf. Yāqūt, *Geog.*, III, 413, 917.

[88] E.g., Ṭabarī, III, 1083; Ibn Khallikān, I, 269 (Arabic, I, 94).

came when the balls, on being opened, were found to contain a slip of paper on which was written the name of a piece of real estate, or of a slave girl, or of a set of horses, or of a slave boy, and so forth. The fortunate guest into whose hands one of these balls fell presented the slip to an agent appointed for the purpose and received title to or possession of the gift specified therein. Neither were the humbler guests and the rest of the persons present overlooked; for among these were scattered gold and silver coins, solid balls of musk, and eggs of ambergris.[89]

A mat woven of gold was spread out in the groom's honor, and pearls in abundance were showered at his feet. This scene took place in the harem quarters, where none of the proud and noble-born ladies made a move to pick up the lustrous gems. The wazir, therefore, protested to his caliph: "The pearls were showered in order to be picked up (by the guests)," said he. Maʾmūn, therefore, called on the daughters of the caliphs to honor the host by the gracious acceptance of his gift. It was only then that each of the princesses reached out and picked up a single pearl. The rest of the gems, as they flashed and gleamed on the golden mat, reminded Maʾmūn of one of the many wine songs of the departed Abū Nuwās. "Allah be merciful to Abū Nuwās," said the caliph. "One would think that he had seen this very sight when he described the bubbles which cover the surface of wine when mixed: 'The little bubbles and the

[89] Ibn Ṭaifūr, p. 210, Ṭabarī, III, 1083–84; Ibn Athīr, VI, 279; Masʿūdī, VII, 65; Khaṭīb, VII, 321; Ibn Khallikān, I, 268–69 (Arabic, I, 93); *Fakhrī*, pp. 306–7; Suyūṭī, *Taʾrīkh*, p. 121, and translation, p. 321.

great resemble a gravel of pearls upon a ground of gold.' "[90]

The bride, too, had her share of beautiful pearls when her grandmother showered a golden trayful of these fabulous gems on her. But this time Maʾmūn saw to it that not even one of the thousand pearls thus scattered went to any but his bride herself. Once more the lustrous pearls were piled on the golden tray, which Ma'mūn himself now placed on Būrān's lap.

"This is your wedding gift," said he to his bride. "Now, ask of me what you will." But Būrān modestly refrained from any request until her grandmother encouraged her with, "Speak to your lord, and make your wishes known as he has commanded." So Būrān, who had, no doubt, been schooled for this very moment, asked that the former caliph, Ibrāhīm ibn al-Mahdī, be fully forgiven and set free and that the Lady Zubaidah be allowed to go on the pilgrimage. Needless to say, both wishes were graciously granted, along with a third wish, referred to but not specified.[91]

But the royal groom and his family were not likely to let the wazir and his family exceed them in the lavish liberality of the occasion. There was Maʾmūn's half-sister, the wealthy and haughty Ḥamdūnah,[92] who spent 25,000,000 dirhams, while Zubaidah proudly estimated her cash expenditure at between 35,000,000 and 37,-

[90] Thaʿālibī, *Laṭāʾif al-Maʿārif*, p. 73; Khaṭīb, VII, 321–22; Ibn Khallikān, I, 269; *Fakhrī*, p. 307.

[91] Ṭabarī, III, 1074–75, 1082–83; Ibn Athīr, VI, 277; Ibn Ṭaifūr, pp. 183–85, 208; Yaʿqūbī, II, 558; Yāfiʿī, II, 48–49.

[92] Cf. above, p. 157.

000,000 dirhams. She made a most gracious and royal gesture when she presented her reacquired estate of Ṣilḥ, much to Ḥasan's satisfaction, as a wedding gift to the bride. Finally, the ever royal Zubaidah crowned these generous deeds with yet another when she herself adorned Būrān with the historic heirloom—the jeweled jacket of the Umayyad ᶜAbdah.[93] When the celebration and the festivities were over and Maʾmūn was ready to start on the return journey to the capital, he granted Ḥasan that year's revenue of the provinces of Fars and Ahwāz. This more than reimbursed the lavish wazir.[94]

Būrān found favor with her royal husband for the remaining eight years of his life, but no offspring of their union is recorded. She accompanied him on his expedition against Byzantium and was with him at the time of his death near Tarsus, in which latter city he was buried, in Rajab, 218/August, 833.[95] She outlived Maʾmūn by more than half a century and died in 271/884 at the ripe age of eighty. Her long and varied life has contributed several worthy anecdotes to Islamic history which credits her with a reputation for great dignity, charity, and piety, as also for high intelligence and love of poetry.[96] *Arabian Nights'* legends came in

[93] Ṭabarī, III, 1083–84; Ibn Ṭaifūr, p. 208, 210–11; Ibn Athīr, VI, 279; cf. above, p. 12.

[94] Ṭabarī, III, 1083; Ibn Ṭaifūr, p. 209; Masᶜūdī, VII, 66; Ibn Khallikān, I, 269.

[95] Ṭabarī, III, 1140; Ibn Athīr, VI, 304; Yaᶜqūbī, II, 573; Ibn Khallikān, I, 270.

[96] Ibn Khallikān, I, 270; Yāqūt, *Geog.*, I, 808; Ibn Taghrībirdī, II, 72.

time to sing her praises as a most accomplished lady of wit, charm, adventure, and romance.[97]

The fact that Būrān asked, as a special favor, that Maʾmūn allow Zubaidah to make the pilgrimage would seem to suggest that he had perhaps discouraged his stepmother from visiting the scenes of the greatest of her philanthropic activities of some years back. It is first to this phase of her royal career and then to the luxurious innovations of her own court that Zubaidah owes much of her lasting historic fame. To these, therefore, the reader's attention is now drawn.

[97] *The Thousand and One Nights*, trans. Edward William Lane (3 vols.; London, 1889), II, 294 (n. 117), 308–12; cf. ᶜ*Iqd*, III, 452–58; Ibn Khaldūn, I, 16–17.

VIII

In the Hall of Fame

THE lavish mode of life that set in with Mahdī and Khaizurān reached its climax in the court and palace of Hārūn and Zubaidah. The fabulous wealth of the ᶜAbbāsid Empire at this its highest point of material prosperity was expansively reflected in the spectacular and luxurious living of this its most romantic and intriguing royal couple. Blue-blooded Arab nobility and high-ranking officers of the empire, Arab and non-Arab alike, reflected in their turn the splendor of the court. The Barmakids lived royally and dispensed largess and hospitality with such regal grace that their very name worked its way into the Arabic language and its literature as a synonym for genuine liberality and as a rich theme for many a poet. Jaᶜfar is credited with a palace that some thought eclipsed even the palace of Hārūn and roused that autocrat's jealous resentment. On sound friendly advice Jaᶜfar was induced to present his political ward, Prince Maʾmūn, with the magnificent structure and all its sumptuous equipment and furnishings.[1] This same Jaᶜfar provided his mother (step- or

[1] Ṭabarī, III, 672–73; Ibn Khallikān, I, 304–5; Yāqūt, *Geog.*, I, 806–7; cf. Guy Le Strange, *Baghdad during the Abbasid Caliphate* (Oxford, 1900),

foster-) with an establishment on a scale that put four hundred slave girls at her command.[2] Zubaidah, guarding the interest and prestige of her son, Prince Amīn, can be imagined as doing the best in her power to see that his establishments were not overshadowed for long and that the magnificence and brillance of her own palaces reflected to his glory.

There can be little doubt that the urge to hold her own, together with her naturally generous impulses, kept her abreast of Hārūn's magnificent scale of life and royal innovations, for Islamic history credits each of them with a series of "firsts" on which rests much of their claim to worldly fame. One reads that Hārūn was the first in Islam to indulge in polo, in bow-and-arrow and ball-and-racket games, and in chess and backgammon—in all of which his example was followed by his court. Again, one is intrigued by the passage which states that Zubaidah was the first for whom was made the finest of fine brocades costing fifty thousand dinars per piece; the first who organized a body of mounted page boys and palace maids who ran her errands and delivered her messages; the first to use palanquins of silver, ebony, and sandalwood ornamented with gold and silver hinges and covered with sable, brocade, and silk cloth in colors of red, yellow, green, and blue; the first to use slippers studded with jewels; the first to burn candles made of ambergris—the scent being much

---

pp. 243–44; Reuben Levy, *A Baghdad Chronicle* (Cambridge, 1929), pp. 536–37. A "Barmecide (Barmakid) feast" has come to mean in English, through the *Arabian Nights*, an imaginatively sumptuous repast.

[2] Masʿūdī, VI, 407; Khaṭīb, VII, 156–57; Ibn Khallikān, I, 315.

in favor with her and with Maʾmūn[3]—and the first to dress up palace girls as page boys—setting the fashion in all these innovations for high society.[4] To this list of "firsts" others add one more, namely, that she was the first woman to prefer swift camels to asses for use on her pilgrimages.[5] The queen's taste and ingenuity in other phases of palace boudoir and salon life must be gauged accordingly.

Zubaidah's influence in these, as in other, matters spread far beyond the capital and the imperial province as she herself journeyed to pleasure and health resorts along the banks of the Tigris, or joined her royal husband at his favorite Raqqah in northern Syria, or undertook her several pilgrimages to the sacred cities of Islam. She lent her name to several sites in capital and empire, all called "Zubaidīyah" in her honor. Two of these were extensive and choice fiefs in western Baghdad, where the queen's palaces, gardens, and retainers' quarters were located.[6] Another Zubaidīyah was close to Wāsiṭ al-ᶜIrāq, most probably in the region of the Nahr Maimūn Canal, which was dug at her orders.[7] A fourth Zubaidīyah lay farther east on a healthy site in the Persian district of Jibāl.[8] At least three Zubaidīyahs

[3] "Bibliotheca geographorum Arabicorum [*BGA*]," VII, 369; Nuwairī, XII, 54–55.

[4] Masᶜūdī, VIII, 295–99.

[5] *BGA*, VII, 195; cf. Thaᶜālibī, *Laṭāʾif al-Maᶜārif*, p. 15; Ghuzūlī, II, 185.

[6] Khaṭīb, I, 71, 87, 89, 93, 110; Yāqūt, *Geog.*, II, 917; IV, 132, 141; Le Strange, *op. cit.*, pp. 54, 113–17, 124, and Map V.

[7] Balādhurī, *Futūḥ*, p. 291; Yāqūt, *Geog.*, IV, 719; II, 917.

[8] *BGA*, IV, 19, 198; II[2] (1939 ed.), VII, 165, 270; cf. Guy Le Strange, *The Lands of the Eastern Caliphate* (Cambridge, 1905), p. 192.

were located on the Pilgrim Road from Kūfah to Mecca.[9] There were, furthermore, several other holdings and sites which were associated with her personal presence and pleasure. Chief among these was her fief in Wāsiṭ al-Raqqah with its considerable building activity.[10] Her fief of Fam al-Ṣilḥ has already been mentioned,[11] and reference to her holdings at Mecca and Ṭā'if follows presently.

The earlier Arab sources have left no record of any visits of Zubaidah to the distant regions of northern and central Persia. Nevertheless, later Persian sources credit her, very generously, with no less than the foundation of the northern city of Tabriz in 175/791[12] and of the central town of Kāshān,[13] as they credit her also with a Zubaidīyah fief in Rayy.[14] That Zubaidah ever visited these cities may be questioned. However, it is not at all improbable that she did indeed, perhaps, cause a fort or a mosque, a guest house, bridge, or canal to be built in these places—as, for instance, a mosque at Tabriz[15]—to which may be traced some of the later obviously

[9] Cf. below, p. 245.

[10] Balādhurī, *Futūḥ*, p. 180; Yāqūt, *Geog.*, IV, 889, 994.

[11] Cf. above, pp. 230–31 and 234.

[12] Ḥamd-Allah Mustawfī, *Nuzhat al-Qulūb* ("Gibb Memorial Series," Vol. XXIII[1–2]), ed. Le Strange (2 vols.; London, 1915), p. 75, and translation, p. 78; cf. *Lands of the Eastern Caliphate*, p. 161.

[13] Mustawfī, *Nuzhat al-Qulūb*, p. 67, and translation, pp. 71–72; cf. *Lands of the Eastern Caliphate*, p. 209.

[14] Yāqūt, *Geog.*, II, 895; but cf. *Lands of the Eastern Caliphate*, pp. 215-16, 218.

[15] Cf. Mary Leonora Sheil, *Glimpses of Life and Manners in Persia* (London, 1856), p. 92; Eric Schroeder, in *Survey of Persian Art*, ed. A. U. Pope, II (1939), 943, and André Godard, in *Ars Islamica*, VIII (1941), 4.

exaggerated traditions. For Zubaidah is known to have indulged in extensive public works in several provinces, near or distant, of the empire. An earlier Arab source, for instance, credits her with a fortified monastery in the far-distant border city or region of Badakhshān, just west of the river Oxus and famed for its mines of precious stones. But a later Persian source makes her the very foundress of that mighty city itself.[16] The border fort of Warathān in the northern province of Adharbāyjān had been first constructed by the Umayyad Marwān II (127–32/744–50) but fell later to Zubaidah, who saw to its repair and upkeep.[17] Farther west on the Syrian-Byzantine border, Zubaidah had a guest house or wayfarer's inn in the mountain town of Baghrās.[18]

But the queen's philanthropy reached far beyond these endowed establishments on the distant borders of the empire that ministered to lonely soldier, traveling merchant, pious monk, or needy beggar. It embraced major public work projects that were intended to bring comfort and joy to the inhabitants of the sacred city of Mecca, on the one hand, and to Islam's great pilgrim host, on the other. For, over and above such cash disbursement as Zubaidah may have made to both Mecca and Medina,[19] she undertook to give the Meccans and

[16] *BGA*, III, 303; Yāqūt, *Geog.*, I, 528; cf. Le Strange, *Lands of the Eastern Caliphate*, p. 436; *Ḥudūd al-ᶜĀlam* ("The Regions of the World") ("Gibb Memorial Series: New Series," Vol. XI [London, 1937]), trans. V. Minorsky, p. 349, and references there cited.

[17] Balādhurī, *Futūḥ*, p. 329; *BGA*, V, 284; Yāqūt, *Geog.*, IV, 919.

[18] *BGA*, I, 65; *Ḥudūd al-ᶜĀlam*, p. 150.

[19] Khaṭīb, XIV, 433–34.

their annual pilgrim guests, on the way and in the sacred city itself, the great boon of refreshing waters to a thirsty land. In her generous and pious concern for the welfare of the sacred cities, Zubaidah was following a well-established precedent in the tradition of Arab royalty. She had, furthermore, the example of Hārūn to live up to. Nevertheless, her interest did not spring from a mere sense of detached duty or a competitive desire to keep up with the caliphs. For Zubaidah herself traveled the Pilgrim Road and dwelt for some months in the sacred precincts of Mecca. Here she had at least two establishments and some property that had formerly belonged to Jaᶜfar the Barmakid.[20] And, following the fashion of the Meccans, she, too, had her gardens in the near-by resort city of Ṭāʾif,[21] where she undertook the repairs of a mosque associated with Mohammed and adjoining the tomb of the arch-Traditionist, ᶜAbd Allah ibn ᶜAbbās. On one of the walls of the mosque appeared the inscription that recorded her philanthropy: "The Lady Umm Jaᶜfar, daughter of Abū al-Faḍl and mother of the heirs presumptive to the Moslem throne—may Allah prolong her life!—ordered the restoration of the mosque of the Prophet at Ṭāʾif wherein it was accomplished in the year one hundred and ninety-two [807–8]."[22]

[20] F. Wüstenfeld, *Die Chroniken der Stadt Mekka* (4 vols.; Leipzig, 1857–61), I, 319, 328, 330, 462; II, 13; III, 137, 159; Yāqūt, *Geog.*, II, 523.

[21] Hamdānī, *Jazīrat al-ᶜArab*, ed. D. H. Müller (2 vols.; Leiden, 1884 and 1891), I, 120.

[22] Wüstenfeld, *op. cit.*, II, 76; *Répertoire chronologique d'épigraphie Arabe*, I (Cairo, 1931), 66.

Hārūn and Zubaidah were both given to frequent pilgrimages. Hārūn began his reign with an avowed determination to lead in sacred pilgrimage and sacred war in alternate years but was, for various reasons, unable to live up to his intentions. He is, nevertheless, credited with from six to nine pilgrimages in all.[23] Zubaidah has five assured pilgrimages to her credit, with a possibility of a sixth. The first of these was made in 173/790 in the company of Hārūn, who was making the journey on foot.[24] the next one was in 176/792.[25] It is not quite certain that she accompanied Hārūn on that fateful pilgrimage of 186/802, though the great issues at stake and the indirect reference to her displeasure at Jaᶜfar the Barmakid's conduct on that occasion may imply her actual presence.[26] There is, however, no doubt about her pilgrimage of 190/805, when she must have witnessed the effects of recent droughts and the people's great suffering from thirst, which both she and Hārūn undertook to relieve, in part, by increasing the depth of the sacred well of Zamzam.[27]

Perhaps it was the above experience that led the queen to undertake, on behalf of the Meccans and the annual pilgrims, waterworks that were bolder in conception and more extensive in scope than anyone had previously

[23] Ibn ᶜAbdūs, p. 252; *BGA*, VIII, 346; Masᶜūdī, IX, 66–68; *Maᶜārif*, pp. 193 ff.; Yaᶜqūbī, II, 521–22, 526; Ṭabarī, III, 701; Wüstenfeld, *op. cit.*, IV, 179, 184.

[24] Cf. above, pp. 99–101; *ᶜIqd*, III, 350.

[25] Masᶜūdī, IX, 67; Ṭabarī, III, 628–29; Ibn Taghrībirdī, I, 482.

[26] Cf. above, pp. 189–91.

[27] Yaᶜqūbī, II, 519; cf. *BGA*, VII, 43.

considered. The ambitious project included the central waterworks around the Spring of Ḥunain some twelve miles east of Mecca, a number of smaller springs, large water reservoirs, and a subterranean aqueduct that brought the water to Mecca and to the precinct of the sacred territory. Famous among this complex of waterworks was the "Spring of Zubaidah" on the Plain of ᶜArafāt—a veritable and priceless boon to the tens of thousands of annual pilgrims. Equally famous was the Mushshāsh Spring in Mecca itself, which ministered to the inhabitants the year round. The magnitude of the task can be understood only when one considers the extremely difficult terrain of mountain and hard rock that had to be cut through and under before success could be achieved. Neither was success achieved with the first trial. But Zubaidah, once committed to the meritorious task, would not be discouraged by either technical difficulties or excessive costs. She urged the engineers to greater effort and declared she would go through with the project were every stroke of the pickax to cost her a gold dinar. The engineering feat was accomplished at a cost of some one and three-quarter million dinars, including gifts and charities incidental to the occasion.[28]

Work on this project had already begun in the reign of Hārūn and was in progress at the time of his death. Zubaidah, shortly after her arrival at Baghdad from Raqqah with Hārūn's great treasure, left in Ramadhān

[28] Wüstenfeld, *op. cit.*, I, 444–45; II, 33–34, 52; III, 334–35; IV, 185–87; *BGA*, VII, 316; Masᶜūdī, VIII, 297; Khaṭīb, XIV, 433–34; Ibn Khallikān, I, 533 and n. 1; Yāfiᶜī, II, 63; Ibn Taghrībirdī, I, 631–32.

of 193/June–July, 809, for Mecca. She took with her Amīn's gift to the Holy City—some twenty thousand dinars' worth of gold bullion which was used as nails and gilding for the door of the sacred Kaᶜbah. While in Mecca she herself witnessed the erection of fortifications, tanks, and canals in connection with her project, which, however, was not finished until the next year and after she had returned to ᶜIrāq.[29] On the arch over the gate of the reservoir in Mecca went up the following inscription: "In the name of Allah, the Merciful, the Compassionate. There is no God but Allah alone without any partners. The blessings of Allah be on Mohammed his servant and messenger. The grace of Allah (be with us all)! Umm Jaᶜfar the daughter of Abū al-Faḍl Jaᶜfar the son of the Commander of the Believers Manṣūr—may Allah be pleased with the Commander of the Believers—ordered the construction of these springs in order to provide water for the pilgrims to the House of Allah and to the people of his Sanctuary, praying thereby for Allah's reward and seeking to draw nigh unto him. By the hand of Yāsir, her servant and client in the year one hundred and ninety-four [809–10]."[30]

The task accomplished, Zubaidah's chief agents and workmen presented themselves at her palace overlooking the Tigris to render an account of their expenditures. She received their ledgers and promptly cast them into

[29] Yaᶜqūbī, II, 526; Ḥamdānī, *Jazīrat al-ᶜArab*, I, 267; Wüstenfeld, *op. cit.*, IV, 185.

[30] Wüstenfeld, *op. cit.*, II, 33; *Répertoire chronologique d'épigraphie Arabe*, I, 69–70.

the river, announcing regally, if not indeed piously, "We have left the account to the Day of Accountings. Let him who has a cash balance keep it, and he who is our creditor, him we will repay." Then having bestowed upon them suits of honor, she dismissed them, and they departed full of praise and thanks.[31]

Parallel with her interest in Mecca went her concern for the welfare of the pilgrims on the road that she herself no doubt traveled, namely, that from Kūfah to Mecca, a distance of some nine hundred miles. It is interesting to note that, though she did at times undertake philanthropic work at some well-known station on the road, such as Haitham,[32] her main objective seems to have been to minister especially to the poorer or more pious pilgrims who, either from necessity or from choice, made the long pilgrimage on foot. For, as one follows the course of her "stations" on the Mecca Road, it soon becomes apparent that these were located mostly at some "halfway" spot between older established stations and towns. At least nine sites are associated with her activities on the road between Kūfah and the southern junction of Maᶜdan al-Naqirah, where the road branches to Medina and to Mecca.[33] A tenth station, Muḥdath, lay

[31] Wüstenfeld, *op. cit.*, III, 335; IV, 186. Contrast her action with that of Manṣūr, who held the builders of Baghdad to strict account (cf. above, p. 2).

[32] Yāqūt, *Geog.*, IV, 998; for itineraries of this road cf. *BGA*, I, 27; II, 40; VI, 125–34, 185–87; VII, 174–80, 311–12; Ḥamdānī, *Jazīrat al-ᶜArab*, I, 183–85; for identification and mapping of cities cf. B. Moritz, *Arabien* (Hanover, 1923), map facing p. 58; Alois Musil, *Northern Neǧd* (New York, 1928) and *Northern Arabia* (maps) (New York, 1926).

[33] E.g., *BGA*, II (1937–38 ed.), 40; VI, 186–87; Yāqūt, *Geog.*, IV, 804.

beyond this on the way to Medina.[34] Three of the sites, all in the first third of the road from Kūfah, were named in her honor, the best known of the three being the first.[35] At all these places was to be found at least either a well or a cistern, though some, as at Haitham, had in addition a shelter for rest or prayer and a fortification of some sort,[36] while one station boasted the still further addition of a mosque.[37]

Her philanthropic interest continued throughout her life and took the form of endowments for the upkeep of her establishments and public works and a readiness to supplement these. A touching story is told in this connection. Ma'mūn's governor of Mecca wrote that caliph in 210/825–26 of the need for some supplementary cisterns and canals in the city itself and was told to undertake their construction. The work was completed and the occasion was celebrated with public festivities. When Zubaidah heard of the new project, she was much pained. It was probably in connection with this very project that she was anxious to make the prilgrimage once more and used Būrān's influence with Maʾmūn, on the happy occasion of their wedding later that same year, to secure that end. When she did make the pilgrimage the very next year, the governor came to pay her his respects. She took him to task thus: "Why did you not write to me so that I could have asked the Commander

[34] *BGA*, VII, 176; Yāqūt, *Geog.*, IV, 424.

[35] Yāqūt, *Geog.*, I, 591; II, 917; *ibid.*, II, 61; IV, 585; *ibid.*, II, 98; III, 827, for the three Zubaidīyahs in order.

[36] E.g., *ibid.*, II, 98, 270; III, 732, 827; IV, 75.

[37] *Ibid.*, II, 778.

of the Believers to assign me that project? I would have undertaken its costs as I undertook the expenses of this other cistern so as to accomplish in full my intentions toward the people of the Sanctuary of Allah."[38]

This pilgrimage of hers seems to have been the last occasion on which Zubaidah appeared in public, though she had some six years of life yet to live. Neither does there seem to be any further reference to her private life during this period, in which she, now approaching her seventies, may have been overshadowed by the younger and much-gifted Būrān. Yet, it is difficult to imagine the ever resourceful and readily adaptable Zubaidah as anything but happily active, even though overtaken by old age. Her last call came on the twenty-sixth of Jumādā I, 216/July 10, 831, about a week after Maʾmūn had started on his campaign of that year against the Byzantines.[39] Maʾmūn's absence from the capital may have prevented an elaborate burial for his "mother," such as Hārūn had accorded Khaizurān. The role of the chief mourner fell, no doubt, to her only surviving grandson, ʿAbd Allah, the son of Amīn.[40]

The early records give Zubaidah the briefest of death notices, mentioning neither the cause of her death—which may or may not have been old age—nor yet the place of her burial. The first historical reference to her tomb is given by Ibn Athīr, an early twelfth-century historian whose too short and incidental reference places the original tomb in the general neighborhood of

[38] Wüstenfeld, *op. cit.*, I, 445; II, 34.

[39] Ṭabarī, III, 1104–5; Yaʿqūbī, II, 568; Ibn Khallikān, I, 533.

[40] Cf. above, p. 231.

Kāẓimain. He adds, however, that the tomb was burned, along with those of her father and son among other tombs near by, in 443/1051 on the outbreak of severe rioting between the Sunite and Shiʿite Moslems of Karkh or western Baghdad. Unfortunately, the reference to the original location of the tomb is too general to be conclusive.[41]

It was left for modern travelers and scholars to get on the trail of the tomb of the Lady or Sitt Zubaidah. The first exciting news was given out by Niebuhr, whose travels took him to Baghdad early in 1766 and who, among his observations on that city, published an inscription found in connection with a prominent and beautiful monument near a mosque in Karkh or western Baghdad. The inscription stated briefly, as Arabic inscriptions of the Ottoman Turkish period usually did, that the monument enshrined the tomb of the blessed and forgiven departed, the doer of good deeds, the handmaiden (of Allah) Sitt Zubaidah, the daughter of Jaʿfar, the son of the ʿAbbāsid Manṣūr al-Dawāniqī ("Father of Farthings"),[42] and wife of the ʿAbbāsid caliph Hārūn al-Rashīd, and that she died in the year 216. But a second inscription added that Ḥasan Pashah, Turkish governor of Baghdad, buried his wife, Aishah

[41] Ibn Athīr, IX, 395. The traveler Ibn Baṭūṭah (728/1328) reported Amīn's tomb to be among the tombs of the caliphs in Ruṣāfah or eastern Baghdad. But, inasmuch as he places the tomb of Mahdī along with the rest, when Mahdī was buried at Radhdh (see above, p. 75), one is compelled to question the accuracy of his report at this point (cf. Ibn Baṭūṭah, *Riḥlah*, [2 vols.; Cairo, 1287], pp. 135–36).

[42] Cf. above, p. 1.

Khānum, in this same mausoleum in Ramadhān, 1131/ July–August, 1719.[43]

For over a hundred years after Niebuhr's publication the monument was accepted as the tomb of Zubaidah.[44] But around the turn of the present century, it came to be questioned as such both on historic and on architectural grounds. Scholars like Le Strange[45] and Oppenheim,[46] the first basing his arguments on Ibn Athīr's information and the second on architectural grounds, discredited the association between the present monument and the original tomb of Zubaidah. Massignon,[47] on the other hand, rightly questioned Le Strange's too rigid interpretation of Ibn Athīr's text, while Herzfeld, largely for architectural and sentimental reasons, believes the present monument to have been built as a genuine and fitting commemoration of Zubaidah. He sees in it a thirteenth-century replacement of the original mausoleum of the famed queen.[48] There the academic contro-

[43] Carsten Niebuhr, *Reisebeschreibung nach Arabien* (2 vols.; Copenhagen, 1774 and 1778), II, 300–301. For Ḥasan Pashah and his wife see Stephen Hemsley Longrigg, *Four Centuries of Modern Iraq* (Oxford, 1925), pp. 123–27.

[44] E.g., J. R. Wellsted, *Travels in the City of the Caliphs* (2 vols.; London, 1840) I, 237–38; H. C. Rawlinson, art. "Baghdad," *Encyclopaedia Britannica* (9th ed.); cf. Le Strange, *Baghdad during the Abbasid Caliphate*, pp. 164–65, 350–52.

[45] *Baghdad during the Abbasid Caliphate*, pp. 164–65, 350–52.

[46] *Vom Mittelmeer zum Persischen Golf* (2 vols.; Berlin, 1899 and 1900), II, 244.

[47] *Mission en Mésopotamie (1907–1908)* (2 vols.; Cairo, 1910 and 1912), II, 70, 108–10.

[48] Friedrich Sarre and Ernst Herzfeld, *Archäologische Reise im Euphrat und Tigris Gebiet* (4 vols.; Berlin, 1911–20), I, 239; II, 157, 173–79; Herzfeld,

versy of the tomb rests while the stately, snow-white, honeycombed cone, a perfect specimen of its architectural type, continues to be popularly accepted as marking Zubaidah's final resting-place.

But if the Moslem historians neglected to provide adequate information as to Zubaidah's original tomb and its subsequent history, they have, nevertheless, taken considerable pains to perpetuate her memory and to detail several instances where her originality and philanthropy served as an inspiration to others in the course of the centuries. The queen's first post-mortem anecdote, though made of the hazy stuff of dreams, is nevertheless quite significant: The departed Zubaidah was seen in a dream and was asked about her condition in the other world. To which she replied: "Allah forgave me with the very first stroke of the pickax on the Mecca Road."[49] Dreams apart, the story is an indication of the great value that Zubaidah's fellow-Moslems of the time set on her crowning charity—the pilgrim road from Kūfah to Mecca. The road came to be known as Darb Zubaidah or the Zubaidah Road. It still exists under that name even today, though it is referred to also as the Persian Pilgrim Road or the Sultānī Road—that is, the State Highway.[50]

More tangible testimony to her contemporaries' appreciation of her great philanthropies comes from

"Damascus: Studies in Architecture—I," *Ars Islamica*, IX (1942), 24–25, and Fig. 63.

[49] Khaṭīb, XIV, 433–34.

[50] Cf. Musil, *Northern Neǧd*, pp. 158, 178–79, 205–12; Great Britain, Admirality, *A Handbook of Arabia* (London, 1920), I, 76, 81, 394.

Azraqī's (d. 219/834) well-known history of Mecca, which was in the writing in Zubaidah's day.[51] Having detailed the construction of her waterworks, the historian adds: "It has become for her an honor hitherto unattained by any other, while she herself experienced more satisfaction in this, her bounty, than did any other; for the people of Mecca and the pilgrims owe their very life to her next to Allah."[52]

Jāḥiẓ (d. 255/869, aged ninety) reckons Zubaidah as one of the great personalities of the reign of Hārūn al-Rashīd. "There gathered," says he, "round (Hārūn) al-Rashīd such an excellent and jovial company as was never assembled round any other (caliph). He had for wazirs the Barmakids, the like of whom was never seen for generosity and glory; for his judge, Abū Yūsuf; for his poet, Marwān ibn Abī Ḥafṣah, who was for his age what Jarīr had been for his own time; for boon companion, ᶜAbbās ibn Mohammed, paternal uncle of his (Hārūn's) father; for chamberlain, Faḍl ibn al-Rabīᶜ, the most dignified of bearing and the most given to grandeur; for singer, Ibrāhīm al-Mauṣilī, unique in his day in his profession; for stringed instrumentalist, Zalzal; for piper, Barsaumā; and for wife, Umm Jaᶜfar (Zubaidah), the most desirous of the good, swiftest to perform pious deeds, and readiest in benefactions—she, among her other benevolences, brought water to the Sanctuary, after the supply had failed."[53]

[51] Wüstenfeld, *op. cit.*, I, 443.

[52] *Ibid.*, p. 445.

[53] Khaṭīb, XIV, 11; Ibn Taghrībirdī, I, 549; Suyūṭī, *Taʾrīkh*, p. 112, and translation, p. 294; cf. Farmer, *A History of Arabian Music* (London, 1929), pp. 116 and 9131, and references there cited for the three musicians named.

Fākihī, another early historian of Mecca, writing in 272/885, gives the best and fullest account of her waterworks and sees in their eventual successful flowing Allah's graciousness to all, including Zubaidah, whose endowments still provided for the upkeep of the system.[54]

The blind but brilliant court wiṭ, Abū al-ᶜAināᵓ (*ca.* 190–283/806–96),[55] was much impressed with Zubaidah's royal relation to the numerous caliphs and heirs to the throne from her grandfather, Manṣūr, down to her stepgrandson, Mutawakkil. He compares her in this respect to the Umayyad queen par excellence, ᶜĀtikah, wife of ᶜAbd al-Malik.[56] Some of the earliest records have preserved, on the other hand, Ḥasan ibn Sahl's testimony to the excellence of her wisdom and understanding.[57]

The classic incident of the next century that was to help in perpetuating Zubaidah's memory dates from the reign of Qāhir (320–22/932–34). The story is preserved by Masᶜūdī (writing in 333/944–45), who received it firsthand from an able narrator of history, the Khurāsānian Mohammed ibn ᶜAlī, who was in favor at the court. Qāhir was anxious to learn the true history of all the ᶜAbbāsid caliphs who had preceded him. He called on this Mohammed to give him the historical facts with-

[54] Wüstenfeld, *op. cit.*, II, 33, 35.

[55] Ibn Khallikān, III, 56–61.

[56] Thaᶜālibī, *Laṭāᵓif al-Maᶜārif*, pp. 54–55; quoted in Suyūṭī, *Taᵓrīkh*, p. 120, and translation, pp. 317–18; for ᶜĀtikah see Nabia Abbott, "Women and the State in Early Islam," *Journal of Near Eastern Studies*, I (1942), 349–51.

[57] Ibn Ṭaifūr, p. 210; Ṭabarī, III, 1084.

out any varnish, on pain of death, shaking his javelin at him the while to reinforce his command. Mohammed, having begged for and received the promise of assurance of life, proceeded with his tale, which in due time brought him to the events of the reign of Hārūn al-Rashīd. He dwelt at some length on the glories of that magnificent reign. In the course of his narration, he mentioned Zubaidah briefly as performing the most excellent of deeds in the reign, namely, the Meccan waterworks, the pilgrim road, and her charitable establishments at Tarsus and the Syrian border. He proceeded next to mention, also briefly, the Barmakids. Then, having listed all of Hārūn's "firsts," he concluded his account of that monarch's reign and waited on the caliph for his next cue.

"I see," said Qāhir, "that you have cut short your account of Umm Jaᶜfar's deeds. Why is that so?"

"O Commander of the Believers!" answered Mohammed, "it was for the sake of brevity while awaiting (your) permission."[58]

Qāhir, eyes flashing with rage, reached for his javelin and shook it so that Mohammed thought he saw "red death at its tip." He resigned himself to his fate, not doubting but that the very angel of death had, indeed, come to take his life. However, when the caliph did hurl the javelin at him, Mohammed still had enough wits about him to leap out of its path.

"Woe to you," exclaimed Qāhir. "Are you then at enmity with your own head and weary of your very life?"

[58] Cf. above, pp. 128–29.

"What is the cause of your displeasure, O Commander of the Believers?" begged Mohammed.

"The history of Umm Jaᶜfar. Tell me more of it," said Qāhir.

"Gladly," said Mohammed and continued. "In her deeds and noble conduct, both the serious and the frivolous, she eclipsed (all) others. As for her serious and monumental acts, the like of which was not known in Islam, there is, for instance [here followed a more detailed account of her extensive philanthropies, headed by the Meccan waterworks and ending with her general concern for the poor and destitute classes]. As for the second type of deeds (frivolous by contrast to the preceding)—such as those in which kings take pride, those that make for their enjoyment of a life of ease and affluence, those that insure the safety of their empires, and those that history records of their life and work—they were that she was the first [here followed the list of her 'firsts,' already given, which ended with Zubaidah's girl pages]." This last institution had survived until then, for Qāhir himself was surrounded with a large group of these girls in boys' attire who waited on him. Mohammed's account of the origin and description of Zubaidah's page girls greatly amused and pleased the caliph, who, holding out his wine cup to be refilled, called out loudly and hilariously for a toast in honor of Mohammed's descriptive efforts.[59]

But it was not only for her worldly frivolity that Zubaidah found royal imitators. The mother of Muta-

[59] Masᶜūdī, VIII, 289, 294–300, 304; Wüstenfeld, *op. cit.*, II, 128; cf. above, p. 212.

wakkil (232–57/847–61) took special interest in the water supply of Mecca and on two different occasions came to the rescue of the Meccans.[60] The history of Mecca is replete with references to the interest that royalty and nobility took in the upkeep and repair of the city's waterworks.[61] Of special interest is the case of the Turkish Sulṭānah of the household of the Ottoman emperor, Sulaimān the Magnificent (926–74/1520–66). She entreated the emperor, as a special favor, for permission to undertake extensive and expensive repairs to the water system that seems to have fallen on bad days indeed. Her plea was that, since it was a woman, the ᶜAbbāsid Zubaidah, who had first provided the system, it would be but fitting that a second woman, herself, should undertake its major reconstruction. Sulaimān graciously agreed, and the work was begun in 969/1561 with much publicity and great expectations. But there were several disappointments in store, alike for patrons, engineers, and inhabitants; for the tremendous project, whose very difficulties reflected afresh to Zubaidah's glory, took ten long, hard years ere it was crowned with success in the reign of Salīm II.[62]

"That which history records of the life and deeds of royalty," to quote the historian Masᶜūdī, seems to have been by about his time pretty well ascertained and recorded so far as Zubaidah was concerned. For it is little, indeed, that can be considered of first-rate importance

[60] Ṭabarī, III, 1440; Wüstenfeld, *op. cit.*, I, 398; III, 129.

[61] Cf. Wüstenfeld, *op. cit.*, IV, 248 ff., 309 ff.; Ibrāhīm Rifᶜat Pāshā, *Mirʾāt al-Ḥaramain* (2 vols.; Cairo, 1925), I, 207–24.

[62] Wüstenfeld, *op. cit.*, III, 341–49; IV, 309–13.

that the later historians, geographers, and travelers add to her story. This does not mean that the better informed of all these three classes ignored or neglected the remarkable queen but only that most of them repeat, either in whole or in part, the earlier accounts. The Arabic sources of this later period tend, on the whole, to be brief and factual and are, as a rule, partial to Zubaidah's philanthropies, for which not infrequently they call down Allah's blessing on her head.[63] Some exaggerate her influence over Hārūn in one brief sentence, such as, "Zubaidah had (complete) control over Hārūn's mind and did with him as she pleased."[64] Others, too generously, credit her with *all* the water supply on the Baghdad to Mecca road.[65] There is, here and there, a tendency to associate her famous name with events that perhaps should be credited to some other ᶜAbbāsid princess. A clear case of false association is met with when she is credited with the famous palace of Maᶜshūq, built by Muᶜtamid (256–79/870–92) on the west bank of the Tigris across from Samarrā.[66] Late Arabic sources

[63] E.g., Khaṭīb, XIV, 433–34; Ibn Jubair, *op. cit.*, pp. 208–9; Ibn Khallikān, I, 532–33; Yāfiᶜī, II, 63–64; Ibn Baṭūṭah, *Riḥlah*, I, 102–3; Wüstenfeld, *op. cit.*, II (Fāsī), pp. 32–35; Ghuzūlī, I, 185; Suyūṭī, *Taʾrīkh*, pp. 112–13, 120.

[64] Wüstenfeld, *op. cit.*, III, 115.

[65] Ibn Baṭūṭah, I, 103.

[66] *BGA*, VII, 268 (says east bank); Yāqūt, *Irshād*, V, 476; Ibn Jubair, *op. cit.*, p. 232; Ibn Baṭūṭah, I, 103, 140. Herzfeld, and after him Creswell, identify Maᶜshūq with the still-existing ruins of ᶜĀshiq on the western bank of the river (K. A. C. Creswell, *Early Muslim Architecture* [2 vols.; Oxford, 1932 and 1940], II, 364). Cf., however, Jean de Thevenot, *Travels* (3 vols. in 1; London, 1686–87), II, 60, according to whom there were, in 1664, *two villages* known as ᶜĀshiq and Maᶜshūq, that is, "Lover" and "Beloved" of the oral Arabic tradition; cf. Musil, *The Middle Euphrates* (New York, 1927), p. 53.

of a class different from the above do, now and again, throw in an unsupported off-color comment or anecdote about the queen that is probably yet another sort of false attribution.[67]

In contrast to the late Arabic sources, the Persian accounts of Zubaidah tend to be more exaggerated and given to romancing.[68] No less a statesman and author than the wazir Niẓām al-Mulk indulges in romancing dreams as a preliminary to Hārūn's and Zubaidah's philanthropies.[69] When it comes to Zubaidah's relationship to the Barmakids, the Persian sources stress her enmity toward the family and exaggerate her role in its sudden fall.[70]

Persian and Arabic sources alike were purloined and juggled to provide many an anecdote and basic plot for the several stories that are woven around the magic names of Hārūn and Zubaidah in that entertainment classic, *The Thousand and One Nights*. In these *Arabian Nights'* tales, as in the more solid historical records, Zubaidah, as a forceful and glamorous character, comes out second only to Hārūn al-Rashīd himself. Analysis of these stories of Zubaidah reveal an overemphasis on her romantic temperament, her love of splendor, her influence with Hārūn, and her hatred for the Barmakids.

Too few of the sources under consideration stop either

[67] E.g., Zamakhsharī, *Rauḍ*, p. 223; Damīrī, *Ḥayāwān*, I, 108; Rāghib, *Muḥāḍarāt*, I, 65.

[68] Cf. above, pp. 239–40.

[69] *Siasset Nameh* (Paris, 1891), pp. 126–28, and the translation by Charles Schefer (Paris, 1893), pp. 185–88.

[70] E.g., ʿAbd al-ʿAẓīm Gurkānī, *Akhbār-i-Barāmikah* (Teheran, 1312/1934). This work, written by a modern Persian who has brought several Persian texts together, is typical of the Persian point of view on this question.

to appraise or to characterize the long-departed Zubaidah. One is informed by Ibn al-Ṭiqtiqā (*ca.* 700/1300) that she was wiser than her son.[71] Ibn Taghrībirdī, as an exception to the rule, treats the reader to a brief characterization. "Zubaidah," he writes, "was the greatest woman of her age in respect to godliness, nobility of birth, beauty, chastity, and benevolence." He mentions next the Pilgrim Road and the Meccan waterworks, the hundred girls who chanted the Qur'ān in her palace, her large retinue of servants, and the great pomp of her establishment under all three caliphs—Hārūn, Amīn, and Ma'mūn. "She was," concludes his account, "in addition to being beautiful and glorious, eloquent, intelligent, wise, and farsighted."[72]

Coming down to modern times, one finds that the archeological interest in her tomb is overshadowed by a wider interest, among Easterners and Westerners alike, in her Pilgrim Road and Meccan waterworks. Testimony is given to one, or the other, or both of these projects, by several venturesome Western scholars and travelers who, in one guise or another, either trod the Zubaidah Road or quenched their thirst at her fountains in Mecca and ʿArafāt. Among the earlier references is that of the Spanish Moslem traveler of the first decade of the nineteenth century. Burckhardt, visiting Mecca in the next decade, refers to the initial construction as undertaken by Zubaidah as "a work of vast labor and magnitude."[73] Snouck Hurgronje, visiting Mecca in the

[71] *Fakhrī*, p. 295.

[72] Ibn Taghrībirdī, I, 631–32.

[73] *Travels in Arabia* (2 vols.; London, 1829), I, 194–96. Cf. *The Travels of Ali Bey* (*Badia y Leblich*) (2 vols.; Philadelphia, 1816), II, 53, 84.

middle eighties, expressed the hope that the Turkish governors would continue the upkeep of the waterworks "which have made the name of Zubaidah immortal in Mecca."[74]

Ibrāhīm Rifᶜat Pasha, thrice leader of the Egyptian Pilgrims in the first decade of the present century, details the long history of the important waterworks and concludes his appreciative account with a paean of grateful praise for "Zubaidah's immortal deed."[75]

That so great a blessing as this vitally needed and excellent water should come to be considered as sacred and be associated with miraculous powers is something that can be readily understood. "Sweet water refreshes the soul," cry out the water-carriers of Mecca, alternating with, "Drink of the sacred water of the Spring of Zubaidah."[76] But, on this point, let a genuine Persian pilgrim, "with his thorough English education," and his illiterate Meccan guide, Sayyid ᶜAlī, speak for themselves, on a crowded day at ᶜArafāt:

> On reaching the bottom [of the hill] we turned for ᶜAin Zubaidah. To this spring has been given the power of working miracles: merely dip a black cloth in it, and it will be washed as white as milk. No dye can resist its cleansing property, no stone withstand its charm. I might believe this or not as I liked said Sayyid ᶜAlī; for his part he would demand no greater wonder than that it should quench his thirst—a thirst that was insatiable, he begged Zubaidah Khānum to believe. Throwing himself on his stomach, he wriggled through the crowd to the water's brink; I did likewise; and then having washed our hands and feet and quenched our thirst, we crawled back and

[74] *Mekka* (2 vols.; The Hague, 1888–89), I, 6–10.

[75] *Op. cit.*, I, 207–24.

[76] Hadji Khan and Wilfrid Sparroy, *With the Pilgrims to Mecca* (London and New York, 1905), pp. 14, 224.

said a two-prostration prayer out of the gratitude of our hearts. "God bless Zubaidah!" cried Sayyid ᶜAlī, "may her fountain never run dry!"[77]

For more than eleven hundred years now, the cry of "God bless Zubaidah!" has echoed through the sands of Arabia, the valley of Mecca, and the mountain-plain of ᶜArafāt. One can well imagine it still echoing through the coming centuries and rest assured that "her fountain will never run dry" so long as Moslem rulers strong of arm, enlightened of mind, and pious of heart hold sway in one or more of the lands of the far-flung world of Islam.

Zubaidah's long royal career unfolds, as in the case of Khaizurān, with a series of pictures that pass in review before one's mind. Born to the purple and christened Amat al-ᶜAzīz, or "Handmaiden of the Almighty," the girl grows into a fair and chubby child. She is, for that very reason, nicknamed "Zubaidah," or "Little Butter Roll" by an affectionate grandfather—that simple family man and great empire-builder, Manṣūr. Like all princesses royal (the case of her girl-cousin Bānūqah was a rare exception to the rule), she was kept close within the harem so that virtually nothing is known of her early girlhood.

When next on the scene, she is the lovely, lively young maiden who has captured the heart of the handsome young warrior and royal prince, Hārūn al-Rashīd, her own double cousin and heir to the ᶜAbbāsid throne. So strong and sweet is her hold that Hārūn, influenced, it is true, by the dangers of succession, thinks for a while in

[77] *Ibid.*, p. 237.

terms of renouncing his heirship in anticipation of long and undistracted enjoyment of her company.

The next scene reveals her in pangs of jealousy as some young charmer catches the romantic Hārūn's passing fancy. But the lovable Zubaidah, be it said to her credit, has her in-laws on her side. When these prove her jealousy to be unfounded, a repentant Zubaidah rises with rare generosity of heart to the supremely acid test of a model Moslem wife and herself presents Hārūn with not one but several concubines.

As the next scene unrolls, Zubaidah is seen caring tenderly for ᶜAbd Allah, the orphaned son of one of these very maidens, as she herself, now queen, awaits the arrival of her firstborn. Hers is a joyous motherhood until her stepson's richer natural endowments force themselves on Hārūn's attention to the increasing detriment of her own son, Mohammed. The fair Zubaidah is now caught in a long and steady struggle between the deep-rooted instincts of mother love and a natural sense of fair play. Blood being so much thicker than water, she seeks at different points to shield her young son, "the flower of her heart and the apple of her eye for whom she had much compassion." She is anxious to protect his interests against fancied or real encroachment on behalf of her stepson, ᶜAbd Allah, who might replace Mohammed in the order of succession.

The Zubaidah of the next scene is a troubled mother and resentful queen. She fears the Barmakids because of their tremendous weight in Hārūn's succession plans and she chafes at Yaḥyā's strict control of the movement of the inmates of her own palace. Granting, at this point, the Jaᶜfar-ᶜAbbāsah story, granting even Zubaidah's stated share in its deadly revelation, there still is nothing conclusive to characterize her action as one with malice aforethought. It is, if at all, an instance of hasty words spoken in anger and repented in belated compassion. Thus only can one explain Zubaidah's willingness to brave the distracted Hārūn's fearsome wrath with a petition for the release of the broken and imprisoned Yaḥyā.

In these last distressed and distressing years of Hārūn's reign—years that see several other legal wives in the royal harem—Zubaidah herself is finally caught in an absorbing external interest: the Pilgrim Road and the Meccan waterworks. Liberal by nature and regal to her very fingertips, she stints neither effort nor funds in the accomplishment of the tremendous task *fī sabīl Allah*, "in the cause of Allah," faithfully hoping for a heavenly reward for her earthly charities.

Time passes and Hārūn's sun sets in at Ṭūs, leaving Zubaidah to mourn in the twilight "a master who was never negligent." The dark shadows gather as the relationship of son and stepson becomes more and more threatening. Zubaidah is now seen faced with a hard choice—perhaps the hardest with which a sensitive and loving mother is ever comforted. Was she to continue to shield her son despite his folly and error or was she to cry out for fair play for the distant stepson? Courageously she chooses the second alternative the while she desperately strives to restrain her son. She stays with the latter to the tragic end, despite bitter words that must have cut to the quick. Darker grows her long night as humiliation and defeat bring her at last to her darkest zero hour, with death for her son and captivity for herself and grandsons. She emerges from her long ordeal with sufficient strength to turn aside the tempter's bait of a cry for blood revenge.

The new day is saved as much by Zubaidah's unquibbling submission to, and her sincere regard for, the victorious Maʾmūn as by any of the nobler qualities of that stepson now become caliph. Resuming, in time, the pomp that characterizes her in three reigns, Zubaidah leaves politics alone to attend to her palace, her vast fortune, and her charities. Approaching old age and the pious hope of a reward in the hereafter add further incentive to her lifelong right-regal generosity. So at Māʾmūn's wedding to Būrān, Zubaidah, to do fitting honor to her royal stepson and his bride, parts with a fabulous heirloom, an extensive estate, and a purse that would more than ransom a king. And in her very last public appearance she is seen deeply grieved at the loss of an opportunity to hasten once more to the aid of the Meccans. A cheerful giver is she who has early wakened to the fact that it was indeed more blessed to give than to receive.

When in the last scene the Grim Reaper makes his call, Zubaidah, the Handmaiden of the Almighty, having spent her golden talents to give a cup of water to the least of Allah's pilgrims, is gratefully believed by these to have entered into the joy of her Lord. She is gone but not forgotten. It matters little if her remains rest in that tomb outside East Baghdad that goes by her name or in some other spot, be it ever so humble or ever so great. The spirit of this generous woman of royal romance and splendor, of tact and vision, of head and heart, is confined to no one single spot on earth. Her place is secure in Islam's Hall of Fame for as long as Allah's hosts of pilgrims progress down the Zubaidah Road to their goals of Mecca and ʿArafāt, there to quench a physical thirst at her springs and satisfy a spiritual one at Islam's Holiest of Holies and Allah's Mount of Mercy. Within and without Islam, her memory lives so long as history continues to instruct and the *Arabian Nights* continue to entertain. Cleopatra! Zenobia! Zubaidah! Magic names these to set the fancy free to work and play in the realms of history, legend, and romance.

Index

Index